Value and Circumstance

OXFORD LEGAL PHILOSOPHY

Series editors:
Timothy Endicott and Leslie Green

Oxford Legal Philosophy publishes the best new work in philosophically-oriented legal theory. It commissions and solicits monographs in all branches of the subject, including works on philosophical issues in all areas of public and private law, and in the national, transnational, and international realms; studies of the nature of law, legal institutions, and legal reasoning; treatments of problems in political morality as they bear on law; and explorations in the nature and development of legal philosophy itself. The series represents diverse traditions of thought but always with an emphasis on rigour and originality. It sets the standard in contemporary jurisprudence.

ALSO AVAILABLE IN THE SERIES

Elucidating Law
Julie Dickson

The Right of Redress
Andrew S. Gold

Faces of Inequality
A Theory of Wrongful Discrimination
Sophia Moreau

Coercion and the Nature of Law
Kenneth Einar Himma

Property Rights
A Re-Examination
J. E. Penner

A Theory of Legal Personhood
Visa A. J. Kurki

Imposing Risk
A Normative Framework
John Oberdiek

Law and Morality at War
Adil Ahmad Haque

Ignorance of Law
A Philosophical Inquiry
Douglas Husak

Reason and Restitution
A Theory of Unjust Enrichment
Charlie Webb

Allowing for Exceptions
A Theory of Defences and Defeasibility in Law
Luís Duarte d'Almeida

Why Law Matters
Alon Harel

The Ends of Harm
The Moral Foundations of Criminal Law
Victor Tadros

Conscience and Conviction
The Case for Civil Disobedience
Kimberley Brownlee

The Nature of Legislative Intent
Richard Ekins

Corrective Justice
Ernest J. Weinrib

Value and Circumstance

Justice, Consent, Equality, and Law

TIMOTHY MACKLEM
*Professor of Law and Philosophy,
Queen Mary University of London, UK*

Great Clarendon Street, Oxford, OX2 6DP,
United Kingdom

Oxford University Press is a department of the University of Oxford.
It furthers the University's objective of excellence in research, scholarship,
and education by publishing worldwide. Oxford is a registered trade mark of
Oxford University Press in the UK and in certain other countries

© Timothy Macklem 2025

The moral rights of the author have been asserted

All rights reserved. No part of this publication may be reproduced, stored in a retrieval system, transmitted, used for text and data mining, or used for training artificial intelligence, in any form or by any means, without the prior permission in writing of Oxford University Press, or as expressly permitted by law, by licence or under terms agreed with the appropriate reprographics rights organization. Enquiries concerning reproduction outside the scope of the above should be sent to the Rights Department, Oxford University Press, at the address above.

You must not circulate this work in any other form
and you must impose this same condition on any acquirer

Public sector information reproduced under Open Government Licence v3.0
(https://www.nationalarchives.gov.uk/doc/open-government-licence)

Published in the United States of America by Oxford University Press
198 Madison Avenue, New York, NY 10016, United States of America

British Library Cataloguing in Publication Data
Data available

Library of Congress Control Number: 2024948702

ISBN 9780198948575

DOI: 10.1093/9780198948605.001.0001

Printed and bound by
CPI Group (UK) Ltd, Croydon, CR0 4YY

The manufacturer's authorised representative in the EU for product safety is Oxford University Press España S.A. of el Parque Empresarial San Fernando de Henares, Avenida de Castilla, 2 – 28830 Madrid (www.oup.es/en).

*For Gail Thorson
My beloved companion in everything I do,
inspiring, gentle, passionate and wise,
not to say beautiful, intelligent and true,
from whom I am still tenderly absorbing
the subtlest and most elusive things I know*

Series Editors' Preface

Timothy Macklem's book is an exciting and profound investigation of the interplay between value and the particularities of life.

The roots of the book's approach to philosophy are to be discovered in *Beyond Comparison: Sex and Discrimination* (CUP 2003), *Independence of Mind* (OUP 2006), and *Law and Life in Common* (OUP 2015). Now, *Value and Circumstance* gives his most complete unfolding of that philosophy. It starts in and leads toward a new way of thinking about social life.

At the centre of this work is the thought that values cannot be fully grasped, felt, pursued, realised, in abstraction from the circumstances in which they arise. To understand the word 'and' in *Value and Circumstance*, we have to understand that Macklem is not addressing value and also addressing circumstance; this is a study of the conjunction between them. He interprets the conjunction as a partnership, 'a subtle and fluid kinship', a connection, a dialogue. He argues that it is 'crucial to the project of living well'.

Justice, Consent, Equality and Law give the book its structure. Justice and its tensions with other values could be said to have been the underlying theme of all Macklem's previous work, and he builds on that work here with a study of the drawbacks of treating justice as if it were the only value. The discussions of consent and equality build on Macklem's work on sexual ethics and on discrimination by bringing his focus to bear on the particular, the everyday. The law has been the theatre of the particular in which he has investigated equality and consent and justice. In this book though, law is the outlier: it does not exactly feature *as a value*. Perhaps the interplay of value and circumstance goes on *within* law (within the law, and within the practice of law) –between general decisions and particular decisions. And where law is valuable, he offers a new argument that decision is the good thing that makes it valuable. Decision is essential to authorship (personal and social), and to responsibility, which Macklem explains as 'the account that is to be given of our engagement with value'.

We can learn something from this book about another value: the value *of doing philosophy*. That, too, is grasped and instantiated in an interplay between the ideal and the everyday. And then it seems that any serious pursuit of wisdom will be enmeshed with the personal, particular actualities of the person doing the pursuing – all their experience and action and emotion. Not just what makes the philosopher human, but what makes the philosopher *that particular* human. When we read philosophy, the character and the life of the philosopher can often be glimpsed, like Alfred Hitchcock in an Alfred Hitchcock movie, somewhere thereabouts on the scene. In reading any good book, we always get some fragment of an understanding *of the author*. So philosophers' books often disclose glimpses of the personal.

This book, by contrast, does not offer incidental glimpses. It is totally and explicitly personal, from the Introduction to the Afterword. It is a unique reflection on humanity, and a reflection *of* humanity.

Timothy Endicott
Leslie Green

Acknowledgements

Radically abbreviated versions of Chapters 1 and 2 and a modestly different version of Chapter 4 have previously been published as journal articles, as follows:
 'The Price We Pay for Justice' (2020) 11 Jurisprudence 417–36;
 'Absence of Consent' in John Gardner, Leslie Green, and Brian Leiter (eds), *Oxford Studies in Philosophy of Law* (4th edn, 2021) 210–37;
 'The Ideal and the Everyday' (2019) 10 Jurisprudence 532–51.

Contents

Introduction: The Experience of Value   xiii

1. The Price We Pay for Justice   1
   1.1 Justice and Its Everyday Rivals   2
      1.1.1 All You Need Is Love?   2
      1.1.2 The Absence of Justice   4
      1.1.3 The Many Faces of 'Love': Charity, Generosity, Mercy   6
      1.1.4 False Consciousness   12
   1.2 Justice and Life as a Legal and Political Being   15
      1.2.1 What Justice Is and Isn't   15
      1.2.2 Fairness and the Lives of Children   16
      1.2.3 The Personal and the Political   18
      1.2.4 Just Allocations   21
   1.3 Justice and Its Alternatives   29
      1.3.1 Worlds without Justice   29
      1.3.2 Companionability   35
   1.4 Justice and Respect for Persons   39

2. Consent and Its Absence   53
   2.1 The Problem and the Project   54
      2.1.1 Points of Departure   54
      2.1.2 Missing in Action   56
   2.2 Consent by Implication   61
      2.2.1 Common Views of Implication   61
      2.2.2 The Structural Features of Implication   63
      2.2.3 The Morality and Politics of Implication   65
      2.2.4 The Legitimacy of Implied Consent   72
      2.2.5 Legitimacy and Explicit Consent   75
   2.3 Action and Interaction   80
      2.3.1 Action and Absence of Consent   80
      2.3.2 Interaction and Consent   81
      2.3.3 Acting and Being Acted Upon   83
      2.3.4 Consent and Different Species of Interaction   85
      2.3.5 Negotiating Interactions without Consent   87
      2.3.6 The Unwelcome and the Unwilled   94
      2.3.7 Submission and Consent   96
   2.4 Consent and the Passive   101
   2.5 Law and Consent to the Active   107
      2.5.1 Sexual Offences   107
      2.5.2 The Place of Consent and Its Absence More Generally   109

3. The Goodness of Equality 123
   3.1 Absence of Value and its Rewards 124
      3.1.1 Neglected Lines of Thought 124
      3.1.2 The Betrayal of Equality 128
      3.1.3 The Need to Temper the Claims of Equality 131
      3.1.4 Equality and the Accommodation of Difference 134
      3.1.5 Paradigms of Equality and the Contestability of their Grounds . . . 137
   3.2 Two Troubling Puzzles 141
      3.2.1 The Levelling Down Objection 142
      3.2.2 Levelling Down and Value Pluralism 144
      3.2.3 The Puzzle of Detachment 145
      3.2.4 The Puzzle of Suppression 147
   3.3 (Mortal) Goods and Goodness 152
      3.3.1 The Interdependence of Value and Valuers 152
      3.3.2 The Interdependence of Goodness and Value 157
      3.3.3 The Interdependence of Value and Social Practices . . 158
      3.3.4 The Fallibility of Goods and Goodness 161
   3.4 Commonality in the Modern Era 165

4. The Ideal and the Everyday 177
   4.1 Grounded Worlds and Ideal Worlds 178
      4.1.1 The Problem of Moral Inspiration 178
      4.1.2 The Problem of the Murdered Testator 184
   4.2 The Problem of Living Well 187
   4.3 The Value in Difficulty and Decision 194
      4.3.1 The Problems of Integrity and of Purpose 194
      4.3.2 The Problem of our Times 200

Afterword: A Philosopher's Life and its Worth 203
Index 209

Introduction: The Experience of Value

This is a book that seeks to capture and examine the connections between value and the moment; to investigate all those things that give life its particular flavour in our hands. It takes as its focus four values or apparent values, and related forms of goodness, that have largely shaped the twentieth century, through law and other social practices, and that continue to resonate today. These are the values that we are most well versed in, and that characterize the times and places out of which we have all been made. It follows that we are in a fair position, through the education of our personal experience, to approach these values, and forms of goodness, with a degree of understanding that makes our grasp of them broadly reliable. We more or less know what we are talking about when we talk about them, and that is crucial to successful reflection upon them. The four particular values, or forms of goodness, that I have fastened upon and made my topics here are justice, consent, equality, and collective decision in the form of law. They are not the only values and goods that have mattered in our recent lives together and, what is more, one or more of them may not matter very much, or even at all, to every one of us. Yet they will do, for each of them has a sufficiently strong capacity to speak to the world we live in as to make it a promising candidate for an exploration of the nature of the connections between value and circumstance, as we have known and negotiated them.

Each of the four main parts of the book is designed to make a contribution on two levels at once. Most directly, immediately, and unsurprisingly, the four parts speak to their particular subjects, namely, justice, consent, equality, and collective decision (in this case the decision embodied in law). In doing so, each of the parts represents something of a return to first principles, out of a conviction that many of the significant difficulties that have attended discussion of these topics, as well as their implementation in practice, stem from foundational issues in our understanding of them. We have not reflected as far as we need to, for example, on either the fit between or rivalry among the value of justice and the other values that constitute practical alternatives to it in particular settings, values such as love, kindness, generosity, and mercy. There may be rather more at stake in our choices here than we have generally allowed. The point is not to propose any kind of grand, all things considered conclusion, be that to give priority to justice or to refuse to do so, but rather to enrich our sense of the options before us, individually and collectively, publicly and privately, as well as our grasp of the attendant lives and cultures that those options give rise to. The same is perhaps even more obviously the case in our handling of consent (the topic of the second part), and its connections: to the

Value and Circumstance. Timothy Macklem, Oxford University Press. © Timothy Macklem 2025.
DOI: 10.1093/9780198948605.001.0001

active and the passive aspects of our lives; to our consequent functioning as agents or as patients; to the value that can emerge from each of those contrary, indeed antithetical, modes of being; and, what is often of more practical importance, to the attendant and contrary risks that each of those modes may pose to our flourishing, notwithstanding their possible benefits.

Among the consequences and rewards of a return to first principles is the exposure of certain contingencies, conceptual and practical, that a less probing enquiry would bracket. These contingencies matter in terms of their particular features, but they matter more fundamentally in that their presence, in a form that can be substituted, through the introduction of a different set of contingencies, but that cannot be erased, so as to give rise to non-contingent modes of engagement, suggest a partnership between value and circumstance, the moral and the living, the ideal and the everyday, that is crucial to the project of living well.[1] Goodness is grounded, and could not be otherwise, and both our lives and the realm of value are the richer for that fact. To put it in physical terms, by way of analogy, the Earth embodies possibilities, for life, for beauty, for living well, and more, that came into being only as a function of the Earth and its history, that would not have existed otherwise, and that consequently enlarge the shape of the universe. Something similar holds true for moral life.

There is a second level, therefore, at which each of these parts is designed to function, and that is as a contribution to meta-ethics, as something of a return to first principles in our reflections on the very nature and functions of morality itself. The thought here follows on from the one just expressed, that there is a deep and ongoing connection, and sometimes a dialogue, between the ideal and the everyday, the nature of which is such that each of those things can be fully understood, appreciated, and pursued only in partnership with the other, even in the cases when that partnership is unspoken and unacknowledged, as it is in all the very many circumstances in which we do good and live well by not thinking too much about it.[2] It is, of course, entirely possible for us to dwell on either the ideal or the everyday without any reference to the other, and many forms of living well, as well as reflections upon living well, do just that. Nevertheless, we are able to understand each of those realms more richly, more vividly, and more dynamically

---

[1] See sub-chapter 3.3 in particular for elucidation and explanation of this suggestion. See further sub-chapter 4.2. At this stage, I am concerned to outline the contributions to moral understanding that this book seeks to make, without allowing myself to be drawn, tempting as that might be, into the kind of detail that can only be properly developed and defended in the fuller narrative of its individual chapters and sub-chapters.

[2] I am thinking here of the additional value that can accrue to an action when it is undertaken from deep resources of character, rather than as the consequence of a process of deliberation. See Philippa Foot's example (from John Hersey) of spontaneous rescue in 'Virtues and Vices' in *Virtues and Vices* (1978) or Bernard Williams's famous 'one thought too many' illustration in his 'Persons, Character, and Morality' in *Moral Luck* (1981) (though he had a different target in mind).

through careful reflection upon the subtle and fluid kinship that they bear to one another.

When we instantiate value in our lives, through the various artefacts of our constant engagement with it, from our persons, to our practices, to the material resources that we call upon, from time to time and from place to place, we thereby bring goodness into being, as well as badness.[3] On occasion, and over time, these circumstances actually feed back into the realm of value itself, so as to enhance its possibilities, for better and for worse, even if, as is often the case, access to that enhancement dies with us, as the social practices that connected to and served it wither and are forgotten, so that, as it happens, other valuers never again engage with those possibilities, and our pasts become foreign countries.

In these ways, and others like them, the moral world is steadily, albeit fitfully and unpredictably, enlarged by the manifold and very often relatively mundane contingencies of our everyday engagement with it. We help to construct, even as we draw upon, the realm of value that we must always look to and be answerable to for our flourishing. It follows that our access to value is in many cases rooted in and dependent upon not only the richness of our social practices but on the intricacy, eloquence, dynamism, and, by extension, the imaginativeness of our command and development of those practices, individual and collective. We cannot live well by reference to the ideal alone.[4] Moral comprehension is immanent in experience, so that we learn fully what justice calls for by doing justice, learn to consent properly through an investment in the practical workings of consent, learn just when, in what manner, and in what domains to pursue equality only through engagement with the prevailing equalities, both secured and unsecured, of our particular times and places.

The meta-ethical narrative of this book does not map neatly and cleanly onto its individual parts. The parts are not to be regarded as separate, free-standing parables. Rather there is a thread running through the book, one that becomes more explicit in its final parts, that has two prominent aspects. The first is that there is a distinction to be drawn between value and goodness and, of course, also between the correlative cases of disvalue and badness, which depends upon but also goes beyond the basic fact that the value of any good is always in question. Goods are bearers of value, and so are open to our purposes and to the sense of point that may follow from and accompany the vindication of those purposes. The goods that we engage with and bring into being are always and also characteristically alive to fresh possibilities, fresh purposes on our part and fresh points on theirs, and consequently alive to fresh forms of goodness and badness, that are themselves

---

[3] Again, the distinction drawn here between goodness and value, and the nature of the relationship between them, is explained and defended in sub-chapter 3.3.
[4] So one should be wary of idealism and ideology, for the values they overlook. Compromise may be morally richer, or morally sounder. See sub-chapter 1.4.

instances of value and disvalue, some familiar, some novel. The freshness of any given set of possibilities, itself a product of and a resource for our present purposes, very often presses the boundaries of the realms of value and disvalue themselves, even to the point of altering their scope.[5] In short, the moral world itself is expanding and alive, thanks to engagement with it on the part of us and other valuers. We are the reason that this happens, though we are hapless in the face of it.

That is the second aspect of the book's meta-ethical thread, namely that the relationship between value and circumstance is always bi-directional and open-ended. Neither has a standing priority over the other, and there is no formula that is capable of articulating for our benefit a stable relationship between the two. This means that there is a species of relativity in our relationship to value, not of value to the will, as a good deal of twentieth-century moral thinking would have it, nor of value to circumstance, in the manner of animism perhaps,[6] but of value to circumstance and circumstance to value, so that we both live well by reference to value alone and also have reference to value by reference to our experience of living well, and thus very gradually, as well as both fortunately and unfortunately, enlarge the possibilities of each by reference to the other. Value is for valuers, as Joseph Raz has noted, and that means, it seems to me, that value comes to life only through engagement with life, on the part of both ourselves and other valuers. Once brought to life, in our hands and the hands of others, value gains access to the features of life, such as dynamism, creativity, renewal, and death, and all the particularities of time and place that those features give rise to, for better and for worse.

For what it is worth and by way of introduction, I will offer a brief outline here of the narrative that this book brings to each of the four topics that it considers in detail. Begin, as the book does, with justice and its alternatives. There are many reasons to seek justice and even to permit its prioritization over other values from time to time. Yet when justice is understood as a distinct value (rather than as a name for all that is good), its claims are incommensurable with the claims of the many other values that are alternatives to it and that it may be in competition with in any given setting. That means that while it is often open to us to assign to justice some sort of regulatory oversight of the operation of other values in our lives, the assignment is an arbitrary one, born of a practical need to prioritize what has no native claim to priority. More important, it means that when we pursue justice, as we often have excellent reason to do, we pay a price in terms of the other values with which the pursuit of justice is at odds. Most obviously, we neglect all those values the realization of which depends on not keeping score in the manner that the realization of justice not only calls for but depends upon. To be just is not to

---

[5] See sub-chapter 4.2 for full development of this thought. See also my 'Ideas of Easy Virtue' in *Reason, Morality and Law: The Philosophy of John Finnis* (2017) 346.

[6] I have in mind here the thought that value is innate in circumstance, rather than something that circumstance, if propitious, may be a bearer of. The term animism is here used as a placeholder for that thought.

be many other good things, and much that is important in our lives is lost thereby, such as the practice and pursuit of generosity, kindness, mercy, and love. That is, of course, no conclusive reason not to be just, for the values that are at odds with the pursuit of justice lack any claim to priority over justice, in the same manner and for the same reasons as justice lacks priority over them. We must simply choose in order to go on, in order to flourish, at any given moment and over time, without the comfort of any guiding algorithm, or any assurance of companionship, so that the choice to pursue and prioritize justice that we have more or less consistently made in the modern era constitutes an expression of our character and circumstances, one that describes a culture that is in many ways (the ways of justice) superior to its alternatives, yet in other ways worse. As I have put it below, to shine the light of justice into every corner is to drive the shadows out of social practice, with all the valuable nuances that they give rise to, and all the malfeasance that they conceal. There is no ready answer here as to what we should do in any given circumstance, but there is more to comprehend and to take account of than we have generally allowed. Or so I am proposing.[7]

Consent (and in particular consent to sexual relations) is a more difficult and more troubled topic. It is also a practice that is relied upon in a range of very different settings, personal and political (as those are conventionally understood) and that has been subject to the scrutiny of both morality and law. The tendency to assimilate these several circumstances, and the operation of consent there, to one another has been the source of much misunderstanding and confusion. That may explain why this turned out to be the longest chapter in the book. It has several significant dimensions, beginning with an exploration of the practice of implied consent: its operation; its many vulnerabilities in our hands (to both misunderstanding and exploitation); the record of its role in sexual relations; and the consequent legacy that we are now called upon to negotiate. Almost anything can be conveyed by implication, it seems, in many cases more fruitfully than otherwise, as long as there is a supporting language in social practice that is capable of making communication by that method possible. Yet it is in the nature of implication to be both indirect and ambiguous, and that means that practices of implication are distinctively vulnerable to error and abuse.[8] Given the sorry record of the practice of implied consent in sexual relations, particularly heterosexual relations, and given too the significance of what is at stake there, there is good reason to renounce

---

[7] The problem here is not that the claims of justice are taken to eclipse the claims of all other values, a position that few if any would endorse. Rather, it is that to attend to the claims of justice, to any extent whatever, is to insist, to that extent, on the eclipse of rival claims, claims that are inherently and necessarily rivalrous just because they depend on attention to the very things that justice depends on not paying attention to. See sub-chapter 1.3 for development of this thought.

[8] See sub-chapter 2.2 for development of this claim. It is worth noting that the distinction between the express and the implied is orthogonal to that between the verbal and the non-verbal, so that verbal communication may well proceed largely by implication and for that reason and to that extent be ambiguous.

implied consent in favour of express consent, as we have already done with regard to a number of other cases of implied consent, such as that between patient and doctor. It turns out that if consent is necessary to sexual relations, as the law for its purposes rightly insists, it cannot legitimately be implied, at least not in the world that we now live in.

Does consent have an intelligible role to play in sexual relations if and to the extent that they are interactive, or indeed in the setting of any other forms of action and interaction? The thought pursued here is that consent marks the divide between the active and the passive. Consent is not intelligible when we function as agents; it is vital when we become patients.[9] It follows from this, and from the fact that the law, for its own entirely sound purposes, artificially deems consent necessary to the lawfulness of certain *actions*, and so to the physical contacts that they involve, that we are bound to be lawbreakers in order to gain access to much of the good that sexual relations have to offer. This is not as troubling a conclusion as it might seem, for two reasons. The first is that we are entirely familiar with and well versed in the exercise of responsibility in our interactions with our fellows, and further, that we are normally no less well protected by that exercise than by the practice of consent, artificial as that practice is in the setting of action and interaction. The second reason for assurance is that the law has taken notice of the standing corruptions that are present in certain realms of interaction, and the vulnerabilities that this exposes people to, women in particular, and has accordingly provided an emergency legal brake in those settings, by rendering such actions illegal if undertaken without consent. When no really means no, one word is enough to stop an action, on pain of a possible prosecution and criminal conviction otherwise. Where the sound exercise of responsibility cannot be counted upon, the law does what it can to fill the gap, or at least claims to do so.[10] Perhaps more is possible as well as desirable.

The distinction between value and goodness opens the prospect to a fresh understanding of the possibilities of equality (the topic of the third part): one that among other things places the emphasis on *equalities* and their worth rather than on inequality; one that regards the recognition of an equality as a kind of cultural resource, offering the benefits of solidarity to all those who are picked out by the currency of equality, as that is articulated from place to place and from time to time (as expressions of the local and quite possibly distinctive need for, and rewards of, the fact of solidarity there); one that accordingly regards equality as a collective good first and foremost, and only derivatively and by extension as an individual good. The central role that is played here by the idea of goodness accounts for the fact that this part, more so than its companions earlier in the book, devotes much of its energies to a meta-ethical examination, in this case of the relationship

---

[9] See sub-chapter 2.3 for development of this claim.
[10] See sub-chapter 2.5 for an account of the value that the law's artifice here can give rise to, most directly and immediately in the hands of the vulnerable.

between goodness and equality, and in order to set that up, to an investigation of the idea of equality that is designed to reveal its shortcomings as a value and its corresponding qualities as a good. The point here is to meet the deep doubts about the independent value of equality that have been raised over many years by Peter Westen, Joseph Raz, Harry Frankfurt, and a number of others, and to suggest how and why the various currencies of equality, the concern of the bulk of current academic writing on the subject, have come to matter, dependent as they are on the worth of equality itself.

By its very nature, equality is deeply invested with circumstance, and so must be approached with circumstance in mind, rather than as an ideal. The dimensions of equality, as we have known and pursued them, have become the key commonalities of the modern era, and the special worth of equality is to be discovered in the fact that it has made these commonalities possible, by reason of the very features that make equality troubling when pursued as an ideal. Equality is at once both auxiliary and indifferent to what it is auxiliary to, committed to the act of assistance rather than to the nature of the assistance provided, concerned to vindicate solidarity itself rather than the various things that solidarity makes possible, and in those troubling features lie its worth. Its moral flexibility enables us to call upon it to give voice to whatever species of solidarity our culture and politics may happen to call for from time to time, or more ambitiously and progressively, for the species of solidarity that our culture and politics truly ought to call for, due recognition having been given to the currently prevailing character of that particular culture and politics, namely that it is fluid, liberal, open, and dynamic (and likely to remain so for some time). These are qualities that very largely bar our culture and politics from fostering or calling upon many familiar and long-standing forms of solidarity, the atavistic in particular, yet they are also qualities that make our politics and culture apt for distinctive commonalities of flourishing and prospect that circumstance, decision, and shared ideals have led them to fasten upon, notably the commonalities experienced by women, racial, ethnic, gender, and religious minorities, the elderly, the disabled, and those who are otherwise vulnerable, on grounds that, as things now stand, we regularly and self-definingly add to.

The final chapter weaves two stories together. The first has to do with the difficulty of living well, and the fruitfulness that comes from the fact of difficulty, the decisions that it confronts us with, and the creativity that this gives rise to, a creativity from which flows much of the worth of our existences, both individual and collective. The second story is a story of law and its worth. It turns out that we can only grasp the worth of law properly by having a suitable regard for difficulty and decision there, a regard that certain justly celebrated accounts of law and its worth would rule out of court, so to speak.[11] If the person entitled to inherit under the

---

[11] Most prominently, by the account of law and its worth offered by Ronald Dworkin, in any of its various incarnations.

terms of a will murders the testator, there is a question of whether to honour the bare terms of the will or to treat the murder as a bar to any inheritance by the murderer. Is there a right way to answer that question and should the law be regarded as embodying that right way and the consequent right answer? Or are there a number of right ways to answer the question, and does a social practice, such as the law, embody larger possibilities for the worth of existence, and for our grasp of and contribution to that worth, if and to the extent that it accepts and faces up to the difficulty, and so not only expects and supports but actually embodies the need for decision? If so, then law is the richer for the fact that it is to be identified by its sources rather than its merits, more or less contrary to what one would intuitively suppose.[12]

A last word of clarification, by way of explanation and orientation. A number of meta-ethical positions are advanced and defended in this book (as described above), yet a number are taken for granted, partly because they are broadly familiar, if not universally accepted, and partly because I have expressed my views on them elsewhere. These include the thought that values make demands upon us that we are bound to answer to and that as responsible creatures we can be called upon to give an account of (what might be described as moral realism),[13] and that values differ in kind as well as in degree (what might be described as value pluralism).[14]

I have many friends and teachers to thank for this work and for all that they have contributed to my life, professionally and personally. I would like to single out only Joseph Raz, as both good friend and great teacher, not in a dedication (for I have done that already, elsewhere), but in the form of a brief tribute that I paid to him on the occasion of a recent conference held in his honour, and that I know he appreciated. That will be my last word here, and perhaps anywhere, as the end of my intellectual life inexorably approaches.

---

[12] Two possibilities are being raised here. The more straightforward is that law cannot offer guidance in the absence of decision. The deeper is that law cannot exist without decision, because the moral content that law embodies is a product of decision, and that broadly, not simply in the setting of coordination problems. See also and respectively my *Law and Life in Common* (2015) and sub-chapter 4.3.

[13] For my views on this, see 'Value, Interest and Well-Being' (2006) 18 Utilitas 362 and see 'Human Disability' (2014) 25 KLJ 60, both written with John Gardner.

[14] For my views on this, see *Law and Life in Common* (2015) ch. 3, 'Decision, For One and For the Many' and see 'Choice and Value' (2001) 7 Legal Theory.

1
The Price We Pay for Justice

1.1 Justice and Its Everyday Rivals

1.1.1 All You Need Is Love?

Let me start small. Many years ago now, I saw a documentary on television, one aspect of which involved revisiting the ethos of the 1960s, perhaps it was some twenty years after the fact, to see how it had fared over time. Had the leading lights of that turbulent era held fast to their youthful ideals? 'All you need is love?' the interviewer asked of each of them, more than a little doubtfully. 'Is that really all you need?'[1]

Somewhat sadly, many, perhaps most, of the interviewees said no. They had changed their minds, with age and with experience. Their sense of abundance had become more muted, their understanding of human nature more jaded. 'What you need is justice', they now said.

Not all of them though. The filmmakers came to George Harrison, and he responded in a fashion that, characteristically, although deeply serious, was still faintly cheeky, dry, playful, recognizably Beatle-ish. 'That's what *I* believe [half-beat pause, coupled with a faint grin] and I'm sticking to it.' Or at least, that's the way I remember it, bearing in mind, of course, the tricks that time can play on one's memory.[2]

Yet why did those interviewed feel that there was a choice to be made? Is love unjust? Is justice unloving? Enough so in each case as to be in significant tension with one another, without going so far as to become a contradiction in terms? Why might they not coexist? Do we not think of certain kinds of rule, most commonly those we describe as paternalistic, as just *and* loving? Is that not how many people think of the Christian God? If coexistence is possible in such an image of the good, does that not imply the possibility of reconciliation?

If so, what might we look to in the world, beyond either love or justice, and without turning to scripture, to guide that reconciliation, to teach us how we might love justly, and do justice lovingly? Or have I mistaken the prevailing character of our cultural ideals? Is the reconciliation that we rely on a slightly different one? Is it a wise and loving, rather than just and loving, rule that we think of? And more probingly, is that only when the rule in question is a personal one, so as to embody

---

[1] Thanks to Timothy Endicott for inviting me to contribute to the conference for which I composed the first, more compact draft of this chapter, and to John Gardner for reading the final, lengthy version, and for offering, as ever, acute and yet unfailingly supportive comment. It was the privilege of a lifetime to work closely with him on a number of projects and to share ideas with him regularly. In speaking of the *price* of justice, I am speaking only of what we yield for its sake, not of a currency.

[2] At the time of writing, I was able to track down on the web a clip of Harrison's response, although it has since disappeared. It confirmed that the words I remember and have recorded above were indeed very close to what Harrison actually said.

a personal relationship, or is presented as such? Is there something about the political that would preclude such a reconciliation?

Alternatively, were the interviewees right? Is there indeed a choice to be made between love and justice, or more broadly, between a range of other values that justice is regularly and with good reason preferred to, and the distinctive value that justice secures? The example that I have opened with is both casual and banal. That is part of its point. Nothing much could be thought to turn on it. Yet unless the world it describes is fundamentally confused, it presents a possibility, a possibility that we have largely overlooked in our reflections, perhaps even set our faces against, yet a possibility that is visible in the features of everyday life and our pursuit of justice there. The possibility is that there is a significant price to be paid for the achievement of justice, a price that goes beyond the fact that justice is often arduous, a price that is undoubtedly worth paying in a whole host of situations, none of which will be in question here, yet a price nonetheless. That price has come to characterize the modern world, to shape its politics, and to inform our very conception of ourselves as persons. To be properly aware of that price, to be clear about its shape and significance, of just what it exacts and what it gives rise to, is to have a richer sense of the ways in which justice matters, and of when and why the price it asks of us is a price worth paying, as we regularly and rightly take it to be.

In suggesting these things, I am making a deliberate departure from the contemporary literature on justice. This is not in any sense to disparage that literature, or to discount the status that it accords to justice. Rather it is an attempt to look more closely at what that literature has neglected. It accepts the obvious, that there is real richness of understanding to be discovered in a great many avenues of inquiry, familiar and unfamiliar. Yet different avenues of inquiry are to a significant extent mutually exclusive, the more so the more deeply an avenue is engaged in, so that the gains that may follow from immersing oneself in one set of issues are often realized at the expense of what might be gained from like immersion elsewhere, as well as from non-immersion. In short, and to be clear at the outset, this is not in any sense a project about justice itself, and for that reason will not refer to such projects, or to the literature that reflects upon them. It is a project about those things that the pursuit of justice necessarily precludes, to the extent of the pursuit.[3] It asks and depends upon some degree of patience, open-mindedness, and dedication from the reader, who may initially feel a bit disoriented, but also offers what I hope are concomitant returns.

---

[3] The idea that justice precludes the operation of other values might be thought to be significantly counter-intuitive. I address the most important features of this intuition later: reasons for marginalization and preclusion (sub-chapter 1.2), the lack of companionability between justice and its rivals (sub-chapter 1.3), familiar yet ad hoc accommodations between the two (sub-chapter 1.3), and the extent of recourse to justice and so space for other values (sub-chapter 1.2.4).

1.1.2 The Absence of Justice

I get up in the morning and make coffee, set the table, lay out breakfast. My partner does physical exercises meanwhile. It need not be this way; it has been otherwise. I used to catch a few minutes of extra sleep while she got things ready. The patterns of our mutual support shift as the demands of our separate lives shift. We each try to think, as best we can, of what we can do for one another in the circumstances that we find ourselves in, from time to time, day to day, year to year. Our conclusions fluctuate, often to our surprise.

The same is true of various other dimensions of the contributions that each of us make to our life together. When we started out as a couple, as a family, she paid the mortgage; now I do.[4] A dependency that used to run in one direction now runs in the other. We have responded accordingly, roughly aligning our relations so that ability shapes contributions, needs shape withdrawals, without any attempt to calibrate either of those functions precisely, so that they have come to be informed as much by their expressive implications for our relationship as a whole, and the desire that it be as rich and successful as possible, for each of us and for both of us, separately and together, as by their fitness for their particular financial or other context. Part of what makes the relationship a rewarding one is the intuitive, spontaneous manner in which it evolves, so that everyday living, and the various ways in which it is negotiated, is an ongoing, constant reflection of what we happen to mean to one another in all that we do, just by chance and as we turn our minds to other things. Our relationship is articulated and advanced in terms that embody an understanding that we ourselves not only do not grasp but probably could not grasp, at least not consciously.[5] Or so it seems.

What each of us contributes to our relationship in these ways, then, and how that changes over time, is not something that we consider explicitly, let alone deliberate over. In our case, as it happens, we do not sit down together to discuss our relationship, as some others do. Indeed, it is not clear that we could do so and remain who we now are to one another. As I have said, our life together is something that evolves organically, in the same way that we evolve, so as to become different people in a different relationship than the people we once were in the relationship that we started out in. In fact, of course, that evolution is constitutive of both our characters and our bond, as those exist from time to time. What we are, to our distinct selves and to one another, is on the whole not something that we decide to be. Rather it is something that we find that we have become. There are certain exceptions, of course, some of them quite prominent, but they are not categorical,

---

[4] True at the time of writing. The mortgage is now paid and as a consequence our respective contributions have adjusted once more.

[5] In speaking of a grasp that is not conscious, I do not have in mind the realm of the unconscious, but rather the many and various factors that routinely shape our character and conduct without our consideration, including those of acculturation.

or something that we could foresee and sensibly plan for. What seems to happen in practice is that we occasionally experience a blockage in some aspect of our relationship, find ourselves at an impasse as a result, and then resort to deliberation, almost always awkwardly, semi-articulately, and with a good deal of difficulty, in order to move forward, as we are bound to for lack of an alternative. It could be otherwise, but as it happens, it isn't.[6]

In none of it do we keep score, as justice would require. In none of it are we either transparent or accountable. Our evolution is guided in ways that are only semi-conscious, and that fact is fundamental to our life together. What exactly is going on here? Isn't it essential that our relationship be one that can be shown to be just? Without that safeguard does it not risk the licensing, perhaps even the valorization, of exploitation? How can we legitimately refuse justice, or otherwise set it aside?

Perhaps some story about liberty and its legitimizing force might be told here, about our freedom to do things that we should not do, to have relationships that we should not have, to live unjustly, at least within certain limits. Yet that story assumes that we are doing what we should not do, in the manifold ways that we both constitute and conduct our relationship, day by day, year by year, very largely without reflection or deliberation, the value of liberty aside of course. That assumption is profoundly untrue to our lives as we understand them. What is needed here, to account properly for what the two of us are about, is some explanation of the good that we see ourselves as engaging in or, more precisely (since it is at least possible that we are mistaken in thinking that our lives are good), of the fact that we can think of ourselves as engaging in a good when we refuse justice, or otherwise set it aside, whether or not we are actually so engaging.

Another possibility is that we are operating in the special realm of the supererogatory. Each of us is trying to do more than our share. Yet that too seems inconsistent with the facts. To try to do more than one's share is possible only in light of some sense of what one's share looks like, and that is not present here. It hasn't just been neglected; it has, as I have said, been set aside. It is true that some such sense of appropriateness is surely present somewhere in the background, yet as far as it is possible to make out, only as a rough parameter. Within certain broad contours that it would never occur to either of us to breach, we articulate the terms of a life

---

[6] For lawyers (like myself, once upon a time), the process at work in this description is recognizably akin to the interventions that legislation is sometimes called upon to make in the development of the common law. When the courts cannot work something out by evolution, Parliament has to intervene. Significantly, when it does so a different set of social practices is engaged, involving different modes of decision, animated by different principles, none of which is compatible with the organic evolution of the common law. The difference between the evolution of the common law and that of a personal relationship, of course, is that the common law is at heart a matter of deliberation and decision, as the relationship that I have described is not. Where the two are alike, however, is in the way in which the fabric of the common law gradually, almost invisibly, emerges from decisions that are not directly dedicated to its development, just as a relationship emerges largely unbidden from day-to-day decisions that are not taken with its character in mind.

together without reference to fair shares, and whether those should be respected or exceeded.

It is not that our relationship couldn't be rendered in terms of justice, or indeed that it shouldn't be. It might well be so rendered, and rightly so, particularly by onlookers. Yet while there could certainly be good reasons to do this, concerns over exploitation for example, they would be reasons of justice and, as such, alien to the unanalysed, largely non-deliberative, non-transparent, and organic character of the relationship. That is why certain onlookers might well have better access to those reasons than we two are capable of, as ongoing participants in the relationship, embedded in its terms, so as to make it constitutively a little difficult for us to know ourselves otherwise. To see our life together in terms of justice would be to construct, rightly or wrongly, a relationship that was largely at odds with the one that we were actually living. Most obviously, our interests would have to be abstracted and opposed, rather than synthesized, at least for the purposes of assessment and whatever followed from it. Indeed, that would be the point of the reconstruction: to expose what it took to be our false consciousness and to release us from that fact.

Once again, the example offered here is everyday, mundane, and yet that is part of its point. What it suggests is a possibility that we are familiar with without quite consciously acknowledging or even recognizing, a possibility, moreover, that is embedded in the everyday, namely, that there is a realm beyond justice, in which justice has no place, to which it is a stranger, perhaps even an enemy, and that this realm includes many things that may be fundamental to human flourishing. To recognize this is to move beyond the binary, in which absence of justice is *ipso facto* injustice, and wrongful as a result. On an alternative, perhaps rival view, embodied in the terms of a relationship as I have described it, we can refuse justice without thereby becoming merely unjust. Indeed, it is possible that we may be right to do so.

1.1.3 The Many Faces of 'Love': Charity, Generosity, Mercy

What follows is something of a digression, necessary though it may be. I have spoken so far in quite simple terms, of a contrast between the claims of love and those of justice. That strikes me as a good way to begin the story, because that familiar means of distinguishing justice from its alternatives is one that can be well captured anecdotally, in vivid illustrations that nearly everyone will recognize and be able to evaluate, just because they form much of the substance of so many lives. Yet to speak that simply is also to risk overstating the contrast between the claims of justice and those of love, and further, to risk oversimplifying exactly what is at stake in the pursuit of justice. The life we live is neither easily binary in this respect, nor constructed in all-or-nothing terms.

The aim of the present section is to look beyond the idea of love, so as to examine the full range and variety of the contrasts that the pursuit of justice can give rise to. What other values are in tension with justice? In what ways is their proper realization incompatible with its pursuit? The point here is to show the multidimensional character of the limits of justice. A simple contrast between justice and love, if left at that, is all too apt to be identified with a contrast between the public realm, in which justice holds sway, and the private realm, in which something like love should prevail. Yet that view of matters understates the reach of both justice and its rivals. The claims of justice cannot be barred from the private realm, while the claims of other values may well displace justice in the public realm. The roots of that thought are what need to be teased out here. Those who find themselves at all impatient with this modest interruption of the main narrative can move straight on to the next section.[7]

To elaborate slightly then, to describe a domain of love (or care, or relationships, to pick some other familiar candidates for alternatives to justice) in terms that take that domain to be nothing less than whatever territory is not the preserve of justice, so that love is understood as justice's other half, is a perfectly good way of speaking of things, but is also to describe love in the broadest possible terms, terms that might be valuable rhetorically in virtue of their inclusiveness, yet that are of limited assistance in illuminating the idea of justice and what it offers and asks of us. If love is simply what justice isn't, then love has little to teach us either about itself or about justice. However, if one turns instead to a narrower, more precise understanding of love, as one should, then one needs to specify what other distinct values in the world are apt to exhibit the kind of tension with the claims of justice that this precise kind of love can give rise to. To move beyond the broad notion of love, one must unpick the various strands of that broad notion, so as to reveal the variety in what it subsumes. What is more, in doing so one must be careful not to neglect the extent to which it is possible to participate in both values in any given setting, that is, to satisfy the claims of both justice and its rivals, different in character as those claims may be. There may be real tension between these several ways of engaging with the world, but there is no fundamental impasse. I will not attempt to offer anything like a complete picture at this stage, or to suggest what principles such a picture might turn on, but I will expand the story, so as to offer a rather more nuanced sense of what is at stake, by drawing attention to certain rivalries with justice that have little to do with love.

Take charity first, a virtue that, though much honoured for the many good objects that its support has in practice proved critical to, is also widely suspected of too often being a reactionary substitute for the modes of allocation that distributive justice would call for. What can charity do that justice could not do better? Does

---

[7] The need for this part of the argument was pressed upon me by John Gardner. As my language indicates, I inwardly felt faintly impatient at the diversion, although I ultimately took his point.

justice not feed the hungry, tend to the sick, relieve the suffering, and so much more, in the same degree as charity but with greater respect? Does justice not buttress human dignity where charity undermines it? Do we not turn to charity only because injustice is ineliminable, and because it is better in that case to relieve suffering less well (because unjustly) than not to relieve it at all?

Sometimes this is certainly the case. Concerned people are driven to act charitably because they find themselves in a world where justice is flagrantly denied, other people are desperate as a result, and charity can do something to mend the failing. Human psychology is such, it appears, that people who are unwilling to pay the necessary taxes, or otherwise acknowledge the fullness of their responsibility to others, will donate, often quite generously, when confronted with images of suffering. Yet is charity just this, nothing other than a second best? Is the raising and distribution of funds the only thing that is good about it? Or is that to see charity through the eyes of justice?

One of the notable features of many forms of charity, and the focus of much of the criticism levelled against it, is the startling extent to which the charitable enterprise is detachable from any direct concern for the objects that it is supposedly dedicated to. Much of charitable endeavour takes place at a good distance from the front line, so to speak, largely sheltered from actual engagement with the grimness of suffering and need at its most acute, and is all the more recognizable for that fact. Charity does not get stuck in (at least in its initial stages), as justice generally must. Instead people very often engage in charitable enterprises for the sake of the engagement, to such an extent that the accumulation and disbursement of funds become secondary to the fostering of the charitable enterprise, both as an end in itself, and as a vehicle for the public expression of what are taken to be the right kind of attitudes towards one's fellows. Many communal endeavours, from church fêtes, to sponsored walks and runs, to the growing of moustaches in November, and even the dousing of oneself with buckets of ice, are pursued with the charitable community and its ethos as much as or more in mind as is famine, or cancer, or Lou Gehrig's disease. We want to be able to know one another as relieving people as much as we want to relieve. It is true that certain practices of hypocrisy are supported in this way, but there is rather more to it.

Charity is rightly about more than its immediate consequences for its objects. People who act charitably build charitable communities, the effect of which is not simply to cultivate a standing tendency to act charitably in the future, but also to cultivate the virtue of charity, a virtue that embodies and expresses acknowledgement of a particular kind of responsible attitude towards the predicament of other people. Part of the point of charity is to cultivate a charitable disposition, and possession of that disposition is intrinsically valuable, although it can also, of course, be over-cultivated, so as to become a species of vanity.

If one is inclined to doubt the existence or worth of any such virtue of charity, one need think only of those who refuse to be animated by anything other than justice. Sometimes those who pay taxes as they should and are then approached for a donation to charity take the view that the payment of taxation exhausts their obligation to offer relief to their fellows, at least in principle. If the taxes owed are not high enough to provide as much relief as is needed, then taxes should be increased, and that response is taken to be enough to answer, at least in principle, the claim of any charity upon one. All too many people think like this. One notices that very few people ever take the opportunity to pay more tax than they are asked for, although that option is open to us all.

To the extent that one has reservations about this stand against charity, one has reservations about the adequacy of justice, and correspondingly has reason to prize the value of charity for the things that it can do that justice cannot do. Both charity and justice are significantly detached from the circumstances to which they speak, for practical reasons if for no other, but justice might be thought to be the more worryingly so, in that it fails to nourish the very roots of the response that it seeks to give effect to. Charity sometimes goes too far in the other direction, of course, so that well paid people sit around in a room debating sums that are much smaller than the value of their time. Yet charity is right to pay attention to the special virtue of being charitable, and to the species of responsibility that it evokes.

By the same token, of course, but in the opposite direction, one is bound to recognize that while the pursuit of justice may neglect the attitudes that charity promotes, it correspondingly takes much more seriously than does charity the people whose lives are the object of charity, and in doing so exhibits a degree of respect for the persons whose circumstances give rise to charitable claims that charity itself is unable to exhibit. Justice, as will subsequently become clear, takes persons seriously as persons. So, the sense that the practice of justice expresses a greater respect for people than does the practice of charity is an entirely accurate one, it turns out, although just what gives rise to it is an issue that will need to be explored later.

I have dwelt on charity, partly because it is something quite different from love, notwithstanding the apparently interchangeable usage of St Paul, and partly because its operations often shade companionably into those of justice, as those of other rivals to justice do not. Charity and justice have many of the same objects in mind and show similar concerns towards them. Yet charity very often supports conduct that justice would condemn, in at least two ways. Charity is undoubtedly concerned that its objects be genuinely charitable, but once having satisfied itself of that fact it is thereafter relatively indifferent as to its objects, just because all of them bring out the virtue of charity more or less indifferently. Not so justice, which is as concerned with the identification of its objects, as common bearers of commensurable claims for relief, as with allocations within them. What is more, and relatedly, charity is infused with several distinct species of charitable impulse, so that one may commit oneself charitably to charities of rather different kinds, including ones that are more or less partial. This means that one can be properly charitable in ways that justice would regard as inappropriately self-serving. Concern for the local, the communal, the familial, need not be justified impersonally in each case, as justice would standardly demand (for example, by some showing that impersonal reasons of justice are better satisfied from a position of connectedness than otherwise). From the point of view of charity, positions of connectedness are part of the very virtue of charity, part of what it means to be charitably disposed, and so require no further impersonal justification. On that view, partiality is central to moral life, and is as impersonally justified as is impartiality.[8]

Two further rivals to justice, in much briefer terms. The significance of these is that they are less companionable to justice than is charity, so that their rivalry runs more to conviction than to approach. Take generosity first. When we are genuinely and properly generous, we part company with justice, not only in the shape of our response to other people but also in the very identification of the objects of our largesse. For the truly generous, goodness resides in the giving, in the fundamental selflessness of the attitude that one has towards what is given, whether that be something material, such as money or goods, or something immaterial, as when we speak of generosity of spirit. Those who act generously do so not as people who have resources towards people who lack them, but as people who treat resources as being as much for others as for themselves, who derive just as much satisfaction from the realization of life in other hands as in their own. Justice takes for granted attachment to oneself, and then insists on a recognition of the presence of other selves, and like attachments with like claims upon the same resources.[9] It makes no sense to justice, as it does to generosity, to give to persons more well off than oneself.

---

[8] This account of the contrasts between charity and justice adopts a particular perspective, inevitably, as but one illustration among many possible: it has a particular dimension of concern (that of distribution), a particular prospect (that of the distributor), and a particular scale (large). As always, things are rather more complicated than that. As and when any of the elements of that perspective change, so too may the roles of charity and justice. On a smaller, more local scale, for example, charity can be quite as concerned with its objects as is justice, perhaps more so. Indeed, that may become part of its point in such a setting, where the beneficiaries of charity are no less members of the charitable community than are their benefactors, just because they too manifest the virtue of charity, thanks to a setting and a practice in which beneficiaries and benefactors operate in close partnership. Yet the contrasts between charity and justice remain, and with them a prospect of rivalry to the point of mutual exclusion: between engagement and detachment, between partiality and impartiality, between putting allocation after other concerns rather than before them. (See sub-chapter 1.2.4.)

[9] Consider a couple of familiar cases of the sharing of food. When dealing with children (about which more later), it is quite common practice to have one child cut the cake (or whatever) and another child pick the first slice. That is the mode of justice, and children understand it well. It satisfies their almost primal demand for fairness. In a loving relationship, however, if one person makes, say, scrambled eggs for breakfast, he or she may well seek to ensure that the other person gets the more attractive portion. That is the mode of generosity, or more broadly, of love. Far from seeking to make the portions indistinguishable, it seeks from the outset to make one portion more attractive than the other, so as to create the opportunity to be generous with it, though not so much more attractive as to undermine generosity, by failing to observe a basic level of concern for the well-being of the donor, and so failing to value the donor as the recipient would want him or her to be valued, and what is more, failing to attend sufficiently to the fact that the recipient is complicit in the act of generosity, so that the generosity has to be something the recipient can conscientiously accept. The mode of justice avoids these perils; that is its value.

Yet are there not a great many good reasons to wish that we lived in a world that was animated by generosity rather than justice, or at the least, was more so than it is at present? Might we not then lead lives, and have relationships with the objects of our responsibility and our concern, that were in many senses better than they are now? Is that not in fact how we typically lead our lives whenever we are directly engaged in the vindication of our responsibilities, so that we come to fuse our responsibility to ourselves and to others in social practices that we learn to pursue for their own sake, without bringing any kind of analytic eye to the relative distribution of rewards? One can call this lovingness, and so recognize it as a feature of loving relations, broadly understood, while also noticing that it is just as antithetical to much of love, most obviously to *amour propre*, as it is to justice.

Mercy is a tricky case of rivalry, because it is both more and less of an alternative to justice. What is largely tacit elsewhere is explicit here. Mercy exists only in the shadow of justice. It is possible to be charitable or generous, or to exhibit any one of a number of other virtues, such as kindness, without ever turning one's mind to the question of justice. Not so in the case of mercy. To be merciful is to speak to what justice speaks to, but to do so by tempering in some way the impositions that justice would otherwise call for. That is not to suggest that mercy and justice embody incompatible demands, to suggest that it is in principle impossible to be truly merciful without thereby gainsaying justice. Many would jump to deny that. On one relatively familiar view of the world, justice very often presents us with a significant range of permissible outcomes, from among which the merciful select those outcomes that express compassion.[10] It is only if one were to think, quite wrongly, that justice is both precise and categorical, that would one be tempted to conclude that what mercy asks of us is inherently unjust. So justice and mercy are often congenial companions.

All this may well be true. Yet even so, it shows only that the rivalry between justice and mercy is not a fundamental one. That much has been assumed from the start. It does not show that the rivalry is not real. On one weak reading of that rivalry, if justice leaves latitude for mercy, it is only because justice has arrived at a point at which it has nothing more to contribute to the determination of an outcome, although there remains something of significance to contribute. That in turn can only be because there remains at that point a range of morally significant outcomes that are not morally significant from the perspective of justice. If that is so, one is then bound to turn to some rival consideration, in this case mercy, to do the further moral work that justice is not capable of doing on its own. In itself that gives us reason to pay attention to values other than justice and to cultivate our capacity to do so.

---

[10] Thanks to John Gardner and Timothy Endicott for reminding me of this.

Yet is moral reality not rather more consistent with a strong version of the rivalry? Is it not the case that the power of mercy includes the power to exonerate what justice condemns? Without such a power, would there be anything distinctive about the character of mercy? One would simply be selecting among just outcomes, in some way that justice found acceptable but that did nothing to disturb justice. Yet is it not frequently and familiarly the case that justice finds itself constitutionally unable to generate the resources that are needed to take certain circumstances into account, forcing us to look elsewhere for relief? Justice is famously blind to certain things, most obviously all those considerations that might prejudice its conclusions. We tend to treat those considerations as morally unworthy because they are unjust, but that is to be conclusory about the priority of justice over other virtues. At the risk of being no less conclusory in the opposite direction, is the blindness that justice relies upon not also moral blindness, that is, blindness to the morally compelling as well as to the morally corrupt, so that one is forced to step outside the domain of justice as and when its deliberately blinkered perspective, for all the good it does, exacts a price that all things considered we may choose not to pay, and be right to do so? In such a case, we have become accustomed to taking the formal step, in certain recognized circumstances, of granting to some competing virtue the moral priority that we normally grant to justice. It is in this way that practices such as the prerogative of mercy have become institutionalized.

Is the weak reading of mercy outlined earlier not best understood as but a back formation from the strong case rather than as a genuine instance of mercy (other than in a broader sense of mercy that is comparable to the broad sense of love)? Some may protest at such a suggestion, call it tendentious even, but whether or not this analysis of the weak reading is correct, it seems to me that on either reading mercy works alongside justice yet in tension with it, to generate outcomes that, at a minimum, justice is incapable of generating on its own, and that on a stronger but no less plausible view, justice might well condemn, and for good reason.

1.1.4 False Consciousness

This brings me back to an issue that was referred to in passing earlier (at the close of the second section), in the course of asking whether a belief in the value of loving relationships that are not accountable to the claims of justice might not be properly regarded as a classic case of false consciousness. After all, certain radical feminists have made much hay out of scorning a famous version of that idea, namely, that the predicament of women is best grasped by reference to an ethic of care. The suggestion I offered earlier was that one needs to show at least prima facie respect to the self-understanding of the participants in a relationship, and so needs to take seriously the possibility that the consciousness in issue is not in fact false. But is that suggestion right? Is it not in need of closer inspection? What is more, might the same charge of false consciousness not be made with respect to any attempt to displace or ignore the claims of justice in favour of some other virtue that is supposed to be no less valid a guide than justice, be that virtue charity, generosity, mercy, or some other? Can it not be plausibly claimed that false consciousness actually resides in a host of settings, indeed wherever self-satisfaction has undermined self-examination?

Charges of false consciousness are very often deployed as a means of foreclosing analysis, and in itself that makes them difficult to address analytically. What is more, in their less bullish versions it is difficult to disagree with them. One should be quite properly sceptical of the soundness of all views one is presented with, particularly so perhaps when the view is embedded in traditions that history and habit have given us reason not to question as far as might be called for by the presence of other reasons. Yet to describe a view as the product of false consciousness is to go well beyond what might be called for by healthy scepticism. That strikes me as a bad move in nearly all cases. Without seeking to reach any profound conclusions on the subject, I want to offer some brief observations that might serve to open the door to reflection rather than close it. On the one hand, I would like to give credit by not dismissing the possibility of false consciousness out of hand and, on the other, to seek credit in return, by offering certain reasons to suspend disbelief that go beyond what the sake of argument would call for on its own. The relatively modest aim here is to keep those readers who are disposed to be sceptical of critiques of justice on board the train, for a little longer at least.

The first brief observation is that a consciousness would have to be quite profoundly false in order to mislead to an extent that the possessor of the consciousness was not aware of, at some level at least. Women surely always knew that they were oppressed, despite the many ways in which the world sought to reconcile them to that fact. Apart from victims of serious psychological damage, nearly all people have a reasonably sound grasp of their predicament in life, however much they may try to cushion that predicament in certain protective delusions, so as to make it seem somewhat less imperfect than they know it to be in fact. This basic grasp of one's moral predicament is the source of the moral understanding that Aristotle relied upon, rather than questioning in the modern manner. For all its flaws, it is the best we have, or can hope to have. What is more, and more Aristotelian, it is all that we could wish to have.

The second brief observation is that even when consciousness is false in this setting, it is false to justice, not to the other values that it prioritizes. What it emphasizes in place of justice can only sometimes be dismissed as sustaining myths, in the manner referred to earlier. There are indeed certain such sustaining myths in the world, that of the value of virginity for example, or that of the uncleanness of menstruation, but they are relatively few in number. After all, were it otherwise, so that rivals to justice were very largely mythic, there would be little of significance other than justice to concern us in the real world. Yet no one who seeks to prioritize the claims of the right over those of the good, as a great many devotees of justice do, can believe that the content of the good is very largely mythic, for in that case the significance of the priority of the right would itself be correspondingly mythic.

Finally, one is bound to notice that the fact of false consciousness inevitably cuts both ways. To believe that the achievement of justice is all gain, that we have nothing to lose but our chains, is itself no less apt to be a piece of false consciousness, the sustaining myth of another culture, than the consciousness that it sets itself against by calling false. What that does not mean is that either consciousness can be said to be false all the way down, so to speak, whether that consciousness serves justice or its exclusion. We all participate in delusions of one kind or another, but that does not make us any the less capable of reflection. It simply means that the fact of delusion, its status, and distinctive perspective, are bound to become part of what we reflect upon, just as the different delusions of others are bound to become the objects of their different reflections. We cannot but see the world in terms of a view from somewhere, and in itself, of course, that is something to be deeply grateful for, given that instantiation is the very stuff of life. We are merely bound to ensure, in order to be true to ourselves as much as for any other reason, that the course of our reflection takes proper account of our predicament, so as to be the thought that it is rather than some other, and more important, to know itself as such.

1.2 Justice and Life as a Legal and Political Being

1.2.1 What Justice Is and Isn't

Talk about justice, as we all know, can be talk about either of two very different things, as Aristotle pointed out so long ago. On the one hand, justice can be understood as embracing everything that is good. A just society, on this view, is simply a good society. So understood, justice is comprehensive, and thus not liable to be contrasted to any other value. On the other hand, and distinctively, justice is a special value, most commonly rendered as fairness. It is the value of ensuring that each person is accorded their due, whether in terms of needs or merits, distribution or retribution, assignment or correction. On this view, justice is essentially allocative. That is not to identify the two. The focus of allocation is not necessarily on justice (one may allocate the hours in the day to different tasks, or to work and to leisure) but the focus of justice is on allocation. There is more to it than that, of course, and for that reason I will return to the question of allocation later. Yet that is enough for present purposes. What matters here is that the allocative nature of justice, which is one of its inescapable features, gives rise to two significant difficulties.

The first is that many good things in life are not susceptible to allocation, so as to make justice a very incomplete guide to a good life. That, of course, is no more than simply what follows from any understanding of justice as a special rather than a comprehensive value, but it does highlight the need to keep justice in its place, so to speak, not to allow it to become too large a concern in our lives, lest it crowd out other concerns that are essential to our flourishing. It also highlights the consequent issue of exactly which particular places in our lives to assign justice to.

The second and more profound difficulty, however, is that the pursuit of justice is inimical to the realization of certain other values, which are not merely marginalized, so as to be eclipsed by justice, but actually precluded by the terms on which justice depends. Put colloquially, if not keeping score is constitutive of certain valuable ways of being, then those ways of being cannot coexist with justice. To be kind, for example, to be generous, to be compassionate, to be loving, is not to keep score. As I said in discussing love, to be any of these things is to reject the claims of justice, at least *pro tanto*, not merely to neglect them. These forms of goodness are constituted, in part, by their disregard for what is due. That is both a good and a bad thing, and it is vital not to neglect either of those facts in attending to the other.

A few years ago, my mother, then in her late eighties, fell while on a visit to London, and broke her femur. She had a steel rod inserted in her leg and spent some time recuperating in St Thomas' Hospital, overlooking the Thames. She said to me one day, speaking of her care by the nursing staff, 'These are people who have dedicated their lives to kindness.' Something in the shape of the observation struck me. To dedicate one's life to kindness is to move beyond justice, although not to move, as we all know, beyond the claims of justice. So nurses today, in a world very largely made answerable to justice, are not so much expected to be kind as to check patients at certain intervals, to monitor a specified list of concerns, and more generally, to behave in ways that can be held to account: has the patient received what was owed to her, and can that be demonstrated? If the nurses tending my mother had behaved like that my mother could not have made the observation that she made.

Something is lost in this, and that something is essential to kindness, which is a virtue that is not only unforced but also unforceable, not susceptible to measure and assignment. Something is also gained, of course, in terms of everything that accountability makes possible on the one hand and impossible on the other, in the needs that can be met and the neglect that can be exposed. The opacity that allows kindness to flourish also screens abuse. To shine the light of justice into every corner is to drive the shadows out of social practice, with all the valuable nuances that they give rise to, and all the malfeasance that they conceal.

1.2.2 Fairness and the Lives of Children

I remember once wearily reflecting, upon hearing yet again, perhaps from my brother at some time when we were both young adults, the eternal complaint that 'It's not fair!', that fairness is for children. It is something that we largely leave behind when we become adult, something that we mostly grow out of, as part of the moral development that Aristotle expected of us. This gives rise to a tempting line of thought which, it seems to me, offers some insight, although it will prove to be ultimately unsatisfying, because it is insufficiently probing.

Many people of my generation made a very conscious decision not to grow up so as to become something like our parents, and in particular not to lose the sense of unfairness, of injustice, that our parents seemed to have lost, and so not to lose the need to protest that injustice, to fight against it, to be constitutively opposed to it. People did not want to become, as they saw it, compromised and inured, to accept the idea that life is not fair (in the sense of being unfair, rather than in the sense of being about something other than fairness). As members of a new generation, committed to the fact of its youth and the insight they took that to embody, people sought to grow powerful without growing up, to discover ways to make their voice count in its own special register. 'Don't trust anyone over 30', it was regularly said, until of course we all turned 30 ourselves, and fell silent on the point. Such people insisted on the binary, that what is not just is unjust. If you're not part of the solution, you're part of the problem.

Put less colloquially, the line of argument ran something like this. If one will but face up to the fact, one is bound to recognize that there is injustice everywhere, embedded in social practices that we have not had the honesty, the courage, or the integrity to question and to challenge, injustice not simply in the broad sense, that the world is not nearly as good a place as it ought to be, but in the specific sense of the misallocation of prosperity, opportunity, security, stability, health, sustenance, housing, and many other vital goods. We must not fail to act in the face of such injustice, it was insisted. This world of manifold injustice is hidden behind self-serving veils that present as virtues what in fact are only devices fostered and promoted by the authors and beneficiaries of injustice. Do not be deluded by appeals to kindness, generosity, charity, or even love. Those are but schemes that a corrupt culture has employed to persuade people to embrace their subordination as a good. The essence of the basic line of thought here was elegantly and incisively captured by Friedrich Nietzsche, and later re-presented with a different target in mind by radical feminists such as Catharine MacKinnon. It became the foundation of a political retort that the determinedly young and uncorrupted made not only or even principally to their parents but to their contemporary counterparts, the hippies and the flower children, many of whose practices, one is bound to observe, were appallingly unjust, as those of us who were straight enough at the time to remember the era properly now recall with a wince. Love is most emphatically not all that you need. In a great many of its forms, it is something to be seen through and exposed.

To see the world in this way is to achieve what appears to be great moral clarity, to reduce the challenges before us to ones primarily of courage and of will. It is also to present the claims of morality as straightforward, non-contradictory, and inescapable. Injustice must be confronted, not avoided, excused, or presented as conflicted, to the warranting of moral inertia. In this insistence, the child becomes the man, as they say, without entirely ceasing to be a child, without losing the youthful commitment to fairness. And yet, it seems to me that although there is real truth in this picture of the impulse to justice it is not quite right. There is more to that impulse than can be explained by the presence of the child in us all. The outlines of a fuller answer are visible in the circumstances of childhood, but transcend them.

Children are moral primitives. When asked to think unegoistically, they are driven to think reciprocally, in terms of the claims of other egos, rather than in terms that reflect a grasp of the fact that the moral life goes beyond ego. In doing so, they become political, not because politics is childish (though in many settings it is and is expected to be fundamentally egoistic), but because politics (whether democratic or otherwise) arrives at similar conclusions as a consequence of different disabilities. It too lacks the capacity for empathy and the values and virtues that depend on empathy, and that is the source of its strength and its limitations. The two impulses, the childish and the political, come together when certain people, alive to the goods that this perspective makes possible, seek to hold at bay the complications (as well as the returns) that a richer perspective would press upon them, the richer perspective towards which many members of previous generations had strained, and so prize justice above other virtues. In doing so, they make a cardinal virtue of what is necessary to politics but is ultimately no less the instrument of a set of correlative moral disabilities, disabilities that are far from inconsequential in many settings, and thus are all too often ground for more than the necessary regret that accompanies hard choices between incommensurables, of the kind that has come to be conventionally, if brutally, expressed in terms of omelettes and eggs.

To put it in other terms, there is a bidirectional scheme of influence here. Certain moral roles entail recourse to fairness, and to the institutions and social practices that the vindication of fairness entails, while those institutions, and the authority and the distance that they embody and depend on, entail the adoption of certain moral roles, the roles of justice. In this way, the dynamic of justice self-fulfillingly describes a moral role and a moral outlook, both self-referential, to the cost of its alternatives.

1.2.3 The Personal and the Political

Another no less familiar and no less tired slogan from the sixties is that the personal is political. What makes this a slogan is that it presents an ambition as a description. The personal can certainly be made political, but at the cost of much of its personality. Some of that personality is better gone, some is worth sacrificing, but some is all things considered to be mourned.

As the popularity of this and other slogans attests, people are attracted to an uncomplicated picture of moral life. In this they are sometimes merely simplistic, whether out of intellectual laziness, or something more malign, or the familiar, unpleasant combination of both those things: think of the politics of Nigel Farage, or of Donald Trump. As often, however, they are wise, for we would live less well if we had to be thinking about everything all the time, if we had no recourse to moral mechanisms beyond our own reflection, not only because we would be overwhelmed by the task of doing so but, more important perhaps, because we would lose touch with the value of what is spontaneous and innate, so as to constitute personal and communal virtue, as well as the value of what is formally determined, and so as best as we can make it, unequivocal, prospective, and relatively stable and reliable.

This gives rise to a picture of moral life that Aristotle would surely recognize. On the one hand, we internalize the claims of goodness, so as to make them part of our character, and our response to them unforced. We do this both individually and as participants in certain shared social practices, from family to community to country to yet broader forms of shared heritage, practices the sharing of which is such as to be constitutive of virtue as we practise it in our lives, practices that constitute what we commonly call cultures. We draw upon these various cultures for much of the goodness that we seek to embody in our lives, as those lives are shaped by the virtue of our persons. On the other hand, once again both as individuals and as participants in shared social practices, we do the opposite, and so externalize and institutionalize the claims of goodness, thereby giving them public and authoritative form, making them the formal burden of some other. Doing this carries with it a significant degree of reductiveness, for better and for worse, both in our understanding of what is at stake and in our modes of response to it. This follows in part from the fact that the pre-emptive reasons on which public institutions depend for their authority operate through the exclusion of other relevant and rival reasons. That is how authorities are able to make up our minds for us, on all matters over which they have jurisdiction, other than the question of the wisdom of recourse to authority itself. In its other part, it also follows from the self-conscious detachment of such institutions from the organic, non-deliberative, non-transparent fabric of our everyday lives.

So there are two broad ways of managing the great complexities and deep contradictions of moral life, and with them two corresponding roles, ancient and modern, one comprehensively just in its ambitions, the other specifically so.[11] Each approach exhibits certain distinctive vulnerabilities: the internal risks being insufficiently critical while the external risks being insufficiently nuanced. In the externalization that inspires justice and lays down the circumstances in which it is to be realized, reductiveness informs both the idea of justice and the extent of the role that reference to authority plays in our lives. How far do we make things matters of justice and of the institutions that determine questions of justice? Do we go so far as to give primacy to justice and to the institutions and practices that embody and secure it?

In the case of children taking the first steps in the development of their moral life, the move to fairness is prompted by moral incapacity of a personal and internal kind, the moral incapacity that comes of an as yet imperfectly developed rationality. In collective adult life, its promptings are incapacities of a different kind, stemming from the different forms of imperfect rationality and, more profoundly, from the impossibility of perfection in the very nature of rationality. They include the size of a community and of its ambitions, the fluidity of social practices, the plurality of value and the diversity of legitimate goals that it gives rise to, and mistrust of the organic coupled with a correlative consciousness of the wrongdoing that the self-justifying, relativizing tendencies of organic practices licenses or at least protects. What these promptings yield include formal institutions and practices of authority, demands for accountability to those institutions, and consequent demands for the transparency that accountability depends upon. From these resources we have built much of the modern world, with all the evils that it has ended, and all the goods that it has made possible. And of course, and by the same token, we have demolished most of the virtues of the pre-modern, and the modern evils that they forestalled.

---

[11] In speaking of ancient and modern, I am drawing a distinction that correlates only in part with the distinction between past and present times. The modernity I have in mind constitutes a culture, one that is common but far from universal in the world we live in, some of which is untouched by it and a great deal of which rejects it.

Questions of justice, and the political institutions that serve them, cut through the complications of moral life, in ways that the modern world has found refreshing and inspiring. It has enabled us to sweep away the organic, the opaque, and the unaccountable. And yet it has entailed huge costs, not only in health care, as suggested earlier, but also, and closer to home for most present readers, in academic life, just to pick an obvious local illustration. One can know how to be a good teacher, how best to explain, how best to assess, in a way that is fully internalized, so as to become a basic aspect of one's professional self-understanding, in a manner that is not susceptible to articulation, and more tellingly, rightly so. One could stop there, defiantly inarticulate, and it would be good to do so. It is not simply that some things are better left unexplained. Rather it is that any attempt at explanation in settings such as this one would undermine what is good about what is being explained. In many universities today, however, one has to be able to account for the quality of one's teaching in ways that reshape the practice of teaching, at the expense of some of its best qualities. So university teachers are now expected to attend to student assessments of their teaching in ways that clearly do not allow sufficiently, if at all, for the fact that the act of learning, at its best and at its deepest, is in many ways an unavoidably unpleasant experience, just as unpleasant as it is properly challenging.[12] There is nothing at all good about pain (special cases of masochism aside perhaps), but many good things can only be acquired painfully, as Joseph Raz has pointed out.

One can similarly know how to be an excellent researcher, in ways that are no less internalized, constituted as they are by deep grasp of a discipline, and acute awareness of its distinctive demands, history, and prospects. Yet once again, in a growing number of countries today, the practice of justice demands that the public funding of academic research be publicly accounted for, and so expects researchers to justify themselves to communities with no deep understanding of the discipline in issue, be they other academic communities, or communities that are dedicated to public goods other than those of academic life. In many cases, it is not possible to meet those demands fully without engaging in a rather different kind of research, less specialized, less cloistered, sometimes less deep. One cannot be as open to the world as the demands of justice would have one be without meeting the terms of that world halfway. Doing so is as apt to foreclose intellectual creativity as to give rise to it. More precisely, it leads intellectual creativity in certain directions and away from others. What is thereby gained in terms of ecumenicism and reach is lost in terms of specialism and enclosure.

Here is the possibility: that we secure a culture in which certain failings, many of them quite serious, are eliminated, at the price of simultaneously and by the same means more or less removing from that culture much of the essence of what made it

---

[12] Thanks to Peter Low for reminding me of the pain that accompanies learning.

valuable. Even if one believes, optimistically, that new values are bound to occupy the space left by the old ones, one is still left with good reason to regret the loss of those values that are no longer accessible. There will be more justice in the world, but correspondingly and consequently less of certain other good things. And if one doubts, as realistically one should, that new values can always be counted on to inform, no less successfully than the old values, what have become new ways of life, one then has even more reason to regret what justice has made impossible, even as one welcomes what it has achieved.[13]

Some of this is down to certain unfortunate, economistic ways of thinking, in which metrics are established so that scores can be given, alternatives can be ranked by number, and choices can be made in what are thought of as rational terms.[14] Yet it is also entailed by the impulse to justice and the allocations that justice involves. The threat here comes not from the values of the private sector, but from those of the public sector. We ask public bodies to behave in these ways partly so that consumers can make choices, but partly because we believe that public institutions ought to be accountable, and further, that accountability requires that the practices of public institutions be rendered in these terms. To fail to do so would be to hold oneself unaccountable. Back to the binary, in which what is not just is merely unjust.

1.2.4 Just Allocations

I have so far spoken very largely in terms of symptoms rather than in terms of the pathology that gives rise to them. In part this has been because it is symptoms that we are most familiar with, and properly so, given that it is the basic function of both justice and its organic alternatives to shape our engagement with the moral world in such a way that moral issues that we cannot resolve through the exercise of our own deliberation are displaced onto issues and modes of decision that yield resolutions for us, resolutions however that we can rely on because and to the extent that we are able to take them at face value, so leaving only symptoms to show for the success of their work. In short, these are the sorts of schemes that succeed only if one does not enquire into them too closely. As a consequence, analysis of them is liable to be both uncertain and puzzling. Yet here again, we typically know more than we let on, and one way to appreciate just how far that is the case is to enquire further into the fact of allocation and the distinctive role that it is called upon to play in the setting of justice.

---

[13] In speaking of new values, I am speaking of values that are new to the society in question rather than values that are new to the world. For an account of how values new to the world might arise and what might be good about that, see Chapter 4.
[14] Thanks to John Gardner for posing this challenge.

I suggested earlier, echoing John Gardner and others, that allocation is central to the idea of justice. I also suggested that there was rather more to it than that. Our lives are filled with forms of allocation that seem to have nothing to do with justice. A few quick examples will make the point clear. At any given moment of our lives, we allocate our time, our energies, our selves, to one activity rather than another (or even to absence of activity), and in doing so shape not simply that moment or that day, but the ongoing evolution of our commitments and our character. That is how we begin to become just who we are. Over time and usually with greater reflection, we further allocate our lives to different goals and to different weightings of the same goals. In doing so, we incrementally develop the narrative of a life. Some of the allocations that we make in this way are relatively conventional, as when we exercise a degree of prudence by saving for our age and its inevitable vulnerabilities. Others may be relatively original in our hands, as when we deliberately drop out of expected life-narratives just because we take issue in one way or another with what they call for from us. All these things are done both on our own and, more commonly, through social practices. Not only at given moments but consistently and over the course of a life, we undertake allocations in conjunction with others, so as to engage, for example, in a division of labour, or of a shared responsibility, so allocating their burdens and benefits.

In none of these allocations do we need to speak of justice. They are guided for the most part by reference to the good, as we perceive it and as it is given to us through social practices. To be aware of these ways of living, as we all are, is in itself to know that justice cannot be easily identified with the fact of allocation. Nevertheless there seems to be something especially allocative about justice, and the question that must now be faced is exactly what that is and how to tease it out. Allocation seems to come first in justice, so much so as to inform the very idea of fairness, where it comes second elsewhere. What might make that the case, if case it really be? It cannot simply be that the issue of justice arises in response to the presence of competing claims between persons, for many, perhaps most, of the claims described in the various quick examples offered earlier were claims regularly made between persons. Such claims are routinely settled without reference to the requirements of justice. Of course, justice may well disapprove of that fact, in certain settings at least, but if so it is on the basis of a moral case for the application of justice instead, not on the ground of an alleged conceptual confusion on the part of those who invoke a different means of resolving conflict.

When we engage with people without referring to justice, we engage with them as bearers of values. Their significance to us as persons is a product of the value and disvalue that they bring to life, at any given moment and over the course of time, and more profoundly, of their status as living creatures (human beings as it happens) in possession of a particular species-distinctive capacity for the realization of value and disvalue. In short, people matter just because and to the extent that they are able to make good (and bad) things happen in the world. One might be tempted to think of this, with a nod to Joseph Raz, as the service conception of humanity. Whatever our human proclivities may be, and whatever sense of purpose may be discerned there, our existence derives its significance from its service or lack of service to the good.

Not so as far as justice is concerned. In the eyes and hands of justice, it is persons who matter, both first and foremost. Their significance is detachable, in practice and in principle, from the goodness that they are capable of giving rise to. Most obviously and immediately, justice is committed to certain familiar forms of moral blindness, and thus is constitutionally committed to a discounting of what full moral sight would recognize and record as morally relevant considerations. More profoundly, however, it calls upon the subjects of justice, insofar as they are subjects of justice, to be in principle detachable from the good, in all those dimensions of the good a degree of detachment from which may be necessary to the achievement of justice. There are no a priori exemptions from this broad demand. This leads justice to take persons seriously *simply as persons*, and to invest them with attributions of dignity and respect that do not derive from moral worth, or at least not from a moral worth that is in any way reducible by reference to the record of its exercise. It is in this commitment to persons that justice becomes recognizable, and in the breadth of the recourse to it that justice becomes modern.

Justice famously takes the distinction between persons seriously, and has claimed much credit for that fact. Yet there are two different ways in which one might in principle take that distinction seriously, which justice conflates. The first is to insist on the individuation of value, so as to register it as value in the hands of some valuer, and thereby honour and give effect to what I take to be the absolutely vital relationship between value and valuers.[15] Thus far justice is fully *ad idem* with most enlightened renderings of the good.

The second way to take the distinction between persons seriously, however, is to give primacy to persons, and to accord them value by virtue of their personhood. It is in this respect that the good and the right (to invoke John Rawls) part company. From the perspective of the good, the value of personhood itself (that is, apart from its actual history in individual cases) is always a matter of potential: we are clearly owed something by virtue of our status as persons, but it is something basic to the species, that the species cannot alter, because it is something that is an inescapable feature of the human condition, invulnerable to the exercise of our everyday moral capacity. To think of it another way, it is a capacity that we cannot

---

[15] I follow Joseph Raz in thinking that value is for valuers in the sense that without the possibility of valuers there could be no value: value is there to be appreciated. However, value is not there to serve any valuers in particular (although some parts of it will clearly suit some valuers more than others) so that the perspective offered by justice, in putting persons first, is on the face of it a meta-ethical error that does moral good by offering us a way to achieve determinations that morality cannot generate from its own resources, but that the instantiation of morality in human lives makes necessary in many settings. Thanks to Christoph Kletzer for pressing me to expand this point further.

help but exercise, but it is still its exercise, and the value and disvalue which that gives rise to, that makes the capacity significant. On this view of the moral world, the connection between our significance as persons and our service to the good is maintained.

Not so for justice, from the perspective of which our significance as persons is independent of our service to the good. The crucial point seems to be this. Persons, *as such*, are what matter to justice, and they are bound to do so by the very concept of justice, because it is in their name and for their sake, not that of the good, that justice engages in the familiar determinations that it is its function to provide. Justice still and ultimately serves the good, of course, as any human endeavour is bound to, but it does so by serving persons first. Were it otherwise, there would be no need for justice, distinctively understood, so that justice in the strict sense, once pushed, would quickly collapse back into justice in the broad sense. Justice in the strict sense is bound to put persons first, so as to make sense of itself. It can only do justice by taking the person more seriously than the goodness and badness that he or she gives rise to in the circumstances before it, by acting as if the function of value was to serve the person, rather than as if the function of the person was to serve value, as is actually the case or there would be no value to justice, in its distinctive service to the person.

It is important to be entirely clear here that to see justice as a matter of allocation between persons is not a way of returning to the idea that I set aside earlier, that justice is about competing claims between persons. That would be to put the idea of competition, rather than the idea of a person, at the centre of the picture of the allocations that we engage in when we have justice in mind. It is true that we very often think of allocation in that way, but that is simply because we very often think of allocation in terms of justice. Nevertheless, it is clear that one can readily contemplate the idea of treating a person justly or unjustly even if he or she happened to be the last person on earth. It is no less clear that one can as readily contemplate doing oneself justice, or doing an injustice to oneself.[16] Idiom is not in any way deceptive here. It might be initially tempting to think that this is the case if and only if one treats a person, whether that be oneself or another, with some other person, here a hypothetical person, in mind. On that view of the world, one is capable of treating oneself unjustly only because one is capable of being more than one person, or less extravagantly, is capable of thinking of oneself in that way, as is evident from the very locution in which one is driven to describe the action involved, distinguishing as it does between the persons of one and oneself, the person acting and the person acted upon. Justice, one might think, does require that there be more than one person to allocate among, but there is always another person available, and indeed it is the gaze of justice that enables us to envision that person.

---

[16] Thanks to John Gardner for pressing this point upon me.

Yet that is to miss the point. One can undoubtedly act in these terms, but it is not necessary to do so in order to do justice, to oneself or to another. One does justice or injustice by approaching a person with his or her status as a person uppermost in mind, whether or not any other person is on the scene, imaginatively or otherwise. Joseph Raz once spoke helpfully of the mark of incommensurability, as a way of testing for the presence of that fact, and perhaps the idea of such a mark might be as helpful here. The mark of justice, it seems to me, is respect for persons *as such*.[17] It is not in any sense an accident, or a non-accidental but contingent fact, that justice treats the needy with respect while charity, for example, does not. Charity respects needs but not, other than derivatively, the people who have them. Justice respects people, and as a consequence of that respect, respects their needs. It cares about needs because it cares about people, and people have needs. In short, it is as much the point of justice to respect the needy as persons as it is the point of charity not to do so. Thus the value of the mark: justice is revealed by the presence of the attitude of respect for persons.[18]

Justice respects value, of course, for otherwise it would be arbitrary, yet it does so only as and when value is appropriately filtered by the scheme of justice in question, and thus in the dimensions which that particular scheme takes account of. In blocking off direct respect for value, justice quite deliberately blocks off whole domains of good as well as of bad, matters that there is good reason to take account of as well as matters that there is good reason to ignore. In those domains in which respect for value is blocked off in this way, the respect of justice for people is unvarying. If that seems in any way a surprising or implausible conclusion, its accuracy can be quite simply tested by contemplating the obverse. If the point

---

[17] The use of the term 'persons as such' is not entirely a happy one, but it is the most precise that I can think of. One needs to remember, first, that the term is simply a placeholder and, second, that its content in any given setting is to be established by reference to whatever features are excluded from consideration in that setting by the particular form of justice in issue there. It should not be understood as a reference to a particular, fixed set of characteristics, applicable in every case of justice.

[18] Things are rather more ambivalent and overlapping than that of course. This cuts both ways. Respect for the good very often turns on the conclusions of justice, while in the hands of justice respect for persons is as variable as it is unvarying. Were it otherwise, respect for the good would be indifferent to questions of justice and injustice, so that goodness would be bound to respect the unjust no less than the just, while the operation of justice would be impervious to matters of the good, so that we would be bound to deliver justice without any reference to respect for persons in all their particularity and the bases on which that respect is grounded. Goodness and justice would simply have nothing to say to one another. In fact, of course, it is part of the very purpose of justice, and a central aspect of its proper functioning, to mete out treatment to people in accordance with their needs, deserts, or whatever the appropriate metric of justice is taken to be in any given setting. All those grounds are as much grounds of goodness and its absence as they are grounds of justice and injustice. Justice is quintessentially blindfolded, in this case to certain dimensions of goodness, but it does not follow that its conclusions are blind to the good, for the blindfold is only partial, ignoring some bases of respect for the good in order to focus on others. It is a premise of justice, and the ground of its blindness, that assessment of persons and the goods they embody proceeds from an unvarying respect for them as subjects of justice. Value and concomitant respect then flow through the filter of justice, so that in lieu of the variable respect that goodness would call for is respect for justice, and the unvarying regard it has for persons as persons rather than as embodiments of the good, on which its own partial respect for the good is built.

pressed here were misguided then it would follow that the basic respect of justice is variable. Yet it is fundamental to the very idea of justice that its subjects are equal in its eyes.

So to map the contrast, when we allocate with reference to the good, the allocation is made between claims of the good at the instance of persons. The difficulty with this is that it gives rise to problems of indeterminacy in the lives of persons just as often as the claims embodied in those lives are incommensurable, and allocation has, for whatever reason, good or bad, become necessary. As a result of the incommensurability, there may well be a number of legitimate answers to the question of how an allocation of goods (or bads) ought to take place in any given case, and in the absence of an authoritative determination of which of those legitimate answers is to prevail, there will be ample opportunity for conflict between persons on the behalf of legitimate claims. That is something of real concern to the good, of course, but it is not something that the good can do anything about, simply because the resources of the good are incapable of providing the resolution that persons, and the goodness that their existence embodies, are in need of.

In the setting of justice, this pattern is very consciously upended: the allocation is one that is made between persons, precisely so that there can be a determination for persons. Justice exists to yield decision, and it does its characteristic work both by giving priority to the ingredients of decision, and by doing so through a focus on persons. This helps to explain the prominence of its most notable attendant features, allocation and conflict. The reason that allocation acquires a particular prominence in the scheme of justice is that the scheme is designed above all to secure allocation among persons. As far as those persons are concerned, allocation is just what the scheme is about. Goodness is attended to selectively, via procedures and institutions that, first, possess the authority needed to yield decision and, second, are governed by established perspectives on the good that will make decision more likely, through the application of what Joseph Raz has classified as positive and negative second-order reasons. The further reason that the presence of conflict appears to be a precondition of justice is that in practice the inability to secure rationally determined allocations between persons often yields significant conflict between persons, although it is the good of rational determination for persons rather than the draining of conflict between persons that lies at the heart of the impulse to justice.

Allocation and conflict are not the only leitmotifs of justice, of course. The practice of justice also gives rise to a characteristic emphasis on the significance of the will, together with the attendant institutions of power, as well as the attendant virtue of courage, all of which gain much of their familiar prominence in the modern world as functions of the priority of persons in the scheme of justice. Persons instantiate goodness by the exercise of reason, here straitjacketed by the claims of justice, and of the will, here correspondingly enhanced. In the realm of the good, the will—and the courage that may be called for in its exercise—are necessary to the very possibility of goodness, indeed so much so as to become partly constitutive of it. That is because the will plays its moral role and acquires its moral import by virtue of its capacity to instantiate value as goodness (and disvalue as badness). In the realm of goodness, the practices of reasoning and willing support one another in the realization of value in what we do and what we thereby become. On this rendering of the significance of will, the service conception of humanity is once again preserved.

In the hands of justice, however, the fact of the will, and the value of its exercise, comes before the good, in two ways. Most obviously, the practice of justice is itself an act of willing insofar as it is a practice of decision, one that gives priority to the goodness of determination over the goodness in all that is thereby determined. More fundamentally, however, the practice of justice takes the fact of the will seriously in taking persons seriously, for from the point of view of justice, persons are significant by virtue of the significance of those determinations that make them persons, determinations that they cannot always arrive at unaided, and that it is accordingly the role of justice to render on their behalf and in their stead.

Doing these things gives rise to the price we pay for justice. Justice, of course, seeks to align as far as possible the claims of the good and the claims of decision (itself an aspect of the good) but the alignment is as imperfect as justice is necessary. The further that we extend our reference to justice, by extending the practice of justice to domains in which its presence and its role are permissible rather than vital, the more profound that price becomes.

This much I have more or less emphasized throughout, yet there is further. I have spoken thus far as if justice was the only mode of determining moral conflict when that is clearly not the case. Determinations can be arrived at in a number of ways, by lottery even. What is not only distinctive but also distinctively modern about the determinations of justice is the focus upon persons. That means that the price that is paid in terms of the good by the determinations of justice is different in kind from the price paid in terms of the good by other forms of determination. As inhabitants of the modern world we are consciously sensitive to the price that is exacted by pre-modern, organic, non-deliberative forms of determination, yet correspondingly insensitive to the price we pay for justice.

John Rawls has been much criticized for the alleged austerity of his conception of justice, on the part of critics who thought the austerity self-defeating and critics who regarded it as impoverished. Yet it will be clear that the austerity that Rawls sought to capture through the achievement of reflective equilibrium, and subsequently to depict in the spare lineaments of the original position, is at heart a function of the very concept of justice, rather than of any particular rendering of it, a concept that was embraced as fully by the bulk of Rawls's critics as it was by Rawls himself. Those critics, no less than Rawls, give to the person the priority that justice demands by its definition, though they would attribute to that person certain of the mores of particular communities. In doing so, they render themselves doubly vulnerable, first to the price of justice, and second to the price of community and the relativism to which it is vulnerable in prioritizing mores over morals. In effect, they have sought to embrace two rival mechanisms for determination, each of which can only be ultimately successful by understanding itself in ways that are constitutively opposed to the other.

Rawls has also been much credited, as noted earlier, for his insistence on taking the distinction between persons seriously. Yet utilitarians were surely right, despite their placement of humanity at something quite close to the centre of the moral world, in retaining a degree of recognition for the independence of value from persons, the degree that allows utility to reach the condition of other animals, and that prevents utility from taking persons fully seriously. Justice by contrast, proceeds as if value served humanity: it thus takes persons seriously *qua* persons, from which its particular sense of the distinction between them follows. That distinction, of course, famously makes it difficult to justify the sacrifice of one person for the sake of the well-being of others. Yet that is not entirely a matter for congratulation. We can all readily agree that one person should not be tortured to make others happy, yet we surely both feel and ought to feel a good deal less comfortable with the fact that what blocks the warranting of such torture no less blocks, as a matter of principle, any compelled sacrifice of one person's good to the good of others that cannot be explained in terms of justice to the one person.

1.3 Justice and Its Alternatives

1.3.1 Worlds without Justice

There is much more to be said here, about the alternatives to justice, and about the social practices upon which those alternatives depend. Many of those practices are deeply rooted and local, in a way that modernity has set its face against, and that we have begun to miss, perhaps profoundly so. The backlash against globalization is typically rendered and explained as a backlash against neo-liberalism, and so against certain associated economistic ways of thinking, but it is also, and no less familiarly, a backlash against the scrutiny of justice, on grounds that are sometimes pernicious, as their commonly atavistic character plainly suggests, but that are sometimes morally perceptive. That is how, for example, the xenophobic is able to present itself as morally enlightened: there are indeed morally enlightened reasons for attending to what the xenophobic purports to attend to, though not for rejecting what the xenophobic rejects.

These are not things that a child of the modern world, such as myself, is terribly able to speak of, partly because of the familiar but negotiable problem of cultural distance, yet more importantly perhaps, because of the vast and rich variety of local possibilities for social practice, from among which it is difficult to abstract so as to speak in general terms without becoming guilty of what one might be tempted to call a degree of injustice, were one not so acutely aware that in fact and to the contrary the real danger is that of introducing a foreign degree of justice into the picture.[19] For that reason, I will not attempt to offer an account of those special modes of determination that are latent in the practices of relationships and communities in the way that I have attempted to do for justice. Nevertheless, it seems to me that there are a few, relatively safe preliminary observations that might be made in that respect. Beyond that it is probably wiser to stick to the suggestive.

First, it is wrong to contrast universal justice with the communal, or with ordinary virtue, as Michael Ignatieff put it in a recent Fulbright Lecture.[20] That would be to fall into the relativizing trap that justice rightly sets itself against, as well as into something like the now tired opposition of the liberal and the communitarian. The true contrast is with the values that justice and the political are incapable of delivering, or at least, incapable of delivering well. Sometimes those can be identified with ordinary virtue, sometimes not. Conversely, ordinary virtue is sometimes capable of securing the ends of justice or something close to them,

---

[19] As in the previous sub-chapter (see n. 11), my reference to the modern world is a reference only to a particular culture that is common in the world we now live in. For a consideration of that culture and its defining features, see sub-chapter 1.4.

[20] For the full expression of Ignatieff's view, see *The Ordinary Virtues: Moral Order in a Divided World* (2017). Thanks to Michael for his elegant, considerate, and delicate response to the broad comments I made on the central thesis of his book at a workshop dedicated to it at King's College London.

sometimes not. The interdependencies here are complex, though no less real for that fact. Indeed to simplify them, to look for informing structures, is already to adopt certain of the analytic premises of the perspective of justice.

Second and relatedly, it is wrong too to say that justice is the first, or even the characteristic, virtue of political institutions. Perfectionists are right to deny this. But it is not wrong to notice that politics is quite poor at kindness, generosity, love, and a range of other virtues, and that to the extent that we commit ourselves to politics and its particular virtues we diminish our collective access to rival virtues and to the worlds that they make possible. This diminution is simply what follows from the politicization of our collective moral life, something that continues to gather pace even today, ironically all the more so in many ways as it is challenged by an inarticulate backlash that it all too plausibly and in many cases quite accurately dismisses as reactionary.

This is not to say that the very practice of politics is to be regretted, to espouse a romantic return to a supposed age of the pre-political, to fall into the trap of thinking that to make choices in the manner that politicians do is inherently corrupt. In truth, there is no way not to be political, not merely as a contingent practical matter, for example in communities that are large, complex, and fluid, in the manner of much of the modern world at the moment, but because the demands that politics makes of us are demands that we are bound to make of ourselves, and rightly so, in whatever groupings we may be gathered, albeit that in making those demands of ourselves we are no less bound to recognize their proper limits, as well as their cost, which may run to the very existence and value of the social groupings upon which our life as social beings depends.

Many people today aver that they are simply not political, as if that were a possible position for someone to hold. Yet not being political is itself a deeply political position. For all those who possess the capacity for politics (which is something close to all those who possess rational capacity) it is in fact the politics of apathy, or at least of abstinence, and very dangerous things follow from it, as well of course as very disappointing things, as those young people who have decided not to vote have often discovered to their cost, as they have found themselves in worlds that their grandparents voted for on the basis that they would be good worlds for grandchildren, rather than the worlds that they themselves would have voted for, as good for themselves. So, justice is something that we are morally bound to pursue, as part of the moral necessity of politics, while also being something that we have good reason to temper.

Third, therefore, it is wrong to condemn the pursuit of justice, as if the price attached to it somehow made it unworthy as an ideal. On the contrary, we have much to be deeply grateful to it for. What is not wrong, however, is to notice the correlative price attached to it in specific settings, and so to notice that it certainly is not all that you need, any more than is love. They say (perhaps too often) that love hurts, but so too does justice. To speak in my own voice for a moment, spare me from the one who takes justice as their guide, and the niggardliness of their spirit, no less than the one who insists upon the loyalties of love, and the oppressions that go with them.

Fourth, it is wrong to think that there can be worlds without justice, in the sense of there being worlds in which the writ of justice simply does not run. In a sense, to say this is no more than another way of putting the first of these observations. We are always and inescapably answerable to justice, and so accountable to its demands, in the same way that we are answerable to the presence of every other reason in the world. Culture and commitment have no power to insulate us from the claims of reason, no matter how alien, or how disruptive of the good, those claims might prove to be. Yet that having been said, the presence of commitment of any kind subtly changes the shape of the reasons that reason presses upon us, by changing the perspective from which they are bound to be contemplated on and responded to.

I said earlier (in sub-chapter 1.1.4) that we cannot but see the world in terms of a view from somewhere, and that being the case the settings in which we find ourselves have a vital role to play in framing our particular view of the world, and in shaping our relationship to it, in something the same way, perhaps, that one's height does in framing one's visual and physical perspective (think of Alice in Wonderland), although they have no capacity whatsoever to alter the terms of the world that is viewed, or the scrutiny that it receives. One can inhabit a domain, such as the personal relationship considered in sub-chapter 1.1.2, that precludes scrutiny of certain kinds, and the consequence of one's engagement in that domain is that it is thence that relationship, and in particular the specific preclusions it embodies, that forms the object of immediate scrutiny. It is perhaps something a little like the deflection that occurs in the operation of the normal justification of authority. Reason wants to know in that as in any other case why we do not think for ourselves, and of course the answer cannot be given by thinking for ourselves without foregoing any benefit that observance of the exclusionary reason has to offer. Yet when, in proper recognition of that fact, the answer offered is the presence of the exclusionary reason, reason will thence want to know whether the alleged exclusionary reason is a sound one, and it will want to know that ultimately because it still wants to know why we do not think for ourselves, and the reference to the presence of the exclusionary reason has become the only way of answering that question. In short, morality regularly requires us to be relativistic without thereby asking us to become moral relativists.

Finally, one is bound to notice the connection between different values and the social institutions and social practices that they depend upon for their instantiation. One might reasonably ask whether the contemporary world is not overly monochromatic in these respects, notwithstanding its nominal commitment to diversity. One might wonder whether we are insufficiently attentive to the sources of the diversity that we nominally celebrate, not only of cultures but, more profoundly, of conceptions of the good and the conditions for their articulation. We cannot simultaneously be as morally diverse as we need to be to make liberalism fully meaningful in our hands, and as committed to justice as we need to be to make our liberal societies just societies. The best that we can hope for is that we will find a way to be diverse enough to make the palette of our possibilities a rich one, and also to be just enough to preclude significant iniquities in their assignment, that is, to be ancient as well as modern in our understandings of virtue, to couple the (potential) wisdom of age and the (potential) resolution of youth. Realistically, however, what seems rather more probable, on the evidence of contemporary affairs, is that we are likely to do the opposite, resiling from justice for all the wrong reasons, and embracing the communal uncritically. In that struggle, it is plainly justice that we need to hold on to, while being clear-eyed enough to appreciate its limitations and its trade-offs, the role that those two defining features play in its rejection, and the need to envision a future that takes them both seriously.

What then can be said about the social practices that constitute rivals to justice, and the ways in which they guide our pursuit of the good, for better and for worse? Many social practices arise unconsciously rather than consciously, as casual by-products of shared circumstance, be that circumstance physical, cultural, intellectual, or some other, be it played out in terms of landscape, tradition, economy, or patterns of authority. The mutual recognition of their practitioners, if and when it arises (as it may well not), becomes the recognition of the fact of community, not so much in contrast to other communities, for those may be unknown, as in the assurance of itself. There gradually come to be certain ways of doing things that are understood and accepted as the right way to proceed in that setting, sometimes strongly so, as when actions and attitudes are regarded as more or less compulsory, sometimes temperately so, as when they are regarded as permissible. Precisely how this comes to be is not something that is or ever could be spoken of. Yet once it has been secured, the fact of understanding and acceptance acts as a kind of filter, which more or less excludes all other possibilities, be they rationally eligible or rationally ineligible. In this way, a great many, though not all, dilemmas that stem from the lack of rational determinacy are quietly and effectively resolved without any recourse to deliberation, of the kind that justice engages in. The process at work here is something like the process whereby value comes to be embodied in character as personal virtue, although in the communal setting, as indeed in the personal setting, what is embodied is not necessarily virtuous.

It is a common thought that such practices of propriety are designed to exclude. Sometimes the thought is a sound one, but more often it is not, partly because social practice does not usually look like that, and partly because it would work less well if it did. Social practices do not usually look like that because their creation and deployment is, as I have emphasized, usually not deliberate. They tend to emerge as by-products of what we do for other reasons, and of a subsequent alignment of that experience in the minds of those who have shared it that gives rise to what is commonly described as intersubjectivity, if one can use that term happily without subscribing to its anti-realist implications. Furthermore, the good in such social practices, such as it is, is the good that comes from the ability to pursue value in ways that are relatively structured in advance and recognizable after the fact. Doing this can make the realization of value significantly more likely, if more predictable, and make the appreciation of value in the consequent narrative of one's life that much more rich, complex, and intertwined. None of these things depends on exclusion. To know a social practice in these ways is, of course, to be able to distinguish it from others, actual and hypothetical, but to identify that distinction with the very point of the practice (to the extent that there is one) is to mistake the possible corruption of the practice for its worth.

The real moral concern with such practices, and with the absence of deliberation in their creation and implementation, is the familiar one of absence of reflection and self-examination. These social practices succeed just in the ways that they do not call for, or indeed permit, the level of examination that would reveal their moral arbitrariness. The moral price paid is the entrenchment of social practices as goods when what they are in fact is very often empty and even pernicious. Sometimes the emptiness may not much matter, for it may well become something that is merely rococo about the culture, eccentric but not at all damaging. Sometimes even the perniciousness may not much matter, for it may be a price worth paying for a cultural whole that yields other goods, including the good of other aspects of determination, a whole from which the pernicious could not be successfully severed without adopting attitudes that were inimical to the very cultural acceptance on which the authority of the practices depends. As often, however, they are truly to be condemned. When that happens, one response is a turn to justice, although it is far from the only possible response. Vernacular social orders are as liable to be displaced by a turn to autocracy, or anarchy. Those who recognize good reasons to overthrow them need always to be mindful that doing so does not necessarily yield justice, even when the overthrow is undertaken in the name of justice. This is no less true in miniature, when the social practice is relatively local in terms of its duration, extent, or subject matter, as it is comprehensively, when the social practice helps to constitute a dominant territorial order.

I spoke earlier of the problem of false consciousness, and in doing so implicitly accepted the view that such consciousnesses are something to be regretted, and thus to be dispelled where possible and without too large a cost. Yet it is one of the principal functions of organic social practices, and a contributing element in their value, to develop false consciousnesses. Doing so enables practices to trade ruthlessly on the chimerical value of their purported inevitability and completeness, as well as on their genuine stability, for the very real value that acceptance of them as governing parameters in the articulation of lives individual and social can give rise to (the kind of value that is constituted, in part at least, by stability, community, recognition, and the like), and furthermore, for the many kinds of goodness that may emerge from the standing embrace of such value. It is in these ways that we come not only to be tempted by but actually to discover and profit from the unreliable value of the practice of self-deceit, and the supporting value of myth. Self-satisfaction is not always a bad thing, and self-examination not always a good thing, it turns out, central though it is to the practice of justice, and rightly so, to regard them as such.

Built into this approach to the world is a related idea, that of taking oneself much less seriously than the modern world expects one to. In speaking earlier of the possible shape of a loving relationship, I set aside the possibility of supererogation as being inconsistent with the self-understanding of the participants. One can now perhaps see why there was rather more to that move than respect for intuition, or the possibilities for argument that the move enabled. What such a loving relationship expresses is selflessness in a much deeper sense, a sense that transcends rather than sacrifices self. It is in that sense that love might well be thought of as the highest form of human relation, simply because it is the most uncompromised by the pull of interests other than those, if any, that identify with its own worth. The self-abnegation that this involves on the part of the participants, at least as justice would perceive it, is something that is to be concerned about as far as persons matter *qua* persons. In the modern world, in which persons enjoy pride of place, and in which social practices are very largely shaped with persons in mind, it is something to be very concerned about indeed. That does not mean that such transcendence of oneself is not potentially valuable, and that there may not be good reason to pursue it in whatever setting, and to whatever degree, does not undermine the overall capacity of people to take themselves fully seriously as persons in other settings, and indeed to be so regarded by the other people on whom their dignity and their prospects depend. To transcend oneself in such a way is to achieve in one's very being a blurring of boundaries with others, both as persons and as bearers of different values, and more profoundly, a blurring of boundaries between oneself and the world at large, and hence between oneself and the value that one's life gives rise to. This is selflessness without self-sacrifice, selflessness as a way of being.

A second equally brief aside. To recognize this way of approaching the world and its potential legitimacy helps to expose the extent to which our ordinary thinking about social groups trades upon two different notions of a group, the one conceived in terms of justice, the other conceived in terms of relationship as I have outlined it. Many of the difficulties in thinking about groups, and indeed in thinking about social identity more generally, stem from the misattribution of the features of one, usually older, conception of a group to a group that has in fact been identified by reference to the other conception. A conception that is conceived in terms of justice is often thereby called upon to do the kind of work that it is conceptually incapable of doing, and vice versa.

A final brief aside. There is a common confusion in ordinary life and in political discourse as to what constitutes the direction of influence in the identification of the parameters of justice. For any particular conception of justice there is a question of which considerations that conception rightly excludes, so as to acquire distinctive legitimacy as the valid conception of justice that it is. It is those considerations that come to define what people are regarded as equal in terms of as far as that particular conception of justice is concerned. Given that the considerations in question also form the basis of the legitimacy of the conception of justice in question, it is entirely natural, yet mistaken, to search for some basis in the good to drive that exclusion. In fact, however, it is precisely because the good cannot supply that answer that justice becomes significant. The exclusion must, of course, be one that is permissible in terms of the good (for that is the source of its legitimacy), but it is one that by the premise of its very reason for being could not be determined by reference to the good.

1.3.2 Companionability

In a way there should not be anything very surprising in anything I have said so far. Once it is recognized that justice is not simply the name for all that is good, but is rather the name for a particular value, commonly described as fairness, it follows straightforwardly from the fact of value pluralism that there are bound to be occasions when the claims of justice will be at odds with the claims of other values, and being different in kind from those other claims, will not be open to assessment as better or worse than their rivals. To believe otherwise is to believe, at a minimum, in the unity of the virtues, and despite its impeccable pedigree, that belief is not one that can be reconciled with a belief in the depth of value pluralism. Without the unity of the virtues, justice remains but one value among others, competing for our attention and a place in our lives. To know that much is *ipso facto* to know that justice has its inevitable price, as do its rivals. That price is far from straightforward, of course, because all values depend for many aspects of their realization on the existence of certain social practices, so that the pursuit of certain values depends on the presence of compatible social practices and discourages others, while the presence of certain social practices enables the pursuit of certain compatible values and discourages the pursuit of others. It is in this way that the priority of justice and certain social practices that are characteristic of the modern world (fluid, impersonal, detached, and political) have come into being together, flourish together, and fail together.

Left at that, however, the story seems not only residually counter-intuitive but quite possibly neglectful of other prominent available ways of prioritizing the claims of justice. After all, justice and other values are regular presences in our lives, so that there must be at least some good ways of reconciling them, as *modi vivendi* if nothing more. I will consider two of what strike me as the most straightforward of those, before closing.

One common and attractive thought is that there is companionship rather than rivalry to be found in the relationship between justice and its alternatives. We regularly pursue justice in certain domains and allow it to take a back seat in others. According to some, that is because justice is by its nature called for in certain domains (in the public realm perhaps) but not in others (such as the private realm). Or, to put it from the opposite perspective, certain domains call for justice while others simply do not. One would need to be extremely careful about the articulation of such domains, of course, and to be healthily sceptical of the existing boundaries of those that have been bequeathed to us, lest they incorporate injustices that are subsequently passed off by those who they privilege as practices to which justice inherently does not apply. A good deal of the recent history of feminist practice has been notoriously, and on the whole rightly, excoriating about attempts to secure a domain of the private against the scrutiny of justice. Indeed, a tacit recognition of that fact was implicit in the real doubts that I expressed previously (in the second section) about the legitimacy of personal relationships that neglect justice or otherwise set it aside. Yet a warranted scepticism about the existing boundaries of the private is compatible with the possibility that some kind of companionship between justice and its alternatives is available in principle, however fraught the negotiation of it may be in practice.

If there is to be such a relationship, and if it is to be one that is to be in any way relied upon, there must be principles in terms of which the relationship can be described, principles latent in the very idea of justice, and no less so in the ideas that are encapsulated in its rivals. Those principles would have to be capable of assigning all values to related domains of human activity, not always uncontroversially perhaps, for the project could be subject to marginal exceptions, but for the most part exclusively. Yet in fact there is no conceptual algorithm of that kind that could eliminate the rivalry. Indeed, the thought that there is or could be such an algorithm is only really plausible to the extent that one is prepared to believe that all values, here including justice of course, are nothing other than abstract projections of the character of human activity, and hence of the domains into which that activity is demarcated, from place to place and from time to time. Fit with domain would then be a premise of value itself. Yet the disturbing implication of value pluralism, where pluralism is understood in realist terms, is that conflict between the claims of value is an endemic feature of moral life, one that cannot be escaped by reference either to the content of morality or to the particular domains in which particular dimensions of morality are called upon. It can, of course, be moderated by ideas of appropriateness, but it cannot be displaced. That makes life less easy than it might be, yet also much richer and more rewarding, as well, of course, as more overwhelming and more distressing.

So sometimes it is possible to say that this is a place and a moment to be kind rather than just, or vice versa, but that possibility is one that stems from the presence of social practices that have established that sense of appropriateness, and further, that have constituted it as the common sense of the culture in question, according it the status of a moral fact without making it one. As much is as true of the social practices, characteristic of the modern world, in which the priority of justice is embedded. We can turn to those practices to discover the proper place of justice as we know and live it, but we cannot look to justice, or to any other value, to scrutinize or supplant those practices by telling us where justice belongs and where it doesn't. It is this, rather than some logic of harmony and reconciliation, that is inherent to the idea of justice, so as to make it the idea that it is rather than some other. From the point of view of justice, it is not that justice is in principle a value that is bound to run everywhere, so that we should only ever act in accordance with justice. Rather it is the more modest claim, that any scheme of assignment, according to which justice is appropriate in some settings and not others, is itself susceptible to the scrutiny of justice, if not to warrant its overthrow then at least to open our eyes to its very real cost. That means that justice cannot be kept in what is supposed to be its place. Its reach is as broad and demanding as is the reach of reason. We are always and everywhere accountable to justice, although when we render to justice what is its due we may well give up something no less valuable.

Another, perhaps even more appealing, thought is that justice sets a threshold for legitimate social order, past which other values describe courses of human interaction that are consistent with justice without being animated by it. Such patterns of accommodation are not only possible but familiar features of our lives. Yet that is because we very often make a practice of reconciling the irreconcilable, sometimes ad hoc and individually, sometimes by creating and maintaining social practices that constitute working compromises (between the rational and the irrational, or between different kinds of rational claim), some of those compromises morally permissible, some not, some of them morally intelligible in terms of the good that they give rise to, so as to be at least excusable, some not. The fact that we very often get by in these ways might show that we have a reason to get by (as indeed we well may), or that we believe that we do, but it does not show that there is nothing to get by, that justice finishes its work where other values begin theirs, so that conflict between them is not a genuine problem in the conduct of our lives.

There is nothing I can discern in the idea of justice to suggest that its remit is an austere one, that it has nothing to say to the details of the allocations between persons, that its role is exhausted by laying the foundations for the operations of other values. Surely to live justly, as it is admirable to do, is to be animated by justice and answerable to its demands in all that one does. The same, of course, can be said of the values and virtues with which justice is potentially in tension. It is not their place to take as their premise the foundations that justice would lay down. Like the claims of justice, their claims reach in both directions, from the foundational to surface detail, so as to make their voice heard and their presence felt in all parts of our lives. One way to see this, it seems to me, is to remind oneself that value does not exist for humans alone, making it difficult to think that it could be aligned with anything like a threshold in our lives.

In the end, these are different gods with different appetites. Whether we have chosen to worship at the altar of one rather than the other, or whether we are in a dilemma of belief, or whether we are bound to improvise a course among their claims as a sailing vessel navigates a course among the claims of wind, water, and provisional destination, we must recognize that we cannot hope to honour both in the same breath.

1.4 Justice and Respect for Persons

The preceding sub-chapters in this part have sought to explore the relation between the pursuit of justice and respect for persons as such, and what implications that might have for the presence of other values in our lives. Yet that is far from the whole story. What has not been done is to probe the order of influence between those two practices. What if one were to look at the situation from the opposite perspective, so as to approach it from the perspective of respect for persons as such, rather than from the perspective of justice? Is that as likely to be the order of influence in the articulation of justice as we now know it? Does respect for persons as such inspire our present concern for justice? If so, is the price that we pay for justice but one instance of a price that we choose, or at least are prepared to pay, to sustain a world of a certain kind, a world that is based on respect for persons as such, the world that we commonly recognize and describe as modern? If so, what gives rise to this wider price, and in what circumstances might it be thought to be a price worth paying, assuming that we have any real say in the matter? The possibility that presents itself for consideration is that in its respect for persons as such the modern pursuit of justice participates in a broader cultural practice in which it is only partly implicated (given the long and rich history of justice in other settings) and for which it is only partly responsible. Let me approach that possibility by looking more closely at the idea of persons as such, and why that idea might matter.

Derek Parfit left us a great many things to be grateful for, but surely among the most striking aspects of his vivid legacy, and perhaps the one likely to have caused most pain to those who knew him well, or at least well enough to mourn especially his untimely death, and so to mourn the distinctive fact of his being and its loss, is the disruptive idea of the insignificance of personal identity.[21] There is a good deal less to us as individuals, to what made Derek Derek (to paraphrase his way of putting it) than we tend to think. Or so Parfit famously maintained. It was a view of personal identity that was striking in particular for its originality, but also for the extent to which it was, and remains, deeply at odds with the temper of the times, which has been to regard personal identity, first in the Parfitian sense, and then by somewhat problematic extension, in what contemporary practice takes to be individual and collective identities, as being of very great significance indeed. What is more, in the latter, more everyday sense of personal identity, the temper of the times, and the basic respect that it calls for, goes a crucial step beyond what can be rendered in terms of personal identity as Parfit presented it. The present moment does not simply take the distinctiveness of our individual existences to be a significant fact, one that marks out the separateness of persons and their history; it

---

[21] I wrote this in early 2017, and so spoke of mourning Parfit, innocent of the loss of John Gardner, no less a philosophical creative, that lay ahead. I knew, admired, and so mourned Derek, but John was my oldest and closest friend.

further takes those existences to be of great and ineliminable value in and of themselves, and then reshapes and extends its baseline respect for personal identity to that end.[22] That position has as much to do with morality as with personal identity, and so is as susceptible to the insights of moral philosophy as to those of the philosophy of mind.

It seems to me, then, that there is another, no less illuminating route to a semi-Parfitian conclusion. Whether or not personal identity has the substance (or lack of substance) that Parfit claimed for it, there is reason to believe that it does not figure largely in our moral life, and by extension, in the achievement of our well-being. Indeed, it seems to me difficult to discern moral import of any kind in the bare fact of human distinctiveness, be that distinctiveness individual or collective. As I see it, the value of Derek did not lie in his being Derek, strictly speaking, but rather lay in the capacities that he was able to call upon (whether those were distinctive to him or not), the virtues that he was consequently able to attain, and the goodness that his existence ultimately gave rise to in the world, all these, of course, set against whatever were his weaknesses, his vices, and his badnesses. That may seem a small point, yet contemporary neglect of it is crucial to what I have called the temper of the times. Moral respect is properly owed, in Derek's case and in every other, to moral achievement, actual and potential, and derivatively to persons, and that means that it is owed to persons only in virtue of the qualities in them (some of which are universal features of the human condition, others of which are more locally generic) that have given rise to value in the past and/or may give rise to value in the future. What made Derek Derek does not figure in such an account.

To bring the point fully home, as I suppose one is bound to, whatever may be owed to me as a human being has nothing to do with whatever makes me Timothy. My Tim-ness is of no moral significance. To put it baldly, it does not matter that I am me. This is not an expression of humility on my part, or of self-effacement. On the contrary, it is compatible with very real vanity. Whatever there is to be said for and against me, by myself or others, may commonly be filed under the label Tim, but in fact it has nothing to do with what makes me Tim, however special Tim may seem to me. Suppose that I had a doppelganger, Tim^1, a person with the same qualities and capacities as mine but with a different personal identity. Could it possibly be thought that there was value to the fact of being Tim^1 rather than Tim, a value over and above that which would be registered by a proper account of the life that Tim^1 has led and could be expected to lead, which would, by his very definition as my doppelganger, be no different in quality from that of the life led by Tim? What would there be in Tim^1 to give rise to such value?

---

[22] It does so in two stages, moving from the moral significance of persons *qua* persons to the moral significance of certain categories of person, *qua* persons of that category, respect for which continues to be detached from their qualities and their achievements, as persons and as persons of that category.

Consider an analogy between persons and places. Suppose that a morally significant action were to occur in a certain precise place, that is, at a certain longitude and latitude, as indeed actions are wont to. Suppose further that the action in question occurred at a certain precise moment. That place (Paris, say) and time (14 July 1789, say) might be morally significant in consequence, but only as nomers for moral capacities and their deployment, capacities that are in certain instances connected to the qualities of a landscape, or to the physical and cultural possibilities that we associate with an era. There is no more. In themselves, place and time have no capacities of their own that could conceivably give rise to moral significance. As much is true of Tim-ness and the locus that it identifies, whatever that may be, and however it may change over time.

What then of personal identity in the more colloquial, familiar, and character-driven sense? What of the special package of human qualities, be they native or acquired, that makes each one of us the particular kind of person that we are? I recall a group of employees, of whom I was one, being asked once, at an office community-building exercise, to name what we took to be our three notable personal characteristics, and in my case answering, solitary, patient, and restless. Take those three as a useful starting point. The presence in me of those characteristics, such as it is, is an artefact, to be evaluated, not a value in itself. As such, it operates in the realm of goodness and badness, in which characteristics are typically, and special cases aside, morally open-ended, open to being deployed for better and/or for worse.[23] My personal identity in this everyday sense is as morally significant as it now functions, has functioned, and is liable to function, for good or for ill. Its moral significance, in short, is a product of its moral achievement or lack of achievement, and only derivatively, if at all, of its being. To put it succinctly, personal identity in this sense is a candidate for value, open to question, subject to judgement, rather than being valuable in itself (as is also true of the human condition generally).[24] In itself, it has no more value than does personal identity precisely understood, and for the same reason. Distinctiveness may prove to be valuable, if and when it gives rise to value in the world (be that value novel or familiar), but it is not valuable simply by virtue of its distinctiveness. To bring the point home once again, in just what ways has it been and might it prove to be good to be solitary, patient, and restless? That is the question that value poses.

Think here of personal art collections, and the extent to which those who amass them regard them as expressions of their own sensibilities, as valuable for that

---

[23] See Chapter 3 (The Goodness of Equality) for an account of the relation between value and goodness. I say 'typically' and 'special cases aside' because a person can be characteristically kind, and that is always a valuable thing, even though the claims that the kindness gives voice to will often have to be balanced against the claims of other values, and sometimes have to give way to them, in consequence of a decision to prioritize a different claim, in any setting where the practice of kindness conflicts with other valuable practices.

[24] See Macklem and Gardner, 'Human Disability' (2014) 25 KLJ 60.

fact, and so worthy of preservation intact, ideally under their collector's name, as a tribute to the taste and perception that are distinctively those of the collector and, crucially, for the sake of that very distinctiveness, so that the taste and perception that they reflect are recognized as worthy, at least in part, just for the particular flavour of character that they embody. It is not that such character is thought to be important because of the good taste and perception that it embodies, if and to the extent that it does so; rather that the taste and perception in question are thought to matter, at least in part, just because they are characteristic of the collector. Sometimes such collections are individual, sometimes they are municipal, sometimes national. As they pass into subsequent hands, they risk being revealed as empty, records only of the phenomenon of vanity without foundation, unless and to the extent that the components of the collection actually speak to one another in ways that are resonant, ways that may well constitute a tribute to the qualities of the collector, but tribute of a different kind than the collector had in mind.[25]

This is not to overlook or deny the aesthetics of an existence and the expressions it may find. Lives are often things of intrinsic beauty, be that beauty physical, intellectual, or emotional. When, in some brief and passing moment, we find ourselves simply delighted by the very presence of another, or later, perhaps when a beloved older relative dies, find ourselves bereft at the loss of the flavour of that person's being and its peculiar evocativeness, soon to fade, never to be reproduced, a loss not only of a person but of the culture of which they were a surviving fragment, we seem to be responding to the value of a person, rather than to the value that a person may give rise to. Yet the point that is being pressed here is not that the value of a person is instrumental in character rather than intrinsic (and the aesthetic, being non-productive, is a straightforward case of the intrinsic value of a person), but that the value that a person gives rise to, be that instrumental or intrinsic, is not the value of the person as such. To repeat, the person in this aesthetic sense, as in every other working sense, is but a candidate for value. By contrast, the value of the person in the sense that justice speaks to, and that the modern world takes seriously, is the value of a person apart from any account of their goodness and its character, including the aesthetic, the value of a life that we sometimes refer to in terms of dignity, and that we frequently seek protection for under the heading of respect. If there are such persons in the world, to be discovered by shearing our lives of the record and prospect of their moral history and character, altogether or in particular dimensions, so as to place those lives beyond evaluation to that

---

[25] This illustration is rather rarefied. The same pattern is observable in the mix tapes that people used to put together on cassette, for the sake of the music they contained, of course, but also for the personal expression of taste that the selection embodied. Indeed, the pattern is observable in everything that we undertake (in part at least) as an expression of ourselves, not simply because that suits us, but because we believe that we matter in ways that warrant expression, where our mattering is understood as a given, as a reflection and function of our very being, rather than as a possibility.

extent, it is hard to see what sort of intrinsic value there could be thought to be in their bare existence.

Joseph Raz has written illuminatingly of the value of life itself as an enabling value, one that makes value possible without otherwise being valuable in itself.[26] The enabling value of life itself, which is to be found in nearly every human life, stems from the connection, not inevitably present, between certain features of the human condition, sensual, cognitive, volitional, and the creation, realization, and appreciation of value in the world, and even more fundamentally, lest one confine evaluation to the human condition, between the presence of valuers of whatever kind, and their particular capacities for participation in value, and the possibility of value in the world. Even a status as elemental as this one is open to question in any particular case, albeit that the question may in nearly every case be readily answered in the affirmative. That status, elemental though it is, is not the status of the person that the modern world is committed to taking seriously by placing beyond questioning.

So, the person does not much matter and yet we have built a culture around the idea that it matters fundamentally.[27] To put it summarily, the thought here is this, that in the culture of modernity with which we are familiar, the influence of the defining elements of that culture runs in both directions at once, in complex patterns

---

[26] Raz, *The Practice of Value* (2003).

[27] There is an important caveat here, which I have sought to draw attention to at several points but which deserves further emphasis. Person and place matter greatly as the starting points from which our lives must proceed at any given moment. We may become new people in new places, indeed are bound to do so to some degree, even if what we become and in what setting is the product of an attempt to replicate what and where we have been previously, but we can only ever get to there from here. It follows that we can be significantly damaged by a failure to recognize the true contours of our present existence on the part of all those upon whom our flourishing depends. That failure of recognition, be it negligent or wilful, lies at the heart of many forms of wrongful discrimination. Yet the fact that recognition of what we are at any given moment is central to our flourishing, present and future, does not support the conclusion that what we are at that given moment is valuable. It may not be valuable, but we cannot hope to improve upon it, or transform it into something different but no less good, without proper attention to exactly what it now is, proper attention on our part as well as on the part of our fellows.

A further clarification might be helpful at this point, though it is implicit in much of what follows. To be a person of some kind, just as to be a member of a particular culture, or a bearer of any of the features of personal identity that we are currently familiar with (in the everyday sense of that idea), is necessarily to partake in some degree of stability, and that stability may have value in its own right, just because it in turn makes other valuable things possible, such as goals in life, and their sharing with others, as well as practices of self-recognition and community. It remains the case, however, given that the role of stability is always auxiliary and supportive, that the value of stability is contingent on the value of what stability makes possible. It follows that the pursuit and practice of stability is as apt to make things go badly as to make them go well. We know this all too vividly, because we have become all too familiar, particularly in the modern, liberal era, with the sometimes grotesque price that a commitment to certain forms of stability, those that have been (or ought to have been) subsequently recognized as unworthy or worse, has exacted on those whom the stability excluded, internally and externally, as well as on the fabric of the world, physical and moral, and the place and flourishing of other beings there. It is also the case, of course, that *instability* can have value, so that the returns of stability in general, as well as of the particular forms that it may take, are nested within, and hostage to, the returns of the ways of life of which they are constitutive elements. For further exploration of commonality and its consequences, see sub-chapter 3.4.

of mutual support, from the presence of justice (and other like values) in contemporary social practices to the status of the person there (and derivatively and subordinately, to the status of certain categories of persons), and correlatively, from the status of the person or persons to the presence of justice, and its political prominence, that serves to constitute and sustain that status of the person in our social and political relations. This interdependence is not in itself a matter of moral concern. What does matter is the degree to which the detachment that it entails, of persons from value, like the older detachment of value from persons, has the potential to make the pursuit of one destructive of the other, so that we secure the person from the value that makes personhood matter, just as we once secured value from the significance of persons that gave value life (and so once pursued value at the expense of the fact of life, and its instantiation in persons, that provides value with the import it acquires, and the participation in life that it gains access to, through the animating fact of its practice).

Let me unpack that a little. The satiability of the demands of value, and the satiability of the demands of life, on which so much depends, become possible in practice just because and to the extent that value and life each act as a check upon the demands of the other. On the one hand, the project of well-being instantiates the demands of value in life, making those demands finite and productive in the same gesture. On the other hand, the quest for value in life instantiates the demands of the person as such in an account of goodness and badness, which serves to record the distinctive richness and meaning of a person's life, its successes and failures, rather than its bare existence. When value and persons, persons and values, are detached from one another, a price is paid for the detachment. When value dominates, lives are sacrificed; when the person dominates, value is sacrificed.

That way of putting things is still abstract, not entirely easy to penetrate, and slightly overstated. It invites expansion and expression in more approachable terms. Just how exactly, in everyday terms, does the alleged sacrifice of life to value and of value to life arise? Is the concern set out here merely an abstract one, with little practical import? I think not. My sense is that the concern stems from the very nature of the practice of value. Put another way, it is a quintessentially practical problem, rather than an abstract one that we might choose to overlook. Let me begin with a sketch of the practice as we currently know it, and of the challenge that it poses for us.

The detachment of persons from value, or value from persons, is not some cultural accident. Rather it is a widely approved cultural ambition. It is often said in the world today that people are not actually equal but must be treated as such. In the same spirit, the modern era characteristically detaches the practice of respect from the bases of respect, so as to generate respect for persons as such. This is taken to be a fundamental status, owed to all, for which no one can be called to account, and from which other subsidiary and nested forms of status, conceived along similar lines, are derived. Its endorsement involves an inversion of the standard relation between values and persons, so as to treat failures of respect in certain particular domains as failures to acknowledge the presence of a status that is unquestionably present in us all. What is sought is respect for persons without ground and without differentiation.

Where is the harm in that, one might ask? Consider this. Joseph Raz once made the claim that the values that lie at the heart of well-being are all diminishing and satiable.[28] That means, in effect, that the pursuit of value in our lives is regulated by the demands of well-being. It needs no other check upon its claims to bring it into service of every life in any setting. Well-being is something that we can approach and achieve, and the same becomes derivatively true of the presence of value in our lives, as long as that value is harnessed to the achievement of well-being. It becomes possible to know whether and to what extent people have enough value in their lives, and derivatively, how far they fall short and what sort of claims upon their fellows that might give rise to. Goodness is not simply an aspiration, an ideal, that can never be brought fully down to earth, so as to come within our grasp. It is something that can be achieved, that can generate satisfaction in those who pursue it. The interesting possibility is that this phenomenon is bidirectional, so that diminution and satiation flow not only from well-being to value, in the way that Raz drew attention to, but from value to well-being, and further, that the phenomenon stems from the interdependency of value and valuers, rather than from some special fact about human well-being. If that is true, then the practice of respect for persons as such poses a threat to the value of our lives, as paradoxical as that may seem.

Let me begin by sketching the traditional case, for the disabilities of the past are easier to recognize than are the disabilities of the present. Take a familiar practice, still relatively common in the contemporary world without being characteristically modern. All too often persons, sometimes individuals, sometimes groups, are sacrificed in the name of collective ideals, be those ideals religious or political. Ideals that are called upon to play this role are characteristically formed out of combinations of values that would otherwise lack easy affinity, so as to create packages that we commonly describe as ideologies, historical artefacts that embody compelling and culturally characteristic recipes for the combination of incommensurable values. This is by no means a bad thing. There may well be value in the recipe and its realization, value that could not be obtained otherwise. Ideologies are not necessarily irrational, as their pejorative treatment too often assumes they are. Yet the priority that they claim for themselves, over other less structured ways of being as well as over other ideologies, is achieved not merely at the price of other values, but at the price of all those persons and groups of persons whose interests and commitments, and hence whose well-being, is formed of those other values, a price that often rises to the level of persecution. Even as we see reason to support such

---

[28] Raz, *The Morality of Freedom* (1986), 240ff.

ideologies, we are bound also to recognize their shortage of humanity. Even at the lowest level, in the construction and deployment of political binaries such as left and right, people are excluded, diminished, denied respect, not taken seriously, regarded in overly blunt terms as either fools or villains. The more strongly drawn those binaries are, the more strongly they exclude and diminish, ultimately to the point of denying full humanity to all those who fall on the wrong side of them.[29]

Continue with a more local case, one formed from similar materials. Commitment to value in the life of any person may be sufficiently single-minded as to pose a threat to well-being, in that person's life and in the lives of others. Trivial instances of this abound. Scholars absorbed in thought of a certain kind go out of doors without thinking to put their coats on. More seriously, they commonly neglect the claims upon them of members of their family, friends, colleagues, not to speak of strangers. Meals grow cold, appointments are unkept, the welfare of others is not taken sufficiently seriously. Even in their own lives, the single-mindedness of certain scholars, and others like them, imperils persons, because its essence lies in a conscious or unconscious neglect of well-being, starting with that of the person who practises it, but very often running to that of others.[30] Value that is pursued single-mindedly in this manner becomes non-diminishing and insatiable just because and to the extent of the distance between the quality of its pursuit and the well-being of all those who are shaped by the pursuit. Lives and their well-being are thus sacrificed to the pursuit of value, in whole or in part.

Now consider the converse situation, more common in the present day, more characteristic of what we think of as modernity. At least three familiar strands present themselves, affecting value in our own lives, in those of other human beings, and in those of other creatures. The first of these is the one that I have spent the bulk of this chapter exploring. In the conduct of our personal lives, we regularly confront insatiability in settings in which the pursuit of justice proves to be imperfectly satisfying in our hands, so that people receive the justice they have sought and yet in doing so remain unfulfilled. There are two possible reasons for this. First, the resolution that justice yields is necessarily at the price of all those other values with which the terms of justice are in conflict, other values the claims of which upon the persons in question are undiminished by the achievement of justice. This is perhaps the least troubling species of insatiability, because it involves a familiar trade-off between the achievement of one value and failure to achieve all those other values with which that value is incompatible, a trade-off that is bound to occur, within or without a practice of respect for persons as such. Satisfaction is available here, albeit that one species of it is obtained at the expense

---

[29] Like any other value, justice may become the focus of an ideology, and thereby put whatever value justice secures before the well-being of persons, but when it does so it operates in a pre-modern rather than modern manner.
[30] Macklem and Gardner, 'Value, Interest, and Well-Being' (2006) 18 Utilitas 362.

of another. The expense gives us ground for real regret without thereby becoming an all-things-considered reason to have acted differently.

Second, however, it is often the case that the answer given by justice is not satisfying because it answers to a conception of the person that even justice cannot sate. If and to the extent that an ideal of the person as such becomes the focus of a project of justice, to which justice must answer, justice can never offer satisfaction even in its own terms. This follows from the fact that respect for the person as such is, by its very terms, unqualified by any engagement with or accountability to value, including the value that justice secures, whatever that may be in any given setting. The demands of a person as so conceived cannot be captured and expressed in terms of particular values and the extent to which they are satisfied or unsatisfied, and so cannot partake of the richness and satisfaction that those values have to offer. What cannot be diminished cannot be satisfied either. Well-being is the inevitable casualty, for the straightforward reason that there can be no well-being in a setting in which respect for being (in the form of the person as such) has been quite carefully detached from questions of wellness (questions that turn on the richness and distinctiveness of the values that make each person or group of persons the creatures that they are and enable them to matter as they do, and the extent to which satisfaction of those values amounts to flourishing).

Apparently still more troubling are situations in which a commitment to respect for persons as such becomes the ground for a commitment to a range of evaluative currencies (justice, equality, respect, status, and others) all of which are insatiable. The larger the role that these currencies play in the shaping of our lives, individual and collective, the more that we become unsatisfiable in the living of those lives, and the less likely we become to achieve anything like well-being. This happens to the extent that our investment in such currencies cuts us off from all those values the pursuit of which requires the priority of their claims over the claims of the person as such. The more modern we are in this sense, the more insatiable we become. Yet appearances notwithstanding, the ultimate risk, of what one might think of as a complete corporate takeover of the person by the person as such, of the satiable by the insatiable, seems quite low, partly because there are strong countervailing tendencies to pay attention to well-being, and partly because the claims of the person as such, whether they are expressed through justice or otherwise, embody their own forms of partial reference to the good and in so doing are in a strong position to secure some portion of well-being. Nevertheless, the possibility of a significant failure of satisfaction on these grounds seems real.

The price of tribute to the person as such is highest in interpersonal relations. The difficulty in this setting stems from the fact that the person as such is not always a universal figure, expressing the respect owed to every human being *qua* human being. It is also a local figure, expressing the respect owed to human beings of certain special kinds. In addressing questions of respect for persons of any particular kind, we are bound to adjudicate the claims of different kinds of persons as such, claims that will be at odds with one another just as often as those persons differ from one another and seek respect for that fact as well as in spite of it. Yet the priority of the person as such removes the currency in terms of which such claims could be adjudicated, in whatever domain the priority is established. When we think in terms of need in this way, for example, the sense of need that is invoked is derived, not from a process of self-examination, self-understanding, and consequent grasp of what is called for in one's own case and/or that of one's fellows, but by a perception of status that is abstract and other-regarding, of wanting something, though nothing in particular, just because others have it, or more precisely, given the fact that strictly speaking there is nothing for those others to have that would mark them out to the extent that they too are regarded as persons as such, because they appear to have it. When people ask in this spirit for respect for their person (and for its needs), what they ask for is not something that could ever be instantiated in response to the details of their condition and what those details call for. Rather it is something that partakes in all those things without being composed of them, and so without being satiable through them. The consequence is that the demands of the person as such become both undiminishing and insatiable, and when they conflict, which is just as often as persons as such are distinguished from one another, so as to pit the claims of one kind of persons as such against another kind, lack all capacity to speak to one another, as one human being would standardly do to another human being otherwise.

Nor are human beings alone in the world in terms of participation in reason and in value. Other living things and even non-living things give rise to goodness and badness through their existence. The Earth itself is a good thing and has reason to be, as well as to be better rather than worse. Yet the claims of the person as such leave no room for the recognition of valuers that are not persons, and so amplify the predatory tendencies that the modern world displays in its relation to the global environment and the place of other participants in value there, from other living creatures to all else in the world that is capable of faring better and worse, however severely limited and non-cognitive may be their own role in contributing to those possibilities. What binds human beings to the non-human features of the world is common participation in value. The sun does not shine for us alone, nor the earth bear fruit, and it is only through the recognition of that fact that we are able to acquire a proper sense of our shared role, and the mutual support it entails, in responding to the demands of value, in the construction of a world that is not simply detritus in space, but something with the capacity to be rich, beautiful, and good, albeit and inescapably no less complex, troubled, and vulnerable. Which brings me to what is perhaps the crucial point.

It will be apparent from what I have just said that the patterns of value and vulnerability that arise here are not some function of the human condition, but rather products of the basic relationship between value and valuers. As Joseph Raz has pointed out, value depends upon the possibility of valuers. Without that possibility there could be no value. Value is there to be appreciated. Yet it is even more straightforwardly the case that valuers depend on the presence of value for everything that might make their lives matter, individually and collectively. That fact is what gives our existence its richness and meaning, but also its necessary vulnerability. Painful as it may seem, value and vulnerability to its absence are in fact mutually dependent. Without that vulnerability there would be no possibility of value in our lives.[31] This pattern of mutual dependency is what constitutes the fragile venture in which we are all engaged, a venture that is precisely as fraught as it is potentially rewarding. Value and vulnerability to its absence are inseparable partners in securing the meaning and worth of our existence. We cannot hope to embrace one without embracing the other, avoid one without avoiding the other. When we insist upon the invulnerability of respect for persons as such we insist upon a condition and status that is also immune to the possibility of value and to the significance that value makes of our lives.

Yet if that much is true, and more or less straightforwardly so, why should the practices of modernity be thought to be so misguided as to seek to avoid the unavoidable? The question here is not a psychological one. Special cases aside, people do things in the belief that doing those things is supported by the balance of reasons, and the reasons that guide people accordingly are unavoidably candidates for the good. What is the candidate for the good here, and is it a sound one? The answer, it seems to me, is that this is a case of securing value by indirection. Good can often be achieved by attributing respect where respect may not actually be warranted. Doing so prevents, or at least discourages, the discounting of human beings, and so ensures that we remain alert to the other dimensions, and other moments, in which those human beings may warrant our respect, dimensions and moments that the overall discounting of human beings, directly or indirectly, in whole or in part, might otherwise lead us to overlook. This, it seems to me, is unquestionably a sound ambition, as well as a very familiar one, but only up to a point. The difficulty that it can give rise to is a consequence of the tendency to take a project of respect without warrant too literally, and thus too far. Doing so creates its own vulnerabilities, some of them more damaging than those that they foreclose.

So, we are careful not to discount the very young or the very old on the basis of rational frailty, the mentally or physically disabled on the basis of their disability, the genders on the basis of their gender, and cultures on the basis of their cultural idiosyncrasies. Yet in doing so we often find ourselves reminded, in setting

---

[31] It is possible to imagine an ideal world in which the presence of value in the lives of valuers was completely assured, so that vulnerability to its absence did not arise. There are two reasons to prefer the rather less than ideal world that we actually live in. The first is that many values are constituted, at least in part, by vulnerability to their absence. Access to such values depends on a willingness to expose ourselves to that vulnerability. The second is that our engagement with value is open-ended and creative, so as to enlarge the possibilities for value that would have existed in an ideal world. That carries risks. See in particular sub-chapter 4.2.

after setting, that we may not be doing the objects of our concern any real favours thereby. What matters in the end is that we make the proper allowances for people, the allowances that will promote their flourishing no less than ours, not that we make sure not to make allowances for people on certain bases just because the practice of making such allowances carries with it a significant risk of making allowances that are unwarranted. Respect for persons as such is the most extreme case of a refusal to discount, in that no allowance of any kind is to be made for either strengths or weaknesses in any particular dimensions in which people are open to being respected and not respected. Instead, people are to be respected without differentiation, in every dimension and at every moment.

There is undoubtedly real good to be found in this, as I have noted. Yet the cost of pursuing it can be no less real, when respect for persons as such fails to be attentive to the case-by-case claims of value that it ultimately remains its role to serve, albeit indirectly rather than directly. The cost can even be runaway, as when the failure of attention to the claims of value is either comprehensive or critical, whether that be for a society (unlikely as that is, as indicated earlier) or for particular people.

The problem is one of a good idea taken too far. It arises whenever respect for persons as such claims or is accorded basic priority over the demands of value in the lives of valuers, without attention to its ultimate basis in value. That is to say, the problem arises whenever a practice of respect for persons as such fails to register some set of social practices that functions to ground respect in value and in wellbeing, as those things play out in the life of each one of us, social practices that can, of course, include the practice of justice, as and when justice is directly linked to value. It is that linkage to value that is crucial to the ability of justice to serve the cause of value personified rather than the cause of the person as such.[32] Even if the likelihood is small of the cost of inattention to the specifics of value becoming runaway, the likelihood of it being critical in the lives of certain people is significant. When that happens people are respected but not valued.

A final, modest aside, on the pursuit of the insatiable, its rewards, and its price, and on the supporting modern practice of respect for persons as such, with its consequent blindness to what an evaluation of their particular character and predicament might call for in any given setting. In the previous discussion and at points earlier in this chapter I have consciously neglected (so as not to digress from the problem of justice) what is perhaps the most straightforward, some might say the boldest, modern instance of a suppression of the linkage to value distinctively

---

[32] That is why justice does not have to look like this or present this vulnerability. One familiar way of containing the claims of justice is to channel them through the institution of the law, and thereby not only to restrict them to the ambit of the law's domains, but to limit their vindication to what is permitted by the specialized, even quaint workings of the law, with its many limitations on comprehension and its no less limited remedial constraints, and the consequently confined resources available there from which to craft a just outcome.

understood, and of the corresponding substitution of an insatiable currency of value for a satiable currency (one that would be satiable because of its linkage to well-being), namely the case of economic value, in which the presence of value in the world (of whatever apparently distinctive kind) is in principle open to being understood monistically and in monetary terms. A few observations on this practice of neglect and substitution might be helpful before closing.

First, and most obviously, there is no reconciliation possible (although there are obviously working accommodations) between the recognition of economic value and the recognition of values more generally, for economic value depends for its operation and import on a denial of the fundamental incommensurability in terms of which the disparate values that are said to give rise to it are apparently composed, and that according to pluralists are actually composed (given that it is the incommensurability of those values that defines and sustains their distinctiveness and diversity). Each account of value claims primacy over the other, and that fact is central to the understanding of either. If a value cannot be ultimately captured in monetary terms, then monetary terms are but an imperfect proxy for that value, and vice versa.

Second, the linkage of economic value to the insatiable (say, to the satisfaction of desires) is on the face of it highly attractive to many, for it gives rise to a currency of value for which demand is in principle unlimited, creating prospects for like increases in value (so understood), consequent wealth, and the well-being that those things are presumed to give rise to, not least of course on the part of those in a position to generate the demand and consequent value, but not confined to them either.

Third, the picture of economic value at work here is also rationally appealing, and frequently justifiable, in terms of value more generally, for the connection between the two species of value, though not inevitable, is in practice entirely sound in a great many settings, all those in which economic value is a more or less satisfactory medium of exchange for value otherwise understood, as when food is bought and rent is paid. Yet, and as we all know, the genuine connection between these two profoundly contrasting practices of value is always elusive and often absent; it precludes a wide range of values, all those that are insusceptible, or at least resistant, to economic exchange; and it is often realized more readily by some than by others (most obviously by the poor, though one has to be careful here not to identify the categories in play with those who are understood in terms of economic value in the first place). Most fundamentally, if there is any substance to values other than economic value, then economic value has different implications for value in different hands, just because and to the extent that the needs and desires that underpin it are not actually fungible, despite the returns in terms of value that can follow from treating them as if they were. It is not so much that a dollar means more to some than to others; it is that for any given person or at any given moment a dollar may mean something entirely different or nothing at all.

For these reasons and more, the pursuit of economic value is a practice that is at once productive of value and all too often merely beguiling. The cases in which schemes of economic value do not even begin to deliver the value they promise are notorious, ironically often in regard to those whom they nominally most benefit. Sometimes, of course, this is but a matter of poor design or execution, yet at other times and perhaps more recognizably it is a matter of constitutional incapacity. Notice here, once again, that Joseph Raz believed that the values that lie at the heart of well-being are all diminishing and satiable, despite the fact that much of what we pursue in life is not, making much of that pursuit a matter of mistaking of an insatiable value for a satiable counterpart, as in the case of pleasure and happiness.[33] The pattern at work in the case of economic value will be familiar from consideration of the case of justice because it is, once again, a characteristically modern instance of a good idea, one that is indirectly capable of being productive of real value, and often to a high degree, simply being taken too far.

---

[33] See *The Morality of Freedom* (1986), 240ff, referred to earlier at n. 28.

2
Consent and Its Absence

2.1 The Problem and the Project

2.1.1 Points of Departure

Not every project is bound to begin with intellectual orientation, by setting out the scholarly context for its argument, but it helps. We all want to get straight to the point, so as to spend time with it, but we need also to remember that getting to the point is a matter not simply of describing a destination, however richly and persuasively, but of appreciating exactly what it will take any particular reader to reach that destination, from whatever position they may happen to be in, which is not necessarily or even typically that of the writer. It almost always matters as much where we are coming from as where we are going. To neglect that fact is apt to render the destination inaccessible, perhaps unintelligible, to many of those who would otherwise be drawn to it.

I want to talk about the meaning of consent, in ways that have been very largely bypassed in the literature, and yet in doing so I need to say a little something about the bypassing, to help orient those versed in the literature, because that is where any extended thinking about consent, in the world we now live in, is bound to begin. I say these things in particular tribute to my late friend, John Gardner, who never forgot in his writing that his project was to take others with him on his journey, and who never failed to be supremely accomplished at doing so.[1]

So philosophers who have reflected upon the question of consent, and there have been many, have been a good deal less forthcoming than they might have been about the meaning of consent, and have dwelt instead upon its conditions and its consequences. Two relatively recent cases will serve to illustrate the neglect that I have in mind. According to Peter Westen, consent is a matter of acquiescence.[2] So far so good, but one is bound to ask how helpful it is simply to state that without going further. Apart from the obvious worries about overbreadth, it seems

---

[1] The tribute here is entirely sincere yet also incomplete. Much as I admired John's writing, and strongly as I sympathized with its ambitions, my pursuit of a different, more solitary path was not simply a personal idiosyncrasy, though it undoubtedly had idiosyncratic roots, but rather proceeded from an awareness of somewhat different, rather less visited destinations, a sense of the kinds of understanding that might be secured there, a certain belief in my capacity to arrive at those understandings, and some corresponding doubt about the potential returns, in my hands at least, to be discovered in territory that had been so long and so thoroughly explored by others who were at least as able as myself. When John and I wrote together, it was out of mutual respect for the different rewards of our different approaches and shared hopes for the possible fruits of their combination. We would take turns at the keyboard, depending on who was freshest, who most animated, one dictating, the other typing and editing, switching roles when we ran out of steam but also in response to our different abilities, so that as it happens and as is relevant here, John would begin, and so set the intellectual context, and I would then continue with ideas and examples from the everyday, the two of us constructing the arguments together, in response to one another's doubts. I am here stepping briefly into John's shoes for these few introductory pages.

[2] Westen, *The Logic of Consent: The Diversity and Deceptiveness of Consent as a Defence to Criminal Conduct* (2004).

merely to postpone the question of meaning. After all, just what does acquiescence involve? Can we understand it adequately without understanding consent? As in his earlier and celebrated consideration of equality, what Westen has to say about consent is both intellectually and politically provocative, yet it leaves us none the wiser as to the practical situations in which consent might matter. Our grasp of them is simply presumed. That is fine in itself, of course, because it is up to Westen to choose his topic, but it is only fine because the question survives intact for others to address.

According to Alan Wertheimer, the ontology of consent (in other words, that which determines what consent is) is to be understood in terms of the constitution of consent, whether as a mental state, as a token, or as some hybrid of those two things.[3] Yet all three of these possibilities take for granted that we already have a sense, however acquired, of what exactly it is that might be constituted in one of those ways. The possibilities speak of the form in which consent may be embodied rather than of just what it is that is being embodied. For all that Wertheimer has to teach us, and that is a great deal, we still do not know what consent is once we have grasped what he takes to be its ontology; we know only how it is to be manifested.

None of this would much matter if there was no real possibility of controversy, if our understanding of consent was both natural and, so to speak, uninteresting, uninteresting because nothing much turned on any questions that an uncertainty about the meaning of consent might give rise to. Yet in fact consent is conventionally called upon in domains where a great deal is at stake, and the record of its negotiation in those domains has been so fraught, not to say tainted, that it becomes hard to escape the conclusion that a failure to enquire into the meaning of consent might well matter hugely. Given that the meaning of consent determines the applicability of consent as a practice, it becomes impossible to be confident of the proper application of the practice of consent without some degree of confidence as to its meaning. My sense is that some kind of return to first principles is called for here, and the balance of this chapter is dedicated to an exploration of the dividends of such an approach.[4]

---

[3] Wertheimer, *Consent to Sexual Relations* (2003), 144ff.

[4] The obvious exception to this narrative of oversight is John Gardner's 'The Opposite of Rape' (2018) 38 OJLS 48, and his discussion of agent/patient asymmetry (in section 3, 'The Passivity of the Consenter'). That is because John and I discussed the issue in the course of our weekly outings to Bermondsey Market, at a time when the two of us were both in the course of thinking and writing about consent and sexual relations, albeit from different starting points. John's paper acknowledged our exchange (at n. 43) without going fully into its details, and I will follow suit here, partly out of reciprocity, and partly out of respect for the fact that John is no longer in a position to respond to anything I might say. In truth, each of us was ultimately happy to have our ideas taken forward by the other. Ideas are not owned, and what is more, they can often be best advanced in the hands of others. That is part of what it means to share, and sharing ideas lay at the heart of our friendship. It is the reason that we wrote papers together as often as we did. For those readers who care at all, it should be reasonably clear from the differing focus of our two papers which of us was the source of which of the several ideas that appear in both places.

2.1.2 Missing in Action

Let me begin, in the manner of most reflection, with a puzzle, in this case a puzzle drawn from everyday life rather than from the library. It is a commonplace, embodied in contemporary ideals of gender, that consent is an essential element of legitimate sexual relations. In the most extreme, disturbing, and politically charged case, sexual intercourse without consent is rape. What is more, in this particular respect, the most extreme case is not in any sense an exception. Absence of consent makes otherwise legitimate sexual encounters of whatever kind criminal. Nothing more need be shown. Or so the criminal law of most jurisdictions maintains, to widespread professional and public approval. Yet it seems to be the case, in everyday life as opposed to the law books, that most people, and here I have to include myself and my partner, seem to enjoy whole lives of sexual fulfilment without ever consenting to sex, formally or informally. How can that possibly be? It is surely not that most people are outlaws at heart, as is recognizably the case in certain familiar, everyday settings, such as that of crossing the road on foot at places where such crossing is forbidden for example. On the contrary, the instinct to believe that the law is correct in its stand on consent, and should be strongly supported in that stance, is just as powerful in us as is the instinct that what the law expects of us here has nothing to do with a good life as most people actually live it. We simultaneously subscribe to the need for consent and to its absence in practice, both at a very deep level. Or so it seems.

Perhaps, however, the experience of everyday life is misleading in this regard, not to be relied upon. The scarred history of sexual relations, and particularly of gender relations, might lead us to be rightly suspicious of ordinary perceptions in this domain. The law on consent, as it has been carefully elaborated and detailed over many years, itself the product of bitter experience, profound moral debate, and extended political struggle, might be thought to be rather more perceptive, less self-delusional, than the experience of everyday life. Perhaps, then, one's everyday sense that good sex[5] need not, indeed typically does not, involve consent is simply an illusion. That illusion might take one of two familiar forms, both ultimately troubling, both demonstrably illegitimate, though the first is perhaps less obviously so.

Consent might be present in our sexual relations in ways that we have been conditioned not to notice. It might be implicit in certain of our gestures, our attitudes, or even, though less plausibly, our roles. The fact, if fact it be, that consent is most commonly secured in this way, by implicit rather than explicit means, might be explained and warranted by the capacity of implicit consent to license our conduct, and our sexual relations in particular, in a manner that we have good reason

---

[5] I borrowed the compact and useful term 'good sex' from John Gardner.

to keep in the background, most obviously because doing so leaves us free to focus our attention on the other more creative, more expressive dimensions of intimate physical contact with another human being, so as to generate, when things go right, the happy illusion of having achieved a human interaction that transcends what are in fact (at least according to this explanation) the necessary mechanics of mutual permission. In short, it might be that we have very good reason to hide the practice of consent from our everyday selves, thereby ensuring that our everyday experience is not a very good place to look for its presence.

Alternatively, our impression that good sex need not and typically does not involve consent might be deeply sinister rather than perhaps forgivably fanciful and romantic. Consent might indeed be absent from our sexual relations, but just because and to the extent that those relations are in fact more or less standardly non-consensual, making the illusion that we suffer from the illusion of good sex, rather than the illusion of the absence of consent. On this view, absence of consent, explicit or implicit, would lie at the heart of a deeply ingrained scheme of sexual oppression and subordination, in the manner that certain radical feminists have sought to draw attention to. Our sexual practices would be fundamentally bad, dressed up to look as if they were good, and our everyday sense that they were sound and healthy would be a paradigmatic case of false consciousness.

It seems to me that there is truth in both these positions, but that the truths in question are contingent and qualified. It is undoubtedly the case that many of our sexual relationships and encounters involve a troubling degree of self-deceit, troubling because of the capacity of self-deceit to serve the bad no less than the good. All too often we are not the lovers that we take ourselves to be, and our pretence to the contrary, while sometimes productive, sometimes innocent, sometimes merely foolish, undoubtedly has the potential to cause significant harm in certain settings. It is also the case that too many sexual encounters are rather less mutually assenting than we present them as being, not only to ourselves as individuals and as sexual partners but to ourselves as a society.

And yet, it takes a fairly dedicated commitment to grand theory to believe that our everyday understanding of good sex is as fundamentally misguided as the latter, more negative reading of our lives would have it. For that degree of scepticism to be sound in this setting we would need to be mistaken about the goodness of our sexual lives not merely in part, but comprehensively, for it would not be possible otherwise to believe, as we seem to, that good sex need not and typically does not involve consent. That is a claim about the very nature of good sex, not one that trades illegitimately on the moral ambiguity of certain of the supposed instances of good sex. If we are wrong about the very nature of good sex, in this way and to this degree, so that even upon considered reflection we are unable to perceive the truth of the matter, then it is difficult to see just how we could begin to go right, or even to think about doing so, to know just where we could look for even the genesis of an untainted perspective and how we might hope to gain access to it, other than indirectly and over the very long term. If that were true, there would be much to discover but, for the time being at least, little to reflect upon or to speak about in our approach to good sex.

That being the case, in what follows I will bracket for the time being (though I will also return to in closing) the possibility that what we take to be good sex as a matter of everyday experience is standardly non-consensual, not simply because it strikes me as implausible (even the most radical feminist believes that good sex is possible, at a minimum in those settings unaffected by gender relations, such as same-sex relationships, and yet is liable to share the perception that good sex, so understood, is seldom characterized by explicit consent) but also and more pertinently because that possibility is one that would compel us to leave the nature and significance of consent unexamined, because we would not be fit to examine it. The thought in response to that kind of grand theoretical doubt is the familiar Aristotelian one, that our everyday experience may well be misunderstood by us in all kinds of ways that are sometimes forgivable and sometimes not, in part because not thinking too deeply about our actions, hazardous as it may be, is in many settings essential to living well, but that everyday experience is nevertheless more or less morally sound, or at least morally informed. While our lives are filled with moral error, even when conscientiously directed, they are not lives of moral incomprehension, and if they were and if we were as a result so benighted, it would not be possible, simply by an act of political will, to comprehend them morally, whether in whole, or in the part that concerns us here, with respect to the significance of consent and its presence or absence in our everyday lives, and in our sexual relations in particular.

The possibility that I want to explore in the balance of this chapter grows out of (though it will ultimately depart from) what strikes me as the more plausible of the two illusions just described, that practices of consent are designed so as to conceal their operation from us, their practitioners. That possibility raises two issues. First, is our everyday sense that good sex need not and typically does not involve consent is an accurate one, so that consent really is as absent as it appears to us to be, or is it an illusion, so that consent in this setting is something that we have hidden from ourselves in deeply ingrained patterns of implication? In order to answer the latter question one would need to be sensitive to the ways in which and the extent to which consent might genuinely and legitimately be implied. What exactly can implication do for us, and is the practice of consent, and sexual consent in particular, one of those things? That will be the subject of the next section of this chapter. Does it make sense to think that if consent is essential to characterization of an act as intercourse rather than rape, it is something that is capable of being implied? On the face of it, there would seem to be a lack of fit between what is at stake here and the means by which its legitimacy is secured. Is that a deep problem or a superficial one?

The other dimension of possibility, of course, is that the seeming absence of consent in everyday sexual relations is no illusion. In that case, just what is going on? If consent is not implied in those cases where it is not explicit, what does its absence from good sex tell us about the nature of good sex, and indeed about human interaction more generally? How can we hope to govern and police our engagement with our fellows, so as to secure our autonomy, our dignity, and our integrity, among other values fundamental to our well-being, without the assistance of the special, close to talismanic device of granting or withholding consent? And finally, if consent is not a feature of good sex (and possibly of any other form of human interaction), just what is its function in licensing human exchange, something that we routinely call upon it to do in a host of settings, in many of which a great deal is often at stake in terms of our well-being? That is a function that consent inarguably performs (once again assuming that we are not suffering from deep false consciousness), indeed must perform if it is to have any function at all (assuming still that it is not a feature of human interaction).

The thought that I will seek to articulate and develop in the rest of this chapter is that consent is typically the wrong candidate for the work that we nominally expect it to do in sexual relations, and that is why in practice we seldom call upon it. Interaction with others and its sound governance is simply not the proper place or role for consent. Rather it is a role that we have assigned to consent on the assumption that if consent were not present in such transactions human exchange in general and human sexual relations in particular would *ipso facto* be non-consensual. Since we see so little evidence of explicit consent in our sexual lives, and yet believe that our sexual relations are typically consensual (or more precisely, not non-consensual), we conclude that the presence of consent must be implied.

That may be too quick a conclusion, however. To anticipate, at least in outline, the position that I will need the entire course of this chapter to make a sound and careful case for, there is available to us a ready and familiar alternative to the protective oversight of our person that is thought to be provided by consent, in the basic and abiding bidirectional moral responsibility that we have towards one another as human beings, and indeed with the world at large. Our exercise of that responsibility is shared with our fellows, but is no less real for that fact. On this view, the boundaries that mark us out as, first, human (and so distinguish us from other living things) and, second, as individuals (and so distinguish us from other human beings), including those that define the significance of our will, our psychological identity, and our physical integrity, which is to say the very boundaries on which the practice of consent is thought to rely, and more important, to help to sustain, are real but not profound. Moral responsibility simultaneously describes and transcends what is in reality the fundamentally provisional and contingent shape of those boundaries, lends them their significance, and yet expects that significance not to be overrated. There is much that is distinctive about the domains in which we have traditionally looked for consent, but nothing that is distinctively vital to the flourishing of our lives. It all depends.

We tend to think otherwise because of our attachment to certain boundaries in particular, in contemporary culture most obviously those on which autonomy not so much turns, but can be most readily articulated and defended in terms of.[6] We then seek practices, such as consent, that appear to have the power to give those boundaries the significance we take them to have, by offering or appearing to offer the sort of protection that this special significance would warrant. The mistake we fall into here is the all too common one, of making things seem simpler than they are, tidier than they are, easier to decide upon, readier to police, of fitting life to the demands of explanation rather than explanation to the demands of life. We often have more at stake in other encounters that do not track these boundaries and less authority over the ones that do. We are more on the line more of the time, more dependent on others and also more in charge. That is what it means to be a human agent, where the ascription of humanity is an ascription of existence as a social being, one whose flourishing is indissolubly entwined with the flourishing of his or her fellows in social practices, like sexual relations, where the flourishing of each participant is dependent on the flourishing of another.

Consent has other work to do, important work but nothing to do with human interaction. Consent, the thought runs further, matters when and if we move from the active to the passive, from the role of agent to that of patient. Those two roles are not always distinct in the practices of human exchange, including the practice of sexual relations, so that consent may be necessary on occasion or in relation to particular aspects of good sex, just as and when we move from the active to the passive. That is a plausible view, it seems to me, of certain forms of sexual relation, but not about them all. Consent may be a minimum condition of certain kinds of good sex, those in which the passivity of one or more of the participants in one or more of its aspects is a feature, but it is not in any sense a necessary condition of good sex, nor even a paradigmatic one.

---

[6] On the connections between consent, autonomy, and personhood, see, most prominently, Heidi Hurd, 'The Moral Magic of Consent' (1996) 2 Legal Theory 121.

2.2 Consent by Implication

All this is but a sketch, the various elements of which will need to be fleshed out and examined carefully if they are to be sustained. Assume then, for the time being and as the first step in that process, that the proposal just outlined is yet to be established, that what appears to be absence of consent in the everyday experience of good sex is but an illusion, and that what in fact makes the sex in question good, at a minimum, is the presence of implied consent. How might consent be implied, and in the setting of sexual relations, by what sort of means? Put more generally, just how is the distinction between explicit and implicit communication of whatever kind, including but not confined to that which conveys consent, to be drawn? A few familiar working notions of the nature of implication can, it seems to me, be readily set aside. These need to be addressed and examined in some detail in order to determine whether consent to sexual relations can ever be legitimately implied.

2.2.1 Common Views of Implication

It is sometimes thought that implication functions as a non-verbal rider to what is expressed verbally.[7] She said she believed him, but her eyes told a different story. She said she admired him, but her tone suggested otherwise. Many implications do indeed operate in this way, perhaps because of the tendency to have recourse to words when one wants to be explicit, in the belief that words are capable of greater precision than are other forms of language. If one believes that the realm of words is the realm of the explicit, then one might be tempted to the further belief that the realm of what is left unspoken is the realm of the implicit. Sometimes that conclusion is entirely correct, for the reason just given, among others. Yet it is perfectly possible to be explicit without using words, and just as possible to use words that in themselves convey an implication, simply by the way they are chosen and arranged, as many everyday situations make clear.

To be explicit without using words is such a familiar part of our experience that attention hardly needs to be drawn to it. Suppose that we want to express approval of another's action. We may say well done, but we are just as likely to give the thumbs up instead. Suppose that we wish to express resentment of another's action. We may say exactly what we think of their behaviour, but if we are both rude and reckless we may choose to show them a finger (or two, depending on our culture). There is something specially pithy and direct about non-verbal communication that prompts us to call upon it when we want to make a blunt point and

---

[7] See, for example, Peter Westen, *The Logic of Consent* (2004), 326.

then move on, without engaging in the niceties, or generating the likelihood of an unwanted reply, that words not only make possible but raise an expectation of.

To convey an implication by using words is slightly less familiar perhaps, because in such cases the implication is often so tightly bound to the words in question, and their particular arrangement, as to generate the perception that what might otherwise have been implicit has been subsumed in the explicit and so become it. Text and sub-text can sometimes be difficult to distinguish, so that we may take things too literally, overlooking implications or according them a status that was not intended, as most of us have found to our discomfiture, though perhaps less so as we get older and more practised in the art of communication. Children often struggle with implications that are readily accessible to adults.

Yet such difficulty in perceiving the implication latent in words is not always or even typically the case. Verbal communication is very often used to imply something other than that which it nominally sets out to convey, and when it is so used we well understand the implication in what is being said, just as we are intended to, unless of course the speaker has miscalculated. To take a familiar case, many things that are too rude to say explicitly are implied instead. Indeed, this is a notorious feature of certain practices of studied understatement in British English, in which true incivility is dressed up as civility. It is worth noticing at once from this example, because it is of central importance in the functioning of any implication, that implications that are conveyed in that manner depend for their success both on the existence of such settled practices and on familiarity with them on the part of the addressee, or perhaps even more commonly, on the part of some third person, to whom the implication may have been quite deliberately addressed over the head of the unwitting nominal addressee, who has not been schooled in the relevant practice, being from another culture perhaps, or another social world. That is very brave of you it will be said, meaning that it is utterly foolish. I'm sure it's my fault, meaning that it is anything but. Sorry, meaning get out of my way. How kind of you. One needs to be reasonably familiar with British idiom and conversant in its practices to participate in these implications at all.

It is sometimes further thought that implications are uncertain just because they are imprecise, or at least more approximate than words. There is clearly truth in this, because implications do lack the fine-grained modularity that words lend themselves to, but it is again a bit too quick. Implications can be entirely clear when the words they are associated with are quite unclear. One can be unsure as to exactly what someone is saying, whether in words or otherwise, and yet be quite clear as to its import. Perhaps there is something threatening about it, perhaps something seductive. In such a case, the implication survives the miscarriage of the explicit communication. This happens most commonly when a standing resource of the kind that is constituted in British understatement has not yet developed, so that a speaker who is unwilling to say what he or she wants to say, because it is socially unacceptable to do so, is forced to mumble or otherwise to cloud what cannot be articulated explicitly, and then to rely on implication to get the message across, which implication must do all the more clearly because it is then being called upon to carry the rational burden of communication entirely on its own, without the support and counterpoint of the explicit, other than as inarticulate structure.

2.2.2 The Structural Features of Implication

Misdirected as they may be, these common views of implication in fact tell us, albeit in spite of themselves, most of what we need to know about the practice. To return to an Aristotelian mode, there is good reason for people to have reached such conclusions. The only shortcoming in the conclusions is that they are insufficiently probing of a genuine condition to generate the kind of deeper understanding that the grasp of certain problems requires. Put broadly, implication operates as a modifying undertone to whatever is being said explicitly. That is its essential function, and that fact helps to explain why it is natural to think of implication as something unspoken. This ancillary role in the practice of communication has two principal features. First, every implication depends on an active partnership with the explicit. It is not possible merely to imply. Every implication necessarily resides in what is not being implied. That is why it is easy to overlook implication, either by not seeing beyond the explicit, and so missing the implication altogether, or by misinterpreting as explicit certain instances of what is in fact intended to be implicit, so missing the status of some portion of what is being said, a status that may be important to the nature of the message as a whole. Second, the function of any implication is to modulate what is otherwise being said explicitly, in one of two basic ways. Implication may either extend the content of the explicit or it may subvert it. (Of course, it may also do both of those things at the same time.)

Extensions of meaning that are conveyed by implication function as a kind of shorthand in our everyday communication, ways in which we are able to understand one another fully, and so to rely upon one another properly, without having to spell everything out. When one agrees to look after a child for the afternoon, one implicitly agrees to live up to whatever circumstantial requirements that responsibility may entail on a particular occasion, not only the basic concerns that are embodied in the very idea of looking after a child, the idea that is rendered explicitly, but whatever concerns looking after the child may happen to mean for that child and for its parents, and indeed for oneself as a carer, in whatever circumstances may happen to arise on that afternoon. Suppose that it rains unexpectedly, or that the child is injured at the playground. One has implicitly undertaken to deal with those circumstances, whether or not they were foreseeable, and is to be held to account for one's success or failure in doing so.[8]

---

[8] Thanks to John Gardner for the example, which reflected his experience of responsibility for the welfare of a fellow philosopher's child.

Subversions of meaning that are conveyed by implication operate to temper the explicit, so as to communicate what could not be communicated explicitly, or could not be communicated quite as effectively. Perhaps the message is only legitimate, either in principle or in terms of local practice, when communicated *sotto voce*. Irony is the most obvious example, but many other species of qualification and ambivalence are communicated by implication, genuinely or in tribute to a social expectation. To be explicit is to be blunt, and there is often good reason not to be blunt, good reason to be kind and show delicacy of feeling as much as reason to be cutting and show absence of feeling, reason to convey criticism in a manner that is shaded, and so protects a person from certain of the most destructive effects of criticism while enabling them to benefit from it, and so on. The many complex practices of human exchange exhibit deep familiarity with the scheme of operation at work here, and almost endless inventiveness about ways to make best use of it. Different cultures often have different levels of commitment to the practice, so that certain cultures are committed to communicating nearly every important matter indirectly by implication, while others make a virtue of directness. Strangers to those cultures, who have not been educated in their local practice, are liable to generate incomprehension if they proceed by forms of implication that are not practised in that locale, or to cause great offence if they are explicit about matters that are expected to be addressed by implication there. Some things are not to be talked about explicitly, and it is all too possible to mistake that fact in either direction.

This last observation about cultural norms leads to a more general point. Implications can function only as a standing resource that is rooted in social practice. That means that they are bound to be understood and to be assessed in terms of the local social practice in which they are embedded and through which they function. What is more, they are not just a social practice but a special kind of social practice. *Mutatis mutandis*, they constitute a language like any other, and so are subject to all the governing conditions of language, although of course those conditions have rather different consequences for the implicit than they do for the explicit, consequences that necessarily play an important part in framing our moral evaluation of the practice of implication in any particular setting. The language of implication cannot be coined for an occasion, any more than can the vocabulary, syntax, and grammar of any other language. It must exist as a standing resource in advance of its exercise. Implications come encoded so to speak, in the social practice in which they are embedded, and upon which they depend for their functioning. The social practice in question may be very local, may indeed have arisen, accidentally or by design, within a setting as confined as a domestic relationship. Nevertheless, however restricted the community in which it is sustained, the language of implication must be fully familiar to all of its participants if it is to do its work.

This means that when we seek to assess implications in terms of their value we are bound to do so in and through the vehicles in which they are embedded.

A significant part of our assessment of a practice of implication will be of its vehicle. Words, by partial contrast, are much less likely to have moral import in themselves, simply as linguistic vehicles, unless and to the extent that the very ideas that constitute them are morally freighted (and if truth be told, there are some very bad ideas in the world that can be quite effectively captured in a word), and so are to be judged largely by reference to the ideas that are conveyed by their combination with one another on any particular occasion, rather than in terms of their standing as words. The language of implication has a special further moral burden to meet. We must always ask whether a practice of implication is morally fit to convey the idea that we are asking it to convey in constituting it as a social practice. The social practice in question may not be able to bear that burden. Sometimes, of course, words are to be judged in this way too, for example when they amount to terms of abuse, but when that is the case they are quite often being judged for what they imply. Implication must always be assessed in this manner. To invert the old saying, in the case of an implication it may well be right to shoot the messenger. There is clearly nothing wrong with saying yes or no to sexual intercourse (at least, provided that children or certain of one's close relatives are not involved), but there may well be something wrong with doing so by implication.

2.2.3 The Morality and Politics of Implication

These structural features necessarily shape our moral assessment of the practice of implication as it is undertaken on any particular occasion or in any particular setting. If one asks what it is possible in principle to communicate by implication, the straightforward answer is that it is possible to imply any content that can operate to extend or contradict whatever is being expressed explicitly. The breadth of that response is significantly limited, however, by the special moral vulnerabilities to which the practice of implication is subject. Implication carries with it distinctive although not unique opportunities for error and for exploitation, and that special moral vulnerability may render certain practices of implication illegitimate, otherwise effective though they might be in the project of conveying meaning. Those opportunities for error and exploitation stem from the basic fact that implication operates as an undertone to the explicit, and so cannot be articulated with anything like the same degree of precision as what is expressed explicitly, leaving a good deal of room for misapprehension, both innocent and wilful. That is not an inherent failing on the part of implication, in need of correcting. On the contrary, much of the value of implication derives from its capacity to shade meaning rather than convey it directly, thereby enabling a speaker to say something without quite coming out and saying it, to commit without quite committing, and so on. Yet that value has its price.

Take an illustration from the law and morality of sexual relations that will be familiar to everyone, that no means no rather than yes or maybe. If one were asked to evaluate that assertion simply as an assertion about the bare capacity of those two words to bear certain implications, independently of the particular practice of implication that can take place in the setting of sexual relations and has so often done so, one would be bound to recognize that no is entirely capable of implying yes, just as yes is entirely capable of implying no. The bare capacity of those two words to imply precisely the opposite of what they explicitly stand for is a well-known feature of social exchange, as is the extent to which the possibility of such an implication in the use of them is often misunderstood or exploited, so as to read in a subversive implication when it is not present or to ignore it when it is. In some settings, of course, the stakes are relatively trivial, so that the cost of misapprehension does not give rise to any moral concern. On the other hand, it is in fact hard to imagine a setting that does not have the potential to become morally troubling on some occasion when no is wrongly taken to imply yes, or yes to imply no. Even apparently trivial instances of politesse and its mishandling may need to be taken seriously. In the case of sexual relations, of course, experience has taught us that the implications are not to be tolerated even if, as the case may be, they have the potential to play a part in a worthy scheme of sexual exchange.

Most of us have had the experience, at many points in our lives, of finding ourselves pressed to take a second helping of some part of a meal at a friend's house. It might be more potatoes or more pudding. Sometimes what is being pressed upon us is something that we would very much enjoy more of. Sometimes it is something that we really struggled with our first helping of. Perhaps I am here betraying an old-fashioned upbringing, but I take it that it is generally considered to be good form to demur at such an offer, perhaps so as not to appear to be greedy, perhaps so as to see if the offer is genuine and not a matter of courtesy by a host who has already made room in the refrigerator, in anticipation of the next evening's dinner, for what is now being offered for form's sake. How far one should demur is a nicety of the social practice in question that is not clearly defined. Some feel that one refusal is enough, others feel that two refusals are required. In both cases, but particularly in the latter, there is ample opportunity for misapprehension, and the cost of that misapprehension, while generally trivial, may be enough to mar the occasion for one person or the other. Speaking for myself, I have missed out on extra helpings of some pretty nice puddings, rather to my consternation, either because I mishandled my refusals or because my host deliberately chose to misinterpret them, having other destinations in mind for the extra pudding. I have also had more than my share of extra potatoes, again perhaps because of miscalculation on my part, but also, and here I am reasonably confident of the motivations of certain of my hosts, because the person making the offer was well aware that my refusal was genuine but was determined to dispose of the potatoes by means of my plate rather than have them take up precious space in the refrigerator, so as to make the leftovers my responsibility, not theirs. However, the motivation need not be so mean-spirited. It can also be the case that a host is simply very generous, wants the occasion to reflect that fact, and so needs to express generosity in ways that involve insensitivity to the fact that the guest really does mean no when he or she says no. In such a case, it is the guest who might be accused of being mean-spirited in refusing, say for the sake of a diet, to engage fully in the kind of occasion that the host is quite reasonably seeking to create. The host wants the guest to have more for that reason of generosity, and is assisted in realizing his or her goal by reading in an implication of acceptance that is not present, as the host knows or strongly suspects. So, misapprehension of refusals is common and its cost can run in either direction.

As trivial as this illustration is (special cases aside) in terms of the concerns it raises, it exposes the fault lines, the morality, and some of the politics of implication as it is practised in a particular setting. Implication by its nature provides fertile ground for error and for exploitation. A proper moral response to either of those two failings is bound to turn on the impact that they have on the particular goods that are at stake in that setting. Most obviously, there may be an immediate cost in terms of human well-being, but no less important will be the long-term consideration of any distinctive vulnerability of the person affected to the miscarriage of an implication of this kind. The politics consequent on that morality will involve either a renegotiation of the terms on which implication is undertaken in that setting, so as to reduce the likelihood of error and exploitation, or if such a renegotiation appears to be either unfeasible or morally undesirable, a wholesale rejection of the practice of implication in that particular setting. In other words, we might try to make sure that we get the implications of yes and no right, or we might decide to insist that in our social and political world those words are henceforth to mean what they explicitly mean, whatever might otherwise have been the case, because our experience has shown that error and exploitation in the handling of them cannot be adequately avoided, and that the cost of their misapprehension in this setting is simply too high.

So to return to the question of the role that implication may play in consent to sexual relations, the first thing to notice is that consent to sex is entirely capable of being implied, in any case where consent is expressed, as an extension to or a subversion of whatever else is being communicated explicitly. Take extension first. It is perfectly possible to agree to one thing and implicitly agree to something more by extension, to accept a certain level of sexual contact and in doing so to accept a further level of sexual contact, say if the experience of the initial level turned out to be a happy one, in the same sort of way that to agree to look after a child for the afternoon is implicitly to agree by extension to a number of other things, should they arise. Indeed, given that the individuation of action has its limits, it seems almost inescapable that to agree to an action is implicitly to agree to everything embraced in that action that cannot sensibly be further individuated.

That is not, of course, to suggest that one cannot change one's mind at any point in the course of an action. On the contrary, a consent that has been given can always be revoked, so that penetration, for example, must cease immediately if such a revocation takes place. Yet the question of revocation is very different from the question of whether further consent is necessary to the furtherance of the intercourse at any particular moment, because to change one's mind does not require special individuation in the same way that further consent does. To revoke one's consent is to alter one's attitude to an action rather than to adopt different attitudes (consent given, consent not given) to different actions, each in need of individuation. One simply withdraws consent to whatever had previously been consented to. Barring revocation, however, in consenting to intercourse one implicitly consents to its normal duration, and indeed to standard forms of its execution. That is what is being consented to, because it is simply not possible to be more fine-grained than that about the object of consent. Consent is bound to embrace as much of an action as is consistent with undertaking the action at all.[9]

What is more, the logical and practical difficulties in individuating action are not the only reasons we might have for implicitly consenting to more than we have explicitly consented to. On the contrary, to proceed by way of implied consent is to create favourable conditions for a range of sexual returns that would be much more difficult to gain access to if consent had always to be explicit. Many of those returns are currently unfashionable, while some others are of dubious value. To be coquettish, for example, seems both dated and unwise. Nevertheless, it is easy to imagine reasons to be less than fully explicit about the quality and scope of one's commitment to a sexual encounter, at certain stages at least. Doing so can make certain kinds of delicacy possible, make certain roles accessible, enable us to toy with possibilities that we are not yet prepared to commit ourselves to. It might also simply be convenient to call upon the shorthand of implication, so as to avoid the burden and the distraction of having to spell everything out at all times. These things in themselves should be enough to suggest that implied consent in this setting is not only logically possible but also morally intelligible.

What is true of extension is also true of subversion. One can perfectly readily say one thing and imply the opposite. No can mean yes and yes no, in this setting as much as in any other. Indeed, we are all entirely aware that that is the case, for if those words could not mean those things there would have been no need for people

---

[9] It must be borne in mind, however, that the moral import of an action is liable to be differently individuated by different people, so that the import of a particular action, and the distinction between it and another action, may not be the same for one actor as it is for another. This means that when people interact, they may well each have a different sense of what is at stake, a difference, furthermore, that may be gendered, so as to have different implications for men and for women. This is because standard individuations are derived from standard cases of moral import, but these almost always have their rivals and are seldom authoritative. It means further, for example, that in consenting to an action a woman may be consenting to something different or something less than a man takes her to be consenting to, even when he is being entirely conscientious.

to campaign against their being used in that way. Someone who attempted to maintain that no meant yes would simply have been treated with incomprehension, as if he had maintained that he thought day meant night. In fact we understand all too well that schemes of etiquette, including the device of saying the opposite of what one means, are as at home in the bedroom as they are everywhere else in the house. Nor is this straightforwardly a bad thing. One may take a dim view of such forms of etiquette, but it is difficult to imagine a world in which etiquette of some kind, including sexual etiquette, did not exist. Were such a world at all possible, it would almost certainly be a poorer world. The point here is not that sexual etiquette is a good thing rather than a bad thing, but that it is often a morally intelligible thing, a candidate for goodness. Yet once one adds subversion to extension, by accepting that no does not necessarily mean no, the conclusion that one is driven to is that some of the most prominent and distasteful instances of implied consent, instances in which people, almost always women, have been taken to have committed themselves to more than they actually committed themselves to, and to things that they had not committed themselves to at all, instances which the social emancipation of women had, or so we thought, finally secured the discrediting of to the approval of virtually everyone, remain fully possible as far as the logic of consent is concerned. On the face of it, that is a deeply disturbing conclusion.

That sense of disturbance cannot be entirely dispelled. Whatever security might lie in the logical impossibility of no meaning yes is simply not available to us. Yet disturbing as it may be, the uncertainty that goes with that lack of security is the kind of uncertainty that fundamentally defines our moral and political lives, as persons and as communities, an uncertainty we negotiate every day and that we have learned to find our flourishing in the face of. It is that flourishing, its rootedness in the values that make our lives go well, and its vulnerability in the face of the various structures that bar to access to value, whether for particular people or for whole classes of people, that we must ultimately be guided by. Our advancement and our protection, as people and as women and men, lie in our moral commitment, in our will to the good, not in the logic of language. The reason that no does not any longer mean yes in this setting, at least in the world that most of us now inhabit, is that we have made a collective decision to forbid that implication, for the sake of the goods that follow from such a ban and, more important perhaps, for the life prospects of the people who would otherwise suffer the costs of error and exploitation that experience has shown to follow from acceptance of the practice of implication in this setting, costs that are particularly high there and that certain people are particularly vulnerable to. Like any other social practice, the use of language, both explicit and implicit, is subject to moral scrutiny and assessment. How far it is subject to our will is, of course, quite another matter.

When no is misapprehended as yes, deliberately or otherwise, the cost of that error is borne by one party or the other, occasionally by both. It is possible to imagine settings in which one says yes to something that one doesn't really want to receive and that the person one is responding to doesn't really want to give, with the consequence that an offer that is not sincere is taken up by means of an acceptance that is also not sincere. Each side is assuming the presence of an implication that is not there. Extra helpings might be a common case. In that setting, both parties are losers, victims of their shared lack of candour. In the setting of sexual relations, however, the cost of misapprehension is likely to fall very largely on one party rather than the other (that is, apart from whatever moral burden is attendant upon a person who is guilty of such a misapprehension). The politics of sexual relations, in which one party has historically been suitor to the other, and in the heterosexual version of which the suitor has usually been a man, have given rise to the consequence that when no is wrongly taken to mean yes, it is a woman who has paid the price, both immediately, in terms of rape, where intercourse is the issue, and in the long run and where other forms of contact are in issue, in terms of her dignity, respect owed, and autonomy.[10]

The same politics, of course, coupled with the logic of implication, lend themselves to a range of further subversive possibilities, however rare they may have been in practice: that no can mean yes, but be mistaken for no (as when a woman wants not to appear overly available, so that a man who misses her implication forbears and the woman is disappointed), that yes can mean no, but be mistaken for yes (as when a woman feels under pressure of some kind to say yes, so that a man proceeds on the strength of that yes and the woman is, once again, the victim), and that yes can mean yes, but be mistaken for no (as when a woman is believed to be responding under an illegitimate pressure that she does not actually feel, so that a man forbears and the woman is, once again, disappointed). These logical possibilities are evenly balanced, but historical social practices have made some of them more telling than others, with the dual consequence that some possibilities are more likely than others to come into effect, and that what is at stake as and when they do so is far higher for some people, namely women, than it is for others. The different weightings that history has given to those different possibilities in the social practices of our culture are thus the foundation of a sound moral response to the presence of implication in any case of consent to sexual relations.

What is true of implications that extend or subvert the explicit is no less true of implications that are read into situations where they are not in fact present. Certain settings inevitably become common homes for certain implications, so that listeners and other spectators become tempted to assume the existence of an implication that has not been made just because it would commonly have been made in that setting, although in fact it was not so made on this occasion. This consequence simply follows from the facts, first, that implication is a language with a recognized vocabulary (so to speak) and, second, that people who present themselves to the

---

[10] In what follows, I will assume a heterosexual perspective, because it is in the heterosexual setting that implication has helped disfigure the status of women.

world, in speech or otherwise, are not in any position to alter the meaning of that vocabulary so as to control its application to themselves, and are thus liable to become the victims of conventional inferences (which may be reasonably founded but also may well not be), for here too error and exploitation are likely. Even explicit denial of the implication as a preventive strategy will not necessarily do the work that is needed. Nearly all of us of us have experienced the phenomenon in some setting or other. One may be speaking without a trace of irony and yet find oneself treated as if one had been ironic, or one may have been speaking ironically and find oneself treated as if one had been speaking literally. Similarly, one may be speaking quite straightforwardly and yet be treated as implying an ulterior agenda. In such cases, one may insist upon both one's sincerity and one's candour, but insistence may be ineffective. In practice and in principle, one is bound to acknowledge the existence of the implication and to negotiate with it as best one can in whatever one says and however one presents oneself, in full awareness that the negotiation may not be as effective as one would like.

This kind of imputation of a conventional implication to a person who has not in any way endorsed it is a familiar and dangerous feature of sexual relations gone wrong. Wearing provocative clothing, or inviting someone back to one's flat to have coffee or another drink at the end of the evening, are both entirely capable of supporting the implications that sexist outlooks attribute to them (or something quite like those implications). When current law and social mores rightly forbid the drawing of any such inferences, it is not because the wearing of provocative clothing (for example) does not imply what sexists take it to imply. On the contrary, such clothing can plainly imply what sexists take it to imply, and what is more, and more troubling, in certain circumstances there is real good to be found in some version of that implication. That is because there are often good reasons to be able to convey one's sexual interest in another person indirectly rather than directly, despite the very real dangers of error and exploitation that are latent in any practice of implication, and because wearing certain kinds of clothing, or arranging clothing in a certain manner, is a reasonable way of conveying sexual interest indirectly. People send out signals all the time, some of them unambiguous, some of them mixed, and there is real value in their being able to do so. Even the presence of a sexual stereotype is a necessary part of this picture, for as I have sought to emphasize, every implication must constitute a language in order to do its work, and the wearing of provocative clothing can constitute the language of implication only if and to the extent that the clothing in question has come to be associated with a social practice that has standardized the specific inferences that are and are not to be taken from its wearing, and in so doing has established that under certain circumstances such wearing can constitute a species of sexual invitation.

One cannot help but feel some revulsion at this conclusion. Yet the question is what the proper source of that revulsion is. Is it to be found in a fresh understanding of what provocative clothing can imply, or is it to be found in doubt about the very possibility of implied consent to sexual relations? Do sexists make a mistake in thinking that interest can be signalled by clothing and its arrangement, or do they make a mistake in thinking that consent to sexual relations can be implied? Which of these should be our target? Implications are a central feature of human exchange, and it seems impossible to deny their potential value in the kinds of communication that constitute sexual relations. Yet clearly there is a significant problem of corruption in the practice of implication in this setting, and the question is whether the corruption stems from the objectionable way in which implication has been practised there (in which case one might address it either by reform of certain features of the practice of implication, such as forbidding the drawing of inferences from the wearing of provocative clothing, as the law has tried to do, or by barring the practice altogether, as indicated above) or whether the corruption flows from the very nature of the project, namely that of giving consent implicitly, in a context in which, given the particular history and circumstances, consent cannot be legitimately given other than explicitly.

There may not seem to be much difference between these two different ways of understanding the illegitimacy of certain implications: between seeing the problem as one of the mishandling of a legitimate practice which has consequently to be suspended, or as one of reliance upon a practice which can no longer hope to be legitimate because of the terrible history of its mishandling. Many of the same facts ground each understanding, but at heart the difference between the two is between an issue that turns on occasion and one that turns on status. When and if the problem is seen as one of occasion, its remedy is logically to be sought in the regulation of implication, through social mores or through the law, in the hope of uncovering legitimate ways of implying consent, and legitimate settings in which to do so. When status is at stake, the fundamental legitimacy of implied consent becomes questionable, because vulnerability of status may wholly rule out the very project of implication in this setting, rather than seek to correct, by whatever means, its misdirection, so ruling out novel instances of implication for which there is no evidence of taint.

2.2.4 The Legitimacy of Implied Consent

Once again, the analysis that follows assumes a heterosexual point of view, because the predicament of women has been played out within, and has gained a significant portion of its import from, women's sexual relations with men. The predicament of women has not proceeded from their sexual relations with other women, and the predicament of gay men has not been a function of their sexual relations with one another. The problems that attend the practice of implying consent to sexual relations are inescapably problems of heterosexuality and must be approached as such, though their ramifications affect us all.

The practice of implying consent to sexual relations has, in the world that we have inherited and have not entirely altered, three special ramifications that are closely linked to the condition and status of women: first, the harms that women in particular have suffered and continue to suffer, physically, psychologically, and socially, as a consequence of the mishandling of implications in this setting; second, the highly loaded context in which implied consent to sexual relations takes place, one that is a notorious theatre for the articulation of the relationship between women and men, and so has over time become suffused with attitudes that draw upon and contribute to the subordination of women, and yet which, given its strong connections to privacy, is in many respects and for good reason free from public scrutiny; and, third, the profound prevailing social and political commitment to the circumstances of autonomy, access to which has become in our world a precondition of dignity and respect, including self-respect, for all people, and yet which it is in the very nature of the practice of implication to undermine, in binding people to meanings that they cannot alter, all the more acutely so when the content of a particular species of implication embodies attitudes that diminish women's dignity and that deny women respect. Put shortly, when implied consent goes wrong, the ramifications are particularly bad for women, in terms of loss of personal security, autonomy, and the respect that is owed to them.

Are there any candidates for the implication of consent to sexual relations that would be free from these ramifications, if not at once and on their own, then over time and with the support of proper regulation, social and legal? Or have all such candidates been effectively discredited in the discrediting of the many inferences that we have come to recognize as damagingly sexist? To be legitimate as a means of conveying consent to a range of activities that is as significant as those embraced by consent to sexual relations, a practice of implication would have to be fit to carry a burden of that particular, prominent import. As indicated earlier, there must be a suitable correlation between whatever is being implied and the vehicle that is being relied upon to convey the implication. We do not, for example, treat consent to surgery as capable of being implied, let alone as capable of being implied by the way one has dressed, or one's presence in the doctor's office. Should we treat consent to sexual relations as something less serious, when its present circumstances are such that getting consent to those relations right may be as significant to us as many forms of surgery?

It is difficult to think of such a candidate, perhaps because all the general types that might plausibly be called upon (relationships, conduct, consent to allied matters) have been effectively discredited in the discrediting of certain of their instances. It becomes difficult to imagine alternatives without venturing into the implausible. Admittedly, given that practices of implication may be very local, and so tied to a particular relationship, a couple might construct an idiosyncratic practice of implied consent for themselves, the contours of which would be hard to anticipate and assess, in advance and from the outside. However, any such private practice would be subject to scrutiny by others as and when a disagreement arose about its operation, and that scrutiny would necessarily remit the matter to more general practices, which it is possible to imagine and assess. So, what legitimate general practices might there be for the implication of consent to sexual relations? It seems to me that there are three governing considerations against which any candidates for such practices are bound to be assessed, which more or less track the three ramifications that the practice of implied consent has for the status of women.

First, a practice that implies consent to sexual relations must be one that has real weight, so as to reflect the level of commitment and the significance of the human interests at stake. This would vary to some extent with whatever aspect of sexual relations was being consented to, but given the significance of sexual relations generally in the articulation of human autonomy, implied consent to any aspect of those relations must be sufficiently clear and robust as not to imperil or otherwise undermine their autonomous character. In this respect, a consent to intercourse, for example, would need to be signalled by a means that was compatible with the serious consideration that such a commitment calls for and the correlative respect owed by the other person to the consenting person's autonomy. Consent to a casual caress might be conveyed by an implication the weight of which was compatible with the relatively fleeting consideration called for by the limited degree of what is at stake in a caress. For example, one might conceivably be whimsical about a caress though not about intercourse. Even if one were unwisely minded to be whimsical about intercourse, one would need to convey that state of mind by means of a language less vulnerable to error and exploitation than is the language of implication, for otherwise one would be liable, when one was not whimsical, to be the victim of an inference based on an appearance of whimsy.

If this particular illustration seems strained, as surely it does, it seems to me that it is because it exposes a fundamental tension between the practice of implication, which is ancillary and suggestive by its very nature, and consent to sexual relations which, given the interests at stake for the person consenting, needs to be sufficiently clear as to be compatible with that person's authority over this aspect of his or her life, and with a reasonable degree of security against the harms that mistakes as to consent inevitably give rise to. Implication is a way of being less than perfectly clear, and it is in that fact that its value lies. Fresh vehicles for implication have no capacity to alter that fact. That being so, the conclusion would seem to be that they cannot meet this threshold of legitimacy.

Second, a practice that implies consent to sexual relations must be sufficiently distant from already discredited vehicles for implying consent as to be free of their taint. Practices that might in principle have been legitimate vehicles for implying consent have by reason of their history become contaminated by the attitudes that they have typically been associated with, attitudes that would inevitably be transferred to new practices that bore any significant resemblance to those predecessors. We have learned not to draw inferences as to consent from dress, deportment, previous behaviour on this or some other occasion, or the nature of a relationship. What is left? Coupled with a commitment to autonomy, this means that there has come to be an inbuilt and warranted scepticism as to the outlooks that are likely to be brought to bear upon any practice of implied consent to sexual relations, together with a concomitant commitment to the idea that neither common nor previous practice should ever be allowed to operate as a reliable guide to present inclination on the part of a person consenting in this domain. Whether by design or otherwise, that commitment is one that sets itself directly against the very idea of implication.

Third, that thought leads to another that is rather more basic, for it calls into question the very possibility of reconciling any practice of implied consent to sexual relations, however refined, with a commitment to autonomy, at least in the case of women. As I have emphasized, practices of implication constitute a language that we must engage with in order to convey an implication at all. It is that fact that prompts us to seek to get the details of that language right, lest those details turn out to be either dangerous or demeaning. Yet the details are but a red herring if the very idea of being bound to the prevailing terms of a language of implication is incompatible with autonomy, at least in this setting and for those people who are especially vulnerable there. This is not to suggest what would clearly not be true, that there is something about the very idea of implication that is incompatible with the realization of human autonomy. On the contrary, it is a familiar fact that autonomy is compatible with acceptance of and integration into a whole range of restrictive social structures, many of which it should be said, including that of the practice of implication, are in truth as apt to enhance autonomy as to limit it. Rather it is to suggest that there may be an incompatibility between practices of implied consent to sexual relations and the autonomy of women, or of some women at least, for whom the capacity to articulate consent to sexual relations on their own terms is central to the achievement of autonomy, and conversely, whose autonomy is particularly vulnerable to the application of a stereotype by a man, harmless as that stereotype might be to other people with other histories in other settings. Implications rely for their effectiveness on the standardization of expectations, and it is that kind of standardized treatment of their character, their capacities, and their desires, that women have sought to escape in order to achieve full dignity and respect. These are autonomy-vulnerable people in an autonomy-sensitive environment. That is not the kind of domain in which a sexual stereotype can legitimately be relied upon.

2.2.5 Legitimacy and Explicit Consent

If all this is true, then there can be no possibility of legitimately implying consent to sexual relations, at least in the world that we now live in. If in addition the legitimacy of sexual relations turns on consent, as is standardly believed (though may not actually be the case), then that consent must be given explicitly. It follows that the people who campaign for the project that yes means yes are, as it appears, quite correct, not of course because yes need always mean yes, but because it must do so in the setting of consent to sexual relations, given the particular history and politics there. If we as a society are to become properly alive to the record of women's disadvantage, of how it has been brought about and how maintained, and if we are to become properly committed to the autonomy of women, to the dignity and respect that turn on the achievement of autonomy, and to women's access to the many goods that are accessible only through autonomy, we are bound to reject as illegitimate any consent that is less than explicit. Sexual relations that are based on a form of consent that is no more than implied are thereby based on a form of consent that the history of gender relations and the proper ambitions of women have rendered illegitimate in this setting, and a consent that has been illegitimately obtained is tantamount to no consent at all.

Yet that returns us to the puzzle with which this chapter began. If most people do not consent to sexual relations explicitly, as appears to be the case, and if any implied consent they might take themselves to have given one another is illegitimate, then it follows that their sexual relations are illegitimate, unless of course those relations have by some means acquired a legitimacy that is based on something other than consent. This gives rise to two possibilities. Assuming once again and for the time being that our belief in the legitimacy of our sexual relations is not an illusion, concealing a dark truth about our sexual relations, and further, that implied consent is illegitimate, and yet further, that we rarely obtain explicit consent (so that legitimate consent is absent), our everyday sense that in practice good sex need not involve consent of any kind, implicit or explicit, would have to be sound. Is it? On the other hand, if our belief in the legitimacy of our sexual relations is indeed an illusion, so that what we take to be good sex is actually illegitimate, it is possible that the illegitimacy flows from the fact that we have failed to obtain explicit consent. The failure of implied consent thus presents us with a dilemma. We must abandon either our sense that we now enjoy good sex or our sense that good sex requires consent. We cannot have both.

Where does that leave us? Most obviously, although to some extent counterintuitively, it does not tell us that we must obtain explicit consent to sexual relations. Nothing in what has been said previously in any way supports the conclusion that the giving of consent is a necessary feature of legitimate sexual relations. On the contrary, the need for some sort of consent has merely been provisionally assumed for the sake of argument, so as to test the proposition that what appears to be absence of consent in our everyday lives is actually a case of implied consent, which we for various reasons have more or less hidden from ourselves, so as to create the illusion of good sex without consent. The failure of that proposition does not tell us that good sex depends on explicit consent; it tells us that if good sex depends on consent, that consent must be explicit. The contingent fact that our history and our commitments preclude any legitimate practice of implied consent, coupled with the fact that explicit consent is untypical, yield the further conclusion that if our sexual relations are legitimate, as we believe them to be, their legitimacy must be sought elsewhere than in the presence of consent. The interesting pay-off is that the impossibility of implied consent in the particular circumstances of contemporary sexual relations may have had the correlative benefit of revealing something important to us about the scope of human interaction.

Or it may not have, because of course the converse is also true. If implied consent to sexual relations is illegitimate, given our sorry history of gender relations and the impact that that has had upon the status and prospects of women, in particular the impact upon the prospect of their leading properly autonomous lives, then it may be, whatever we like to tell ourselves, that our sexual relations are altogether illegitimate as a result. It might be the case, in other words, that it is our belief in the legitimacy of our sexual relations that is an illusion, rather than our belief that good sex does not depend on consent. That would not be the end of the enquiry, of course, because we would want to test that dramatic conclusion by exploring the possibility that our belief in the legitimacy of our sexual relations is actually a sound one, by asking, for example, whether explicit consent to sex, while certainly not illegitimate in the manner of implied consent, is inapt and so in no way a necessary condition of good sex. That would require an examination of the possibility that there is another source of legitimacy available, one that offers a rather more recognizable understanding of good sex as we know and experience it.

It seems to me that there is some immediate promise in that thought, for a commitment to the necessity of explicit consent suffers from a degree of implausibility in two respects. First, it is somewhat implausible that we could be quite so deluded about the experience of good sex, although, of course, it might be the case that we have been more or less innocently relying on the possibility of implied consent, and that we have simply not given enough thought to the matter, so as to see how fraught the practice of implication has become in this setting. Is that indeed the case? If the idea that our enjoyment of good sex is a delusion is an idea that continues to seem implausible after examination it is surely because and to the extent that a great many of us have in fact thought quite carefully about the fraught nature of implication, as the record of our questioning of many once common implications shows, and what is more, because those who have thought carefully about these things have concluded that consent to sex is not something that ought to be implied, so that the root of their objection to those once common but now discredited implications has been the fact that they are implications. That is not a conclusive response, of course, because it settles nothing about explicit consent either way, but at a minimum it leaves the question open, so prompting further enquiry into alternatives to consent.

The second source of implausibility in the idea that explicit consent is necessary to legitimate sexual relations is that it is almost impossible to consent to sex in a way that is not implicit as well as explicit, given the organic, improvisational nature of sexual activity. Imagine a sexual encounter that begins tentatively and ends in intercourse. So far, so conventional. If explicit consent is necessary to the legitimacy of that encounter it would have to be obtained from both parties at every step of the encounter, for if we have learned anything about implication in this setting, it is that we cannot infer consent to a later, qualitatively different aspect of the encounter from consent to a previous aspect. Autonomy and security require that each and every aspect be committed to independently. That means, however, that if explicit consent were all that was available to us it would be necessary to obtain explicit consent to each and every step of the encounter. Yet there is no way that obtaining explicit consent to each and every step can be reconciled with the improvisational, attentive, reflexive, and dynamic character of good sex.

On the contrary, in cases of explicit consent it is essential that we know in advance exactly what we are consenting to, rather than finding ourselves being asked to give broad consent to a course of action key features of which have not been disclosed to us. That is part of what it means to be explicit, as well as to give consent. Implication, by contrast, permits a certain lack of focus in what is being consented to, whether it operates on its own or in partnership with the explicit, so as to establish consent to something that is described broadly in explicit terms and then detailed by implication. Yet that lack of focus is exactly what people object to in implied consent. Explicit consent overcomes the objection by requiring something in the order of a prospectus in order to secure the various goods that it is designed to secure. However well this may work elsewhere, it seems to me that this is simply not feasible in the setting of sexual relations. Sex would not be good sex in any sense that we could recognize if that were the case. It would be rather more like certain species of prostitution.

What next then? The thought sketched at the outset of this chapter was that human interactions are but a species of action, so that it is no more sensible to consent to interactions than it would be to consent to actions. Both actions and interactions are rationally directed in ways that are ultimately spontaneous, even as and when a significant degree of deliberation is involved in them, and that are rationally assessed in ways that take that spontaneity into account. Good sex is simply one very powerful, particularly resonant portion of a good life, the narrative of which is fundamentally fluid, and so endlessly negotiated and renegotiated with the terms of the world in and through which we pursue, and sometimes find, value and goodness.

That world is made up most immediately of other people, with whom our fellowship is particularly strong and our interaction unusually mirroring, but also of other creatures, other forms of life, other material facts, and ultimately of the entire, complex, mutually dependent apparatus of a creation that is itself fundamentally dynamic, chimeric, and morally elusive. One might say, more succinctly, that the world is as mortal and as fallible as we recognize many of its elements to be, and so exhibits all their fragility, and all their growth and decay, physically and morally. Navigating that world successfully is what moral responsibility means. That navigation characteristically follows certain channels, has certain guiding goals, and responds to certain operational directives, but these are only ever provisional and so must be reconciled with the openness and fluidity of the basic project and the various elements of that project in which they play their part.

Consent has a place in that project, but it is not a precondition of it. We do not consent to life; we live it, for life is something that could not possibly be consented to, and in the living of our lives we from time to time consent to something, when somewhat special circumstances are in play. Those special circumstances are that we are for that moment not living life directly, but rather are surrendering our living of it to someone else. We are stepping out of life in a sense, so that we may be in a position to live it better when we step back into it.[11] Consent is not at the heart of life, but rather marks a departure from it, in good sex as much as in anything else.

That thought is somewhat at odds with our fundamental sense that life is something for us to direct and to control, in accordance with our reason and our will, as best we can, and yet it is entirely consonant with our sense of our fundamental continuity with a mutable world, in which the borders of our being are every day established and disestablished, for better and for worse, at our bidding and otherwise. Consent implies a species of control of our existence to which we often aspire but which in our wiser moments we recognize as a mirage, one that misleads us as to the quality of our basic circumstance, and in doing so encourages us to place too much emphasis on the will and what it is capable of imposing, and too little emphasis on the openness of reasons and the various and conflicting things that they call for at all times, on the kind of commitments that reasons encourage or permit, commitments that must always have their qualifications and their alternatives, and on the qualities that reasons expect of us personally, most obviously in terms of the degree of imagination, courage, and independence of thought that must be summoned every day if we are to embrace that uncertain remit successfully. In that framework, good sex is a venture of uncertain character and outcome, a venture that we undertake in partnership with another mind and body, and the goodness of which we thus construct together, reciprocally and reflexively, a venture that we both shape and are shaped by without ever fully controlling, a venture that we are both vulnerable to and uplifted by. Consent may arise in this setting, but only anomalously. Or so the thought would have it. Whether that thought is a sound one is the subject of the next chapter.

---

[11] If we step back into it. In cases of assisted suicide, we consent to our death, because our life has become something not worth stepping back into.

2.3 Action and Interaction

2.3.1 Action and Absence of Consent

Consent requires the presence of another actor, if not physically then in contemplation at least. There must be some agent to give one's consent to. That much is built into the very idea of consent. It follows that there can be no sensible question of consenting to one's own actions. Such an interpolation would be surplus to the explanation of action and, more profoundly, would have the further effect of making one a stranger to oneself, with interests different from one's own that one was in need of protection against. It is, of course, possible to multiply one's understanding of oneself for certain purposes, as where a distinct perspective is brought to bear on the analysis of one's condition, so as to isolate one's will, or appetite, or conscience, but not, it would seem, for the purposes of consent. As a youth, my father used his left hand and a penny to play gridiron football with and against his right hand. I am told, by him, that there were some great passes, great blocks, and some truly great receptions. He had to stop when he met my mother, who insisted, quite rightly it seems to me, that it was not possible to take sides against oneself in that way. The same surely also holds for consent. The very idea of being an agent implies a unity of interest sufficient to distinguish one agent from another. That unity is in some ways arbitrary, for interests are often shared, in principle and in social practice; it is complex, multifaceted, and as a result often incoherent and at odds with itself rather than synchronized; its distinctive response to reason and value is always incompletely determined and so never fully characterizable and consequently predictable, certain psychologies apart perhaps. Yet without it there would be no agent to attribute an action to.

So if one picks up an object, such as a pen, it is not sensible to think of oneself as having consented to that act. But suppose that one picks up a cat, another living creature with interests of its own, perhaps ready to be picked up, perhaps not. Something rather more is now at stake. The existence of the cat has an impact on one's own existence and autonomy of a kind that is different from that of the pen, for the cat is also an actor with the ability to be at least part author of what happens to it in one's arms, and so with the ability to exercise its interests and impose them on one's own. Yet it still seems not to make sense to think that one consents to pick up the cat, unless, of course, another person has asked one to do so, in which case it might possibly be sensible to say that one had consented to do so, because the presence of the other person would have made the idea of consent intelligible in this setting (though not necessarily applicable). If one is alone in the house, and not bound by prior agreement, one simply picks up the cat, or not, without in any way consenting to do so.

Now suppose, finally, that one picks up a baby rather than a cat. Incompletely formed as he or she may be, the baby is from the outset an agent like oneself, with interests that parallel one's own most fundamental interests, as well as a distinct existence and an emerging autonomy that call for something akin to the respect that is owed to oneself, albeit with all the modifications appropriate to the baby's particular stage of development. More pertinent to the issue of consent, the baby's presence in one's life and in one's arms has a profound impact on one's own existence and autonomy, an impact that, rich as it generally is, may not always be wholly welcome or constructive. Yet even here it still seems not to make sense to think that one consents to pick up the baby, and that continues to hold true even if the baby happens to be particularly demanding and one has rather significant other claims on one's attention, so that picking up the baby at that particular moment is in fact contrary to one's interest, not only immediately but quite possibly in the longer term as well, making it something that for very good reason one would much rather not do. One could up the ante still further, so as to suppose that one's autonomy was seriously impaired by engagement with the baby, as many parents will gloomily recognize the possibility of, and yet continue to believe that it is not sensible to think that one consents to actions that one takes in relation to the baby, such as that of picking the baby up. The baby's burden may possibly be an unwanted burden, but it is not for that reason alone something that one can intelligibly consent to in picking the baby up.

2.3.2 Interaction and Consent

In what way might the situation be different when another adult is involved? What would make it so? Part of the answer might be thought to lie in the fact that the other adult is a fully developed agent with a fully realized autonomy of his or her own that is in need of proper respect, and so is not available to be picked up or otherwise dealt with in the manner of a pen, a cat, or a baby, and what is more and, by the same token, has a reciprocal responsibility to respect one's own autonomy that is either not present or at best imperfectly present in the case of the pen, the cat, or the baby. Yet that answer appears to get the order of influence and ensuing concern rather the wrong way round. The question for the moment is what sense it would make to consent to one's grasp of another when that other is an adult like oneself, and so is in a position akin to one's own, and that question is bound to be approached from the perspective of oneself (or the other adult), in the same manner as in the cases of the pen, the cat, and the baby, rather than from the perspective of whatever is being grasped, be that the other adult (from whichever point of view), or the pen, or the cat, or the baby. So what kind of difference might the fully realized autonomy of another adult make to the situation, so as to trigger the need for consent? If and to the extent that the action in question is reciprocal, the answer will apply to each adult, making any need for consent to the action bidirectional. Each adult is in a like position. Neither seems to be in a position to consent sensibly to what he or she is doing. What reason might there be then for either to seek consent from the other for an action that it makes no sense for either of them to consent to?

Take the case of a handshake. One extends one's hand, and rather than grasping an inanimate object, in which case no question of consent could be thought to arise, one grasps the hand of another person. The situation embodies a host of possibilities that need to be carefully parsed. One of those can be quickly set aside. Suppose that two people approach a heavy beam that needs to be moved. Each person grasps one end of the beam, and together they lift it. Their action is cooperative but not consensual. There is no call for either person to seek the consent of the other before undertaking the task. The same would be true if each person were to grasp the end of a stick and then hold it steadily, as part of a ceremony perhaps. The action of each person would not be affected in terms of its quality or character by the bare presence of another's hand at the other end of the stick, although when looked at as a whole the fact that the two acted in concert, both distinctly and cooperatively, would be of expressive value, thereby making the ceremony a rational ritual, and connecting part of its value to each person's action.

Suppose now that the stick is removed, so that each person grasps the other's hand, and again holds it steadily. It seems to me that nothing in the quality of either person's action has changed, as we all would accept if the hand that either person was grasping belonged to a person who was unconscious. Of course, a person who is unconscious is by definition both immobile and unaware. The person who takes one's hand is neither of those things. Yet in itself the fact of awareness seems a distraction in this setting, because it is present in several of the cases under consideration, in only some of which consent could be thought to be an issue. Setting awareness aside, therefore, what might mobility bring to the situation so as to make it one that calls for consent?

Suppose then that what takes place is a conventional handshake, in which hands are not merely grasped but moved up and down in concert with one another. Depending on the particular handshake, nothing at all may have changed. If the actions of the parties are synchronous, the movement of each person's hand will not have been affected by the movement of the other person's hand. Each hand will simply keep time with the other, so to speak, without being operated on to do so. As in the case of picking up a beam together, the two actions are coordinated but not consensual. One action is inspiring but not driving the other. Nothing here could call for consent.

Yet as we all know from experience, some of it bruising, the practice of handshaking is open to many nuances, which may be played out in quality of grip and vigour of movement as well as in duration. In many cases, certain of those nuances will not be reciprocal. So one may grasp a hand, or more to the point perhaps, find one's hand grasped, either firmly or limply, may pump another person's hand in greeting or simply lift it slightly, may engage in a brief handshake or a very prolonged one. Variations of these kinds are ways of communicating one's attitude to the greeting of any particular person on any particular occasion, so as to localize and give particular content to the operation of a general convention. The attitudes expressed thereby are not necessarily reciprocated or even welcome. In this setting and many others like it, the idea of consent might appear to be in a position to obtain some rational purchase.

Suggestive as these nuances seem, however, their analysis remains elusive. It is still the case that one cannot sensibly consent to the taking of another person's hand. Why then does another person need one's consent to an action that it makes no sense for one to consent to? What is one's hand doing differently from whatever it does when it grasps anything else? The conventional picture may make this question slightly difficult to get one's head around, because convention has done much to shape our intuitions here. Nevertheless, it seems to me that one can get the gist of the issue by approaching it in steps. If one picks up an object, be it a stick or a hand, one will notice many things about the object, whether it is rough or smooth, cold or hot, heavy or light, inert or alive. If the object is alive, then one will notice further, as part of noticing that it is alive, that it is warm (usually), active, independent, and distinctively vulnerable. The question then is whether these features of interaction with a living creature are of a different order from the features of the inert in a way that affects what one is doing, that is grasping. The fact of grasping is not affected by any other feature of its encounter with what is grasped. The possibility is that it is not altered by this feature either, unless and to the extent that one is passive in the face of it.

2.3.3 Acting and Being Acted Upon

The most obvious response to the question of what one's hand is doing differently when grasping the hand of another, a response that might seem to have been artificially sidelined in the analysis so far, would appear to be that in cases like that of a nuanced handshake one's hand is grasped as well as grasping, and it is the former that one needs to consent to. In a way that response does help to point us in what I take to be the right direction, but in a way too it begs the question, which is now embedded in the idea of being grasped and what might distinguish that experience, not only from the grasping but also from other forms of engagement with the world, all of which have their impact on one, not all of that impact welcome, a great deal of it not at one's bidding. So what appears obvious also continues to remain obscure, for to notice that one's hand is grasped as well as grasping is not in itself to advance our understanding of the distinction between the two without some unpacking of the idea of what it means to be grasped.

On the face of it, all the distinction shows is that the handshake constitutes an interaction, and so can be regarded from either of two perspectives, in each of which the agent is grasping something outside himself or herself and is consequently affected by that experience in a way that we can plausibly describe in terms of being grasped. It does not thereby show that an interaction is in any sense fundamentally different from an action, apart from possibly being more complicated, more contingent, and perhaps more explicitly intertwined with forces outside oneself, although that will not always be the case. It is true by definition, of course, that in all interactions there are two actions involved rather than one, each of them proximate to the other, each of them influencing the other. That is what makes them interactions as well as actions. Yet what is true of interactions by their definition is also in many respects true of virtually all the actions that one undertakes, whether or not they are susceptible to being formally labelled as interactions. Indeed, when one comes down to it, it is hard to imagine an action that is not at some level an interaction with some aspect of the world. Is there then any deep reason to distinguish the two? What might give rise to a special authority over another's action, in the form of a requirement that the other obtain consent from one, just because an interaction more self-evidently engages with the world in a way that affects oneself as well as others? It cannot simply be that one is acted upon as well as acting, for that can be and very often is true of bare actions, those in which the forces of the world that one engages with do not respond directly to one's engagement yet nonetheless act upon one.

Perhaps it is the active character of what one is grasping, together with the guiding intelligence and potential opposition of interest to be found there that makes consent an issue. Perhaps that sense of an alien point of view is what is comprehended in the idea of being grasped. Otherwise, as I have said, the experience of being grasped would be no different from the experience of grasping. The hand that lay in one's own would feel the same in both cases. The immediate thing to notice about this way of making sense of consent is that opposition of interest was also present in the cases of the baby and the cat, and yet there was little or no temptation to think that it would be sensible to think of one's consenting to pick up either. Indeed one might have shaken the cat's paw, or have put one's finger in the baby's grasp, still without generating the need to alter the picture in which consent has no role to play.

More broadly, however, it seems to me that this perspective on interaction, which emphasizes the adversarial, simply makes more explicit the fact that we function in a world in which our actions are typically shaped as well as shaping. How could it be otherwise? The world is not there merely to be acted upon, not there to align itself with one's interests. It is there to be negotiated with, and that surely is precisely what we do whenever we act, whether our actions are ones that can be formally labelled as interactions or not. In that negotiation there will very often be found a measure of resistance to one's will and so to whatever drives one's will, be that rational or irrational. Resistance makes accommodation necessary, and the accommodations that one makes in the course of negotiation will inevitably not always be to one's liking. Yet that is sometimes a good thing, though also of course sometimes not. Actions are negotiations with the world in pursuit of value, negotiations that may well be both complex and frustrating, and that may well also end in failure, often failure for oneself and flourishing for another, so much so as to prompt in some of us the isolationist thought that one person's failure is the necessary price of another person's flourishing, as if the collective life of all were a zero sum game, rather than the imperfectly conceived, imperfectly cooperative, frequently obstructed, yet frequently rewarding project that it is. The force of another that is felt in a nuanced handshake is continuous with all the other forces that, taken together, constitute the experience of living, and with all the values and vulnerabilities that engagement with any of those forces gives rise to.

What remains in the idea of being grasped, an idea that admittedly does seem to capture, however provisionally and inarticulately, the concern that the practice of consent is designed to address, to distinguish the cases that it has in mind from all the other negotiations that we undertake with a largely indifferent and often intractable world? It appears from the considerations advanced so far that it cannot simply be that the world is apt to be less than fully amenable to our will, apt to push back if pushed, to grasp if grasped, as the attribution of special significance to the bare idea of being grasped might suggest. If that is not the right way to think of things, then might the point of consent be to secure certain of our interests in particular rather than to insulate us from unwanted impact across the board? What might those particular interests be, and does the practice of consent as we understand it succeed in picking them out?

2.3.4 Consent and Different Species of Interaction

It is noticeable that questions of consent are at their most prominent when what is at stake is some aspect of one's physical integrity. That is surely no accident. A persuasive case can be made in support of the view that there is a special connection between one's bodily integrity and one's dignity, between control of one's body and one's autonomy, and underpinning both those connections, that there is special intimacy and special vulnerability to be found in physical contact with another person. That combination of high value and high vulnerability might be thought to call for special protection and, it might sensibly be further maintained, that is just what the practice of consent provides. Consent places what matters most to us most fully within our control. Or so the thought in support of this particular view of the practice might run. The question in response is not simply whether the case for the body as the locus of consent is a good one, but whether it is in fact a case for consent. On both fronts, there seems reason for significant doubt. Central as our physical experience clearly is to the achievement of our well-being, and closely fused as that experience is to all of our other functions, it is implausible to think that it can be happily identified with what is most at stake in the acquisition of our dignity and the pursuit of our autonomy. And as valuable as consent can be, in ways that were sketched earlier and will be explored more fully later, it seems ill-suited to the effective securing of either dignity or autonomy.

In many settings, and more broadly, in certain cultures, physical integrity simply does not have the connection to value, let alone to the realization of autonomy, that this rationale for the practice of consent assumes. We are all too familiar with everyday settings, such as that of a crowded bus or train, or an entrance or exit to a major public event, in which close bodily contact is now routine. In such settings, it is assumed, usually correctly, that one's dignity is not at stake in the aspects of one's physical integrity that are regularly intruded upon there. The reason is that the connection between one's dignity and physical integrity takes its shape in and through social practices, some of which are inescapable, and so are bound to be observed everywhere and at all times, but many of which are rightly regarded as matters for local interpretation and decision. It is open to us, as one particular urban culture, to accept, as admittedly we do with some degree of reluctance, the physical consequences of crowding on public transport, closely though those consequences resemble the very kinds of physical contact that in other settings would trigger a demand for consent. We can do so because the meaning of those contacts is not given entirely by the body but also by the social practices that are articulated and engaged in with the involvement of the body, and by the value that those practices are capable of yielding, directly and indirectly.

This can lead to very different schemes of significance, not only within a particular culture, where meanings inevitably influence and limit one another, but also across cultures, where those restrictions either do not apply or apply only weakly, turning as they do in that setting on the presence or absence of connections between the practices of different cultures. Attitudes to physical integrity, that is, are not only driven by particular settings within a given culture but also come in social packages, the elements of which influence one another so as to give characteristic shape to the package as a whole, with the result that different cultures may come to have radically different instantiations of what is, in its most abstract terms, a universal connection between physical integrity and dignity. As we know, the consequence has been that practices that would be quite unthinkable in one culture can be quite reasonably pursued in another. The heightened value and vulnerability that we associate with the body generally, therefore, and look to oversee by means of the practice of consent, are in fact derivative of the interests and associated well-being of the particular people that we are in the particular place we happen to be in. Dimensions of physical integrity have an important part to play in the development and realization of those interests without being the heart of the matter. In other words, what are ultimately being picked out here are interests rather than the body, constitutive though the body is of certain of those interests.

Yet if it is interests in general that consent is called upon to protect, or at least the most valuable and vulnerable of them, then it will be immediately clear that many of our most important interests, the sites in which our dignity and our autonomy are most at stake, are vested in practices that have little or nothing to do with the body, and just as clear that consent has and can have no role to play in them, in practice or in principle, the latter in part because so many of them are cases of action and its consequences, in which consent cannot figure. This observation has two aspects. The first is that the settings in which we seek value and in which our interests may be vulnerable to the power and perceptions of others are typically systemic rather than discrete. Put in slightly different terms, the discrete derives much of its significance from its connections, connections that are traceable in the discrete but not governable there. This gives rise to a mismatch with the practice of consent, which is unavoidably based on occasion and incident. The mismatch comes of the fact that the systematic devaluation of one's interests, which may well be the most significant challenge that they face, need not be and usually is not rendered in any specific incident that one might be in a position to refuse consent to. Consent is a way of securing personal control, and as a method of securing our most valuable and vulnerable interests it suffers from the fact that any control that might be established over the systemic features that place those interests at risk cannot usually be instantiated in the settings of individual consent.

The second and related aspect of the observation is that many of the worst things that can happen to us, many of the circumstances most damaging to our interests, proceed from aspects of the world other than the presence and influence of our fellow human beings. Those circumstances can be negotiated but never consented to, and a focus on the practice of consent thus overstates the significance to our well-being of both our control and the presence and influence of other people. It is true that we might want to settle for control of what can be controlled, but in doing so we would be bound to recognize that consent is a device that is fundamentally at odds with the attitudes that are needed to advance any suitably enlightened view of one's interests, and that, even were it intelligible, to exercise control through the device of consent over what is only a limited and often marginal portion of the domain of one's autonomy may well prove to be valuable largely as a gesture.

2.3.5 Negotiating Interactions without Consent

Does this not yield the conclusion that actions and interactions are broadly alike in their burdens and responsibilities and thus are to be governed in the same way, making consent as inapt to the latter as to the former? It is only the thought that there is a necessary congruence between one's actions and one's desires and interests that is liable to prompt the further thought that there is a fundamental distinction between actions, where that appears to be the case, and interactions, where it appears not to be. Yet far from being necessary the congruence is largely an illusion. Not only can one all too easily mistake one's desires and interests in one's actions and be better guided in interactions, where one can draw upon the content of another mind as well as upon one's own, but more profoundly one's desires and interests are by and large most fully realized in and through interaction. This suggests that the divide between action and interaction, as between the prudential and the moral, is real but not deep. Indeed, it might be thought, for the reasons given above among others, that properly understood all actions are ultimately interactions with the world, even those actions that involve only one's own person, such as scratching one's head. All are cases of responsibility, in which one seeks to realize value in ways that respect both value and valuers, not only generally but also in the particular case, for engagement with other valuers is part and parcel of our engagement with value, to the extent that one cannot genuinely respect value without respecting valuers, and vice versa. It is that respect for value and valuers in the actions that we undertake that consent so awkwardly and imperfectly seeks to govern. What is needed in its place is a properly sensitive and nuanced approach to the exercise of responsibility, in our interactions as much as in our actions, and to the various forms of negotiation with the world that such responsibility entails.

The only significant difference between actions and interactions in this context is that in the case of actions that directly involve other people (and to a lesser extent, other living creatures), and so are formally labelled interactions, one finds oneself responding to responses as well as to all the other values present there. That makes engagement in such actions distinctively fluid, unpredictable, driven by another person as much as by oneself, and so in many ways as improvisational as jazz. It also and at its best makes the engagement distinctively rewarding, because where otherwise there would have been an indifferent universe there is instead someone like oneself, to whom one's interests are interesting, to put it succinctly. That reward is diminished, of course, by failure to comprehend where comprehension is called for, to recognize where recognition is called for, or to respect where respect is warranted.

All these miscarriages, of comprehension, recognition, and respect, are born of failure to read the signals in another's actions, to take on board the significance of their responses, to be ready to see oneself as grasped as well as grasping, and to find promise as well as vulnerability in both those things, indeed to become alive to and versed in the various connections and interdependencies that tie promise to vulnerability, and vice versa. Fluid and improvised engagements depend for their success on sensitivity to others, and all too often that sensitivity is absent. Insensitivity is born sometimes of indifference, sometimes of misunderstanding, and notoriously sometimes of deliberate strategies of division and exclusion, whether embodied in the ad hoc mistreatment of one or more individuals on a particular occasion, or generalized so as to affect whole classes of people, and so standardly to misshape the course of the interactions between those people and others. Despite their enormous promise, sexual relations have long been a particularly influential theatre for the development and implementation of both individual and generalized insensitivities, thereby damaging both particular relationships and the status of women generally, partly because so much is at stake there, and partly because a high degree of sensitivity is required to draw out all the value that sexual relations are capable of giving rise to, and to recognize and respect the many correlative vulnerabilities present there. Yet special cases aside, the remedying of insensitivities can only be successfully undertaken by means that are compatible with the general character of action and interaction and with the particular forms of goodness that are at stake in their instantiation. That calls for enlightened negotiation rather than consent.

Consider first, however, those cases where things go right. Begin with the sympathetic and collaborative. Suppose that two people, staying at a hotel together, in the course of their evening take to the floor to dance with one another. To preserve the sense of spontaneity, suppose further that dancing had not been part of their plans for the evening, but that the hotel restaurant turned out to have a dance floor, the hotel band was old-fashioned but awfully good, and they said to one another, in the way that people do in these accounts, let's dance. To dance with another person is to move in ways that draw inspiration from the movements of one's partner. Sometimes, as in a close dance in one another's arms, that inspiration is fine-grained and intimate, responsive to the smallest and most individual nuances of one another's physical expression, so building and drawing upon the rewards of a particular relationship and the individual idiosyncrasies, physical, emotional, intellectual, that give that relationship its character. Sometimes, as in a formal dance that involves the execution of an established routine by a number of people acting in concert, the inspiration is communal, and the point of participating in the dance is to dramatize, contribute to, and confirm a certain image of social order, the contours of which will help to shape the future conduct of the participants in other settings. One need only call to mind a supper club or a square dance, minuet, or quadrille. Nothing in this picture is or could be a matter of consent.

That does not mean that things cannot go wrong. On the contrary. One person may lead and lead badly, so that the aesthetics of the dance are impaired or altogether lost. One partner may be insufficiently attuned to the other, so that the resonances that might have arisen from mutuality of understanding are never discovered, and in their place there is only the brutish dominance of one partner over the other, or the self-regarding isolation of a nominal partner who in fact ends up dancing largely by and for himself, or less commonly, for herself. The very form of the dance may have been designed, as in times past, to secure certain general social goods at the cost of personal meaning to its participants. In such cases, the design or conduct of the dance may well turn out to be subversive of the goods that are claimed for it, so as to become a pernicious ritual. Yet the proper regulation of these outcomes is a matter for enlightened social practice, and for steady education in the kinds of consciousness upon which such practice depends. Some of that practice will be very local, as when each partner bit by bit educates the other, and so bit by bit builds a better relationship; some of it will be cultural, so as to design better dances and better attitudes towards their execution. In none of these could a practice of consent be either intelligible or effective. What is more, and perhaps more debilitating of the underlying motives that prompt us to call for consent, in none of them is consent something to be missed. To address the most immediate and most obvious area of concern, its absence does not make us in any way more vulnerable or less respected. We are no less protected by the exercise of responsibility than by the practice of consent because we are no more alone in it. Both phenomena rely for much of their meaning and effectiveness on supporting social practices, albeit the one turning on understanding and the other on authority.

Dancing is all about cooperation and what it makes possible in terms of beauty and intimacy, some of that expressive of a personal relationship, some of it expressive of a social order. The point of looking to dancing as an illustration is to bring out the possibility of negotiating intimacy in a manner that takes full account of all that is at stake there yet that achieves its ends without recourse to the practice of consent. Next consider by partial contrast, as something less directly dedicated to cooperation and so as something that brings out the continuity of action and interaction, the kinds of actions and interactions that take place when one walks down a crowded street. The various people going about their business there have different destinations, different paces, different understandings of the etiquette of avoidance. There are no formal rules for pedestrians, it seems, special settings aside. People move as they see fit. Yet while there are many consequent frustrations, there are few collisions. All is somehow invisibly negotiated. All is more or less cooperative. How does this come to pass? What makes the anarchic broadly harmonious?

In Toronto once, approaching a man coming the other way, I moved first left, then right, then left again, only to end up in his arms. He was, it turned out, Hungarian, one of those who came to Canada in 1956. He held me gently for a moment and then in thickly accented English told me: 'Always pass on the right.' Yet if that is really a rule, few observe it. Instead, we seem to call upon a repertoire of strategies of avoidance and then to improvise as the occasion calls for, for example keeping close watch on the trajectory of the people coming our way, reading the signals they are sending out, and taking account of the particular cultural setting in which they are moving. In London, if walking alongside iron railings, on a crowded pavement, in a particular neighbourhood, in a mildly brutish culture, I leave room between myself and the iron railings, even when several people are approaching me and space is very limited, so that I can move over if I have to. I have learned that it is quite likely that others will not give me the room I am looking for if they can help it. I then observe the approaching people carefully, trying to read them as individuals and as potential bearers of the general social attitude. They, of course, are doing something the same thing as me, the less sensitively the more of them there are, the younger they are, and the more they have had to drink. In New York, where pavements are on the face of it less crowded and so easier to navigate, my behaviour is if anything more defensive, because the other pedestrians there are liable to be rather different people from Londoners, with a rather different set of attitudes. It would be a mistake, for example, to look at them directly. It is better to avoid their eyes. Or so I learned once. Perhaps my lessons need updating.

These, in many ways no less than dancing, are cases of cooperative interaction, not matters of bare action, of my simply walking down the street. Everyone on those streets is at all times engaged in negotiation with everyone else there. Getting those negotiations wrong can have significant consequences, for not every collision is with a person as benevolent as my ruefully remembered Hungarian fellow Torontonian.[12] Yet once again there is nothing to rely on other than the enlightened exercise of responsibility. That is just how we interact with other people successfully, even when those people are strangers undertaking missions that we do not share, missions that may interfere with our immediate interests and undermine our autonomy. Consider the predicament of the elderly or the disabled, whose frailties make the navigation of a crowded street difficult to the point of potentially undermining their autonomy, and who thus every day depend on other pedestrians to recognize and accommodate their predicament, even as those others go about their own business of proceeding through the crowds themselves. We could not inhabit the worlds that we inhabit without becoming expert in what is needed to live up to the demands of the responsible management of our myriad encounters with our fellows there, in all their varieties of character and significance, encounters in which, for all their passing nature, a great deal may be at stake for one or more of those involved, and so which cannot be set aside as typically trivial. That is to say, the enlightened negotiation of our interactions with other people is a crucial aspect in the realization of our dignity and our autonomy, from which much of the richness of our lives flows. It is not, certain special settings aside, something to be afraid or unconfident of, something to be marginalized, limited, unilaterally controlled. It is how we cooperate daily. It is part of what defines us as social beings. It is not a matter for consent, for the unilateral authority of each one of us over the other's actions.

Consider finally sexual relations, as a setting for interactions that are expected to be governed by consent rather than by negotiation. Given what is at stake in that setting, and the history of exploitation that has taken place there, it is vital that those who are exposed to the acute vulnerabilities that can arise in that setting have access to a veto on further dialogue, a way of calling an end to further negotiation,

---

[12] I once half-collided with a Londoner when approaching an Underground station and said 'Sorry' to him, out of what I took to be politeness, rather than out of a sense that I had done something wrong. His response to me was, 'I'll make you sorry.' (My guess is that he was reacting to an implication of British English that I had not intended, that 'Sorry' means 'Get out of my way'.)

a way of removing this particular form of interaction from the realm of responsible exchange that would normally guide and inform it. That is exactly what the law gives them in providing that intercourse that takes place without consent is rape. The ramifications of that provision will be considered later, in the final section of this chapter. The present question, however, is the extent to which the correlative is true, that is, the extent to which the goodness of sex depends on the presence of ongoing consent, and of explicit consent if the conclusions of the earlier discussion are correct. Sex without consent is illegal, and therefore undertaken at risk of legal sanction, but does it follow that it is wrong, other than in terms of the wrongness that follows from illegality? It seems to me that the answer must be that it is not, or at least not necessarily so.

Absence of consent to sex is not only the mark of great wrong, although it certainly can be that, but also and more commonly a precondition of great good. That is at least part of the reason, though far from the whole reason, why debates over consent have been so fraught in this setting. People who have sex together without securing one another's consent are taking a legal risk, and that is as it should be, but they may be the better people for that, not because breaking the law is good, but because the sex that they consequently engage in has a goodness that is incompatible with the practice of consent. They will not be better people, of course, but very much the worse, if the sex that they are engaging in, or the circumstances under which it is engaged in, is such that one of the participants is passive. In that situation, consent, and explicit consent at that, is absolutely necessary, and in its absence what is illegal is also immoral. To put it succinctly, the law's prohibition covers two sets of experiences, one bad and the other good. There may be sound reasons for the law not to distinguish those experiences but we should. That is because we need to be lawbreakers in order to gain access to much of the good that sex has to offer. If we shrink from that fact, we will be in no position to grasp the full value of sex, to understand how we can lose touch with that value, and just as important and more troublingly, how we are liable to abuse it.

What would warrant such a view of good sex? Simply that spontaneity and improvisation, alertness to the details of one another's physical and emotional state in all its richness and contradiction, inventiveness and inspiration in how those details might be responded to sensitively and fruitfully, and much more of that ilk, are crucial features of many forms of sex at its best, and of the personal relationships that those forms of good sex help to constitute. All of these are incompatible with consent. Good sex, as we all know, can be like certain conventional kinds of good dancing, something in which one can, of course, learn the steps and then execute them as prescribed, but it is also and more recognizably something in which people can together make up their own steps, find their own expression, call upon old tropes or discard them, as suits their mood and the occasion.

This is not to be dewy-eyed about the experience of sex. Even good sex can be dull as well as dangerous, can be rather less like dancing and rather more like negotiating with an oncomer on a crowded street.[13] In heterosexual relations in particular, where value is derived in part from dissonance, the kinds of harmony that characterize dancing at its best are liable to be elusive. Nevertheless, and as our everyday understanding of it suggests, much of good sex is not something that one can sensibly consent to, at least not something that one can consent to explicitly. What is more, and more important from the perspective of consent, the same is true of much of bad sex, for a sexual encounter that miscarries retains the ambitions and consequent character of the good sex that has been aimed at, and so remains an inapt setting for consent. Sex may be repetitive, inattentive, and unimaginative, so as to be a pretty poor experience for all involved, the poorer for those to whom it matters most that it be got right (which may characteristically be one sex rather than the other, depending on one's view of the respective sensitivities of the sexes), and yet continue to be an inapt setting for consent. As I have indicated, it is only when the project of sex involves the passivity of one of its participants that consent is not merely intelligible but essential.

There is a crucial caveat that needs to be noted here, at once and to repeat, so that it may be bracketed here and returned to later in considering the implications of the stand taken by the law in insisting upon the presence of consent to sexual relations. Practices of negotiation can often become corrupted, and the kinds of education, consciousness raising, and reform that would be necessary to remedy those practices, so as to ensure that they are by and large consistent with the dignity and autonomy of all who are involved in them, cannot always be counted upon to arise naturally. In that case, the only practical prospect for reform lies in the intervention of an authority that has the power to alter the culture of negotiation, to overturn those practices in their present form, which in this case means the authority of law. Law is seldom sufficient to secure change but it can be its catalyst. Yet the ultimate aim of the law's intervention in this way need not be to establish a substitute order of human interaction, or to displace the significance of the direct responsibility of participants in sexual relations, or to rewrite the scope of that responsibility, let alone go so far as to convert agents into patients, if that is what is at stake in the practice of consent. Rather, and surely more plausibly, it is to offer those who have been and are likely to continue to be the victims of culturally entrenched patterns of tainted negotiations over sexual relations an effective instrument in their defence, and in doing so to disrupt practices that would be unlikely to be disrupted otherwise, in the hope that a more enlightened successor to those practices will over time emerge as a result. Were it otherwise, it would be constitutive of the law's ultimate aim, in part at least, to cut us off from much of what is good about sex, much of what makes good sex continuous with, and a contributor

---

[13] Lest I be taken to be doing anything other than calling to mind an earlier example in using the reference to negotiating a crowded street, I should make clear that I am thinking here of the negotiation that takes place with any person proceeding in a different direction, rather than in pursuit of harmony.

to, our successful functioning as social beings. One should hesitate to conclude as much. If that were what the law was really aiming for, we would have good reason to resist it as well as to respect it.

A final, more general observation. Whatever claims may be made for the special character of the human condition, ours are not the only lives that matter in the world, although we are, as far as we know, the only creatures that are capable of consent. In itself that should make us doubt the dependency of well-being, and of physical well-being in particular, on the practice of consent. Consider in that vein the predicament of all in the world that cannot consent, because of a lack of capacity to do so, yet that is entitled to no less concern for that, not only the other conscious things in the world, who are no less committed than we are to the project of life and the goodness that can be found there, but also those things that are not conscious or even alive yet the existence of which has value, not for them, for they are not valuers (because they are not capable of so being), and not simply for us, as the particular valuers that we are, but in itself and so for the very idea of value and the valuers that (as Raz points out) the idea of value implies.[14] As living creatures and as the specially rational creatures that we are, we have a basic, one might even say an environmental, obligation to our fellow denizens to engage with them responsibly, in our actions as much as in our interactions, an obligation that may sometimes involve the practice of consent but that cannot be identified with it. Indeed, it is that responsibility that consent can serve, when suitably invoked.

2.3.6 The Unwelcome and the Unwilled

None of these things, be it the dancing, the walking in crowds, or the sex, are things that in any sense happen to one, or that happen to the other person involved. Rather they are things that one does and that the other person does, each working with and through the other. Doing them together in this interactive way gives rise to synergies, few of them predictable, many of them volatile, that each person may either participate in to their benefit or be undermined by, without ever being in a position to control outright, not so much because such controlling is impractical, though that is often the case, but because it is incompatible with the realization of the values at stake. All of these phenomena are entirely familiar features of everyday life. What then has led us to think otherwise, particularly in settings where sexual relations are involved?

The most obvious source of a different view is in the idea that something that is unwelcome to you is something that must have been done to you rather than by you, something that you did not will and that consequently must be the product of

---

[14] Raz, *The Practice of Value* (2003). See also and more broadly, Macklem and Gardner, 'Human Disability' (2014) 25 KLJ 60.

another's will, something that you would unwill if you could and that you should therefore be put in a position to unwill if at all possible (which in practice means forestalling the will of another, something that you should be put in a position to do in advance of its exercise, given that history is seldom reversible). Consent is a device that, when properly supported by other social practices that render its exercise effective, secures the pre-emptive force of one's will, on the assumption that one's will is something that can be called upon to forestall the unwelcome.

This conflation of the unwelcome and the unwilled is clearly misguided, for it gives too much credit to the will in the articulation of goodness, and too little credit to the independent pull of the good, in all its complexity, and to the contingencies of the world. Much of our experience is both unwanted and unwilled, and one need not be a Victorian to recognize the goodness that this fact makes possible. We regularly adapt to circumstances that we did not seek and would not have sought, and in doing so gradually come to discover the good in them. Stuff happens, as the idiom puts it, and that is not always a bad thing, entirely natural as it may be to think otherwise in the very moment that stuff is happening. This conflation of the unwelcome and the unwilled leads to a further conflation of certain aspects of the active, those that are unwanted, with the features of the passive, and hence to the remedial importation of the idea of consent, a crucial operator in the realm of the passive, into certain realms of the active, in the belief that consent can perform the same role in relation to the active as it does in relation to the passive, ensuring as far as possible that nothing happens to us that we do not want to happen to us. Interestingly and possibly revealingly, the importation brings with it recognizable shadings of the character that consent has in the setting of the passive, shadings that account for some of the idiosyncrasies of its operation and place in the active.

When one is passive, one's mind retires from the fray, so to speak, in some respect, for some purpose, and for some period of time, other than as an observer, critic, and ultimate judge. What is left is one's physical being, and it is for the sake of that physical being that one is prepared to be passive. That is because the conscious mind cannot itself be passive and so is committed by its nature to action and to interaction. Another person can readily act upon one's passive body, but can act upon one's mind only with and through that mind's participation. This may explain the broader association of consent with bodily integrity. However, quite apart from the doubts one might have about the soundness of that association, passivity itself has a broader scope than that which the practice of consent suggests, for one's physical well-being may sometimes require that one be passive in the face of actions that one does not consent to. What this reveals is that the value of passivity and the value of consenting to one's passivity are distinct and separable. In fact, and slightly surprising as it may seem, in becoming passive one submits, without engaging in any reciprocal action of one's own, to the effect of some other person's action upon one's body, either with or without one's consent, and hence either with or without the legitimation that one's consent confers. To be passive may be valuable in its own right, even though consent is absent.

The further function of the practice of consent to what one passively submits to, and of the legitimacy that it confers upon what would otherwise have been wrongful interference, is to permit the realization of some value or values, not only from the fact of one's passivity but from the supporting fact of one's consent to that passivity, values that would be unrealizable otherwise, values that one has reason to want but cannot will directly, values that depend upon the intervention of another person upon the fact of one's passivity, and that therefore depend upon the licence that makes that intervention legitimate and thus legitimately available.

Finally, in both types of case, but the more particularly when consent is absent and with it the guidance that can be provided through the detailing of consent, the condition of passivity by its very nature entails vulnerability, not merely physical vulnerability but psychological and rational vulnerability as well. These three features of the passive, the physical, the valuable, and the vulnerable, when imported by the practice of consent into a setting such as that of sexual relations, render that importation plausible (because its combination of features is already familiar) and so possibly more effective for that reason, albeit yielding, as has already been emphasized, whatever benefits it may give rise to at the cost of the abandonment of the role and claims of the active in that setting, and of the value that those activist claims can give rise to when properly responded to.

2.3.7 Submission and Consent

These observations may go some way to explaining why the unwelcomeness of certain actions, those that involve the body, its value, and its vulnerability, is characteristically looked to when a rationale is sought for the requirement of consent to interactions. Yet the unwelcomeness of an action and the power of consent to forestall it is ultimately a distraction, the requirements of the law aside for the moment. We have reason to avoid the unwelcome, but it is a reason that we give effect to through our actions. It would be quite odd to try to avoid something by means of refusal of one's consent to another's action were any sound action of one's own available. That is because one's actions are rather more expressive of one's will and usually more effective in implementing it than are the actions of another that one has consented to. This suggests that the practice of consent is properly inspired by something other than avoidance of the unwelcome. It would follow that we have good reason to turn to consent in the setting of sexual relations, but it is not the reason of aligning our desires and outcomes as far as possible through the exercise of our will.

What is in fact fundamental to the practice of consent is the extent to which one is passive, the extent to which, either by one's choice or otherwise, things are simply happening to one. In that situation, a grant of consent becomes the only available vehicle for one's will. By contrast, the fact that something is unwelcome is a sadly familiar feature of the landscape of action. It does not in any sense entail that one is passive in the face of it, and so does not entail a place for consent. Put differently, the distinctions between the active and the passive and that between the welcome and the unwelcome are cross-cutting, not coextensive. The beguiling thought to the contrary is what is so damagingly misleading in the idea of being grasped, an idea that tends to conflate the unwanted effects of interaction with passivity. In fact it is quite vital to distinguish, particularly in the domain of sexual relations, what one does not want but remains active in the face of, physically or mentally, and what one passively accepts. One then needs to further distinguish passivities that are consented to and those that are not. One of the most prominent occasions for the deployment of these distinctions, and a notorious example not only of the confusion that mishandling of them has given rise to but of the cost of that confusion, is the phenomenon that the law describes as mere submission to sexual relations, a phenomenon that appears to have been grasped with somewhat greater subtlety by the appellate courts than by certain commentators.

Suppose that a woman finds herself in the position that if she resists a demand for sexual intercourse she is likely to face physical violence. She might well choose to offer physical resistance as far as she possibly could, unwise as that would almost certainly be. If she did resist physically, it could clearly not be said of her that she had actively engaged in the intercourse. On the contrary, her every action would have been directed to avoiding intercourse. Nor could it be said that she had consented to the intercourse. She would not have given explicit consent and there would have been nothing in her conduct from which consent could reasonably have been inferred. No sound court or commentator would pretend otherwise, at least not any longer, in any society in which feminism has left its mark. The apparent clarity of this conclusion is one reason why some women feel the need to offer physical resistance to sexual assault, so that they may be sure of other people's agreement that they have not consented and, regrettably and reprehensibly, why some of those other people still expect them so to resist.

Once again, however, it is important to notice that what seems obvious is not inevitable. We know that the woman in question is not consenting only because we are prepared to read that fact into her resistance. Yet that is a moral conclusion rather than one that we are logically compelled to by the bare fact of a struggle. For some assailants, resistance is part of the game that they pretend both parties are engaging in, and thus perfectly compatible with willing participation. She knows she really wants to, they say, or this is just play-acting, hard to credit as such responses have now become. Clearly no reasonable person would for a moment accept this line of argument today, but its logical possibility still matters, because that possibility carries over into situations where physical resistance is not offered, and as to which observers are less of one mind in denying the presence of consent.

Suppose then that instead of resisting the same woman chose to submit to sexual intercourse. For some observers, a question then arises of whether by the very fact of her submission the woman consents to intercourse. The present position of the courts, in England and Wales, where I happen to be writing, and in most other jurisdictions, is that mere submission does not constitute consent. A woman who merely submits to intercourse is raped, at least as far as the *actus reus* of the offence is concerned. However, certain commentators disagree. For Peter Westen, a woman who submits to intercourse consents factually to the intercourse, but as the law stands in most jurisdictions her factual consent does not amount to legal consent, because the law has decided that a consent that has been secured by threat of violence ought not to count as legal consent for the purpose of the offence of rape (and certain other offences against the person).[15] Yet the distinction between factual consent and legal consent is not a distinction that the courts themselves draw and it is not at all clear to me why Westen feels bound to draw it. The law does not take the view that a woman who submits to intercourse has in fact consented to intercourse but that this fact is to be ignored. It takes the view that she did not consent, full stop. What might make it a fact, then, one that the law needed to override, that mere submission constitutes consent, as Westen believes?

Clearly submission does not communicate consent explicitly, and any claim that it does so implicitly depends on the soundness and the legitimacy of that inference on the part of the person who draws it. Those are social and moral facts, rather than a fact about the very language of behaviour. That means that it is only possible to decide whether mere submission constitutes consent by interpreting submission as a social practice, deciding whether it is capable of implying consent, deciding whether it has done so on this occasion, and finally, deciding whether any consent so obtained is morally legitimate. When the law concludes, as a matter of principle, that mere submission can never constitute consent, it is because it has gone through this exercise of analysis in order to establish the fact of the matter, not because it has decided to override the fact of the matter for its own purposes.

Yet there is something much deeper at work here, which enables the question to get off the ground at all. What in this scenario gives rise to any question of consent? When a person, in this case a woman, submits to sexual intercourse, she ceases to act, either by way of resistance or by way of cooperation, and becomes passive instead. Passivity raises the question of consent. Without it there would be no such question. However, special circumstances aside, passivity does not *answer* the question of consent, simply because it has little or no capacity to do so. One could say that passivity is inscrutable whereas consent is all about scrutiny. This makes it difficult, although not quite impossible, to derive consent from the fact of passivity.

---

[15] See Westen, *The Logic of Consent* (2004).

If the woman had actively engaged in the intercourse, the question of her consent would not arise, simply because one does not consent to one's actions and interactions, as everyday life bears witness to. (It is true that her consent would arise as a matter of law, but if she had actively engaged in the intercourse the issue would never legitimately come before a court.) It is because she decided to be passive in the circumstances that consent is an issue. What is absolutely crucial to notice and take full account of here is that something more must be shown in order to establish the presence of her consent to intercourse. If all that can be shown is the fact of her passivity, then the only basis for a claim that she consented to intercourse is that to be passive in such a situation is in itself to imply consent to intercourse. Any woman who simply lies down before her attacker, so as to be passive in the face of his conduct, is consenting to his actions upon her by the very fact of her passivity. That is what it means for a woman to lie down in that situation. Or so the argument in support of consent would run. Yet that line of argument involves making her passivity do double duty, at once triggering the question of consent and then answering it, incontrovertibly and in the affirmative. That is almost certainly to misunderstand the significance of passivity.

If and when a person is passive, another person may engage with them only with their consent. The normal patterns of interaction, and the mutual licensing that they embody, have been suspended. Consent is what replaces them, so as to secure, as best it can, the will of the person who grants it, and the various interests that are reflected and instantiated in that will. What is more and by the same token, special cases aside, the consent must be explicit in order to embody the level of detail that is required to guide one person's action upon another when the other is passive, given the importance of detail in the articulation of particular interests and the fact that the interaction that would normally convey that detail is absent. Consent can be legitimately implied only if what is consented to is exceptionally discrete or if the context in which consent is given is exceptionally detailed and self-interpreting, so that the context in which consent is given tells us all we need to know about the content of consent, all we need to know about the will of the person who is passive and what would make that consent genuinely his or her own.

It is just possible to imagine special situations where an argument of that kind might be plausible. Suppose an established relationship, in which a man says to a woman, I want you to lie perfectly still while I do everything to you, and that she lies still and he does it. Whatever one may feel about such an encounter one is bound to wonder further whether it actually involves passivity on her part, and if it does involve passivity whether there is non-verbal explicit consent to it. It seems more likely that the two are interacting, she in a minimalist, he in a maximalist manner. What is not plausible, however, is the general proposition that a woman who submits to her attacker is implicitly consenting to what she submits to, when there is every reason to believe that to the contrary she, like any other sensible person, is seeking to protect herself as far as she can in the circumstances by submitting to the lesser of two evils. That is because, put at its highest, the fact of passivity in that situation is compatible with several meanings, and there is no sound basis for ascribing one rather than another to the woman in question. Where any significant doubt remains, the default position must be that she has not consented.

Leave intercourse out of the picture for a moment and imagine a soldier on the battlefield throwing down his or her arms before a more powerful enemy. What on earth might lead us to think that in doing so, and so formally submitting to death at the enemy's hands, the soldier was consenting to be killed? In both scenarios surely the only reasonable conclusion is that the supplicant is seeking from their assailant something less than the very worst, that is, something less than what would be very likely to follow if resistance were to be pursued any further, physical injury followed by rape in the case of the woman, certain death in the case of the soldier.

The confusion that arises here is a product of the underlying fact that in the law governing sexual offences consent is being treated as applicable to interaction. Courts and commentators alike approach every sexual encounter as an action, and then ask whether that action implies consent. This, however, gives rise to interpretive strain in two directions at once. Where the encounter is indeed an action, the search for consent is inapt, and at odds with the values for which the encounter is normally engaged in. On the other hand, where, as in many of the cases of sexual assault that come before the courts, the encounter involves the passivity of one party, there is normally no question of reading the implication of consent into it, because passivity on its own rarely implies consent. One who lies down on the operating table is placing himself or herself in a position to consent, but just what to is a further question for the surgeon and for those in the health-care system and the courts who have oversight of the surgeon. That is why explicit consent is almost always necessary in the passive, not merely where there is a history of exploitation. By importing consent into the active, the law creates real problems for itself. It could avoid at least some of those problems by recognizing that in certain settings intercourse is legitimately taking place without consent. Or it could insist, as it does, on the presence of consent, so that the active and the passive are continuous in that respect, at the price of rendering much sexual interaction illegal. Before turning to the difficulties that this gives rise to and the benefits that it makes possible, further consideration needs to be given to the value of passivity and the role of consent in securing it.

2.4 Consent and the Passive

For all that our lives are filled with action, and closely as that action is connected to our flourishing and to our self-understanding, sometimes things really do just happen to us, and sometimes too, as when fortune smiles on us, however slowly, that is actually a good thing, so much so that we have reason to identify that special fortune in advance and seek it out, hard as it may go against the autonomous grain of our lives to do so. For a limited time, on some special occasion, and for some special purpose, we yield up our hard-won role as agents, and place an aspect of ourselves and the goodness of our lives in the hands of some other person, or even the fates. We become passive, not only to avoid a harm that would almost certainly be made greater by our involvement, as in the case of victims of sexual violence and others, who to a greater or lesser degree play dead in the hope that danger (or some aspect of it) may overlook them and so pass them by, but also to achieve some good that is inaccessible through our agency, either alone or in collaboration with the agency of others. It is in the latter setting, where passivity is sought out as a way of enhancing our well-being in some respect, one that we can guide and shape but cannot undertake for ourselves, that the question of consent comes into play. What exactly can consent do and not do for us? What kinds of goods does it make possible and what kinds of costs does it exact? What precisely is its moral power? The phenomenon is familiar but its nature is once again elusive.

One thought is that in giving consent one makes another's action one's own, and correlatively, allows the other to make what would otherwise have been one's action theirs, so that the good-making properties of the fact that an action is one's own, such as they may be, flow in both directions through the vehicle of one's consent into and from the action of another, making that action both good for one and one's own. Their action and one's will become fused, for whatever purpose consent has been given to. In this way, the authority of one's agency, physical and moral, is enhanced by the agency, physical and moral, of another. There seem to be at least two ideas present in this thought, one of which can be quickly set aside. The first idea draws attention to the value of collaboration, and to the ways in which one's agency can be enhanced by means of interaction with the agency of others, whether directly or through the mediation of social institutions and practices. Yet consent is not a case of collaboration, and so cannot lay claim to the virtues and rewards of collaboration. The moral power of consent runs dangerously albeit sometimes profitably deeper, so as to shift the very locus of authority over one's condition from oneself to another, however contingently, so that one's condition may benefit from greater reach and scope than one's agency can provide, on its own or in combination, whether through action or interaction.

The second idea present in the thought is the possibly although not necessarily sceptical idea that to confer some dimension of one's agency upon another is to empower that other with the good-making qualities of one's agency, so that the action of the other becomes both one's own and good for one. If another person does something to one with one's consent, the presence of consent cleanses that action of the taint of the force of another's will upon one, and in its place imbues the action with the constitutive blessing of one's own will. Yet that cannot be right either, partly because there is nothing intrinsically good-making about bare agency, so that there is nothing consequently good-making in consenting to another's agency so as to appropriate its moral implications, and partly because in consenting to an action one does not in fact make that action one's own so as to be acting through another (that would be assenting rather than consenting), but rather yields passively to the action of another upon one, so as to permit another to treat one as an object, within the bounds and for the purposes described in the grant of consent.

The truth seems at once simpler and more delicate. In ceasing to be an agent, and in adopting the position of a patient instead, one allows another agent to undertake certain discrete actions upon one's person, those specified by the terms of one's consent, usually physical but also psychological, in order to advance interests, not simply that one cannot, for want of capacity, advance on one's own, for that would be a case of collaboration, but that can be advanced only by the renunciation of one's status as an agent. This is not simply a logical function of what it means to become passive, so as to be a patient rather than an agent. Rather it is an attempt to reconcile the moral requirements of an autonomous life and the virtue of patience. That reconciliation is fraught with contradiction by its very nature, and all too likely to resolve into circumstances that amount to a betrayal of one's autonomy, a betrayal that may well have long-term as well as short-term consequences. One should be very careful about consent, for it is essential to the achievement of an autonomous life that one not merely prefer but give fundamental priority to the fact of one's authority over one's own existence, and self-authorship of its narrative, rather than pursue the benefits that might follow from their surrender, in whole or in part. To consent to the suspension of that project, however conditionally, however temporarily, is to make the opposite choice, to surrender one's autonomy, not so as to improve its character, and alignment with rationality, but so as to obtain the benefits that follow from that surrender. The various constraints that one places and is able to place upon one's consent, however well designed they may be, can never be quite enough (as regular practitioners of consent have long discovered to their cost). They cannot draw out from that surrender the venom of passivity in one's relation to others, and its insidious power to undermine one's independence of mind, together with the dignity and respect that go hand in hand with that independence of mind in a world such as that we now live in, a world that has been articulated in terms of autonomy and the distinctive possibilities for a valuable life that autonomy gives rise to.

One should also be careful, of course, not to be over-protective of one's autonomy. Not only is there good reason to care about matters other than autonomy, for autonomy is not the only way to pursue a good life, dominant though it is in the world we now live in, but autonomy may itself depend for its flourishing on a willingness to place other concerns ahead of it from time to time. We are only as free as we are strong, for example, not in the degraded sense of that claim, namely, that freedom requires force as its guardian and companion, but in the most basic, constitutive sense, that freedom depends for its realization on the infusion of our circumstances with our mental and physical energies, so as to bring to life the possibilities for value there, that we may participate in them. That is an entirely sound, indeed fundamental, reason to give priority to one's vitality over one's autonomy, and so reason to allow oneself, say, to become the patient of a medical practitioner as and when one's health and vitality require it.

Yet to be a patient is not merely or even to gather advice that one can respond to autonomously, but also to consent to actions of the practitioner upon one's person that one is passive in the face of, from the manipulations of a physiotherapist to the operations of a surgeon. At moments like those, one places one's person, and from time to time one's very life, in the hands of the practitioner, yielding fundamental authority over one's condition to another, allowing them to act upon one while one stands by, so to speak. Vital as it is to do so, and to not be afraid to trust the doctor (as some are by reason of a religious belief such as Christian Science, or physical fear, or misguided forms of professional scepticism that lead them to mistake the advice that they can live with for the advice that they are in need of, and also to overestimate the power of their own judgement to distinguish the two), it is no less vital to remain alive at all times to the dangers of placing too much faith in one's doctor, and to the consequent need to monitor, review, and ultimately govern, however broadly and indirectly, the actions that one is submitting to, through the delineation of one's consent, and otherwise through its withdrawal or refusal. Passivity needs careful policing. Even in the realm of medical treatment, which is nominally always governed by the best interests of the patient, we have in recent years gradually become more alive to and better versed in the all too many ways in which allowing ourselves to be patients so that another may be the keeper of our interests can make us victims of the medicalization of our circumstances, at the expense of both our autonomy and our health. More specifically and more saliently, it makes us victims of the ways in which that medicalization can embody bias against particular autonomies, as when doctors undertake treatment of women that embodies attitudes to women that are not defensible, so treating illnesses that women do not have while being insensitive to the ones that they do have, leading to damaging outcomes that run from sedation to sterilization.

It seems to me that there are at least two important things to bear in mind if one is to give consent appropriately, for the moral implications of consent are not quite as straightforward as they seem. In truth, consent does not have the immediate attractions that it appears to have and for which people often turn to it. First, consent does nothing to make the content of an action good. On the contrary, the action is just as liable to be good or bad as it would have been in one's own hands. It is a different action, of course, one that would not have been possible otherwise, but it is no less morally vulnerable for that fact. If it is a mistake to have a certain tattoo, for example, the fact that the tattoo has been consented to does not make it any less of a mistake. In general, an action that has been consented to may well be a wrong action, and that possibility is and remains a moral peril for both agent and patient. It follows that a person who performs an action upon another in reliance upon the other's consent cannot rely on the consent to confer any kind of immunity from the badness of what has been consented to. In such a case, the only reproach that the agent in question will be freed from, and that in part only, is the reproach of the patient, certain dimensions of which will have been barred by the terms of the patient's consent, if the consent is a good one.

Nor does consent make the surrender of one's autonomy good. On the contrary, that surrender may or may not be compatible with one's autonomy, however freely the surrender has been undertaken. It is all too easy to agree to surrender what should not be surrendered, and we are all too familiar with occasions when that has been the case. Consent is only good in terms of autonomy when the action taken by its licence enables one to advance one's autonomy more by that means than by acting for oneself, only good in other terms if a similar pattern holds for those terms. Otherwise, it is bad. Once again, this is a moral peril for both agent and patient. The fact that one has obtained a person's consent to a certain course of action does not mean that one has not wrongfully imposed oneself upon the person of another, for even if the consent has been freely given it may be mistaken. Consent may bar certain avenues of reproach, but it leaves others open, including that of self-reproach.

With these considerations in mind, and others like them, one can ask whether passive engagement in sexual relations is something that can ever be legitimately consented to, even where the giving of the consent has been free, informed, and explicit. What might be the good for which the person giving consent is thereby renouncing their status as an agent, and the dignity and respect that flow from that status, albeit for only a limited purpose and time? If there is such a good, could it be thought to remain good when and if embraced by some person, or some category of person, the agency of whom has been historically devalued, and with it the dignity and respect that should have been accorded them? It is possible that I am unimaginative, or deeply conventional, but I find it difficult to think of what such a good might be. There would have to be something good about somebody doing something to one without one's involvement, and in the realm of sexual relations goodness flows entirely from involvement. Even if one has reproduction rather than pleasure in mind, goodness is constituted in part at least by mutual involvement in conception.

Is this too quick, too reliant on passing reference to observations made earlier? Is it merely stipulative to say that in the realm of sexual relations goodness flows entirely from involvement? Yes and no. The goodness of sexual relations is undoubtedly a matter of involvement but that may not be the entirety of the good to be found in sex. Perhaps there is a good to be found in sex without involvement, sex that is not a sexual relation. Sex with a person who is passive is ambiguous between those two possibilities, nominally relational but actually not so. If it were really relational, it would not be good, for what is apparently conclusory in the claim that goodness flows from involvement is actually constitutive, in all the ways that I sought to set out in some detail previously, in considering sexual relations as a species of interaction. The goodness of sexual relations flows entirely from the richness that the bidirectional character of interaction gives rise to in this setting. If a woman says to a man that she doesn't much feel like it but that he should go ahead, he should decline the offer. Going ahead is not sex with another and it is not good. Sexual relations that do not involve the active participation of both parties are not truly relations, but are more like a case of masturbation by one person who uses the other person as something akin to a sex aid. They cannot therefore lay claim to the value of sexual relations.

Of course that does not quite tell us what we need to know, for once again it might seem question-begging as well as wrong-headed. Sex with one who is passive is not sexual relations only if sexual relations are assumed to be exclusively interactive. That is why the example is ambiguous, relational and not relational at once, obviously not valuable and yet potentially so. Suppose then that sexual engagement with a person who is passive is indeed equivalent to masturbation with a living sex aid. What on earth is not good about masturbation, it might then be asked? What on earth is wrong with sex aids? The short answer is that whatever good there is in masturbation is to be found either in its self-referential character or in its continuity with sexual relations. Engagement with the passive is neither of those things. And while there is nothing wrong in sex aids, there is something very wrong in being one.

In his early, self-deprecating days Woody Allen once observed of masturbation: don't knock it: it's sex with someone you love. Yet the joke succeeds precisely because it is perverse. We know that it is not really true. Masturbation is not sex with someone, and nor is it love. That does not mean for a moment, of course, that there is not good in it as well as physical pleasure. However, it is vital to appreciate that the good in it does not derive purely from the pleasure it gives rise to, indispensable a companion to good as that pleasure undoubtedly is, for pleasure is as apt to arise from what is bad as from what is good. Rather the good in masturbation derives from its capacity to combine the private exploration of one's sexual being and the establishment of imaginative continuity with the goodness of sexual relations. To use another person merely as a sexual aid is neither of those things. It cannot lay claim to either the goodness of masturbation or the goodness of sexual relations. Rather it is a corrupt form of both, a corrupt form of involvement, in which the involvement has become a pretence, for there is in truth no involvement at all, and a corrupt form of masturbation, because imagined interaction, which has value, has become mock interaction, which does not. Such a pretence can only pretend to the goodness of what it pretends to be. It cannot possess it. Without those sources of goodness, the bare fact that a man may derive physical pleasure from sexual engagement with a woman who consents to be passive does not make that engagement good, for pleasure is no guide to goodness.

There are three further possibilities for value that I can think of. The first is that there is value to be found in the very fact of passivity. Yet that is plainly not the case. To become passive is to step out of life and thus out of direct engagement with value. That departure is valuable only if it gives rise to value indirectly, through its impact on the actions of another, either preventing the bad in them or making some good possible through them. If the conduct of a man is not good, then passivity in the face of it is not valuable, other than as a way of forestalling even greater harm. The second possibility for value is in self-sacrifice and corresponding generosity towards the person who is thereby permitted to act unilaterally upon one. Yet once again that value would ultimately depend on the presence of some good in the recipient that the self-sacrifice made possible. Self-sacrifice involves putting another's interests before one's own at the expense of one's own, but the interests in question must be real interests, not bogus ones. To sacrifice oneself to bogus interests, even if mistakenly rather than deliberately, is to lend one's arm to one's own degradation.

It is possible, of course, to seek degradation, and to find value in the experience. Or at least, so I am given to understand, and am in no position to comprehend sufficiently to dispute. However, I am inclined to think that the goodness of degradation is plausible only if nested in a larger package, the overall content of which could be thought to be good, because it was non-degrading. Yet even granted the existence of goodness in certain instances of degradation itself, it seems to me that such goodness is perverse in the technical sense of that word, for it both trades upon and is parasitic upon the fact that the standard answer must be to the opposite effect. If that is the case, then to consent to a passive role in sexual relations, however explicitly and appropriately, is to adopt a position in relation to one's partner that is fundamentally at odds with one's autonomy, dignity, and self-respect, and that one can intelligibly endorse only in conscious pursuit of one's degradation.

2.5 Law and Consent to the Active

2.5.1 Sexual Offences

Where does this leave the law on consent to sexual relations? Are we all rapists in the eyes of the law if we fail to secure consent, as appears to be the case? The answer is, of course, one for the law to provide, and thus one that is to be ultimately provided by the communities to which particular legal regimes are accountable, as those communities go about their constitutive business of delineating the exact contours of consent to sexual relations in the law that they are to be governed by. In providing that answer, it is entirely open to the law, for various kinds of strategic reasons, to construct a special legal reality that to a greater or lesser degree parts company with the moral reality that I have sought to explore in this chapter. Consent to sexual relations may be legally required even though it is not morally required. There is nothing to object to or be concerned about in this. It is often a good thing that the law makes something wrong that would not be wrong otherwise, for the ramifications of that kind of legal intervention in our moral lives may be beneficial to us in ways that would not be attainable without the intervention of the authority of law and its power to stipulate wrongdoing. That being the case, there are many variations in the way in which the law might choose to articulate a requirement of consent to sexual relations, but the most obvious and at the moment the most pressing choice to be made is that between explicit and implied consent. Should the law insist that yes means yes, so that there is no legal consent to sex in the absence of that word?

Suppose then a requirement that consent be obtained explicitly. In the face of such a requirement, all those who engaged in intercourse without ever raising the question of consent, because they were instead interacting with one another in the manner that I have sought to explore and describe, would simply by reason of that fact be guilty of rape, or at least have committed its *actus reus*, and would be preserved from conviction and sentencing for rape only by whatever disinclination there might be on the part of the other person to press charges. On first impression, that would appear to give rise to too wide a disjunction between legal reality and moral reality, just because it would seem to make it difficult for people to conduct their lives in a way that was not criminal, to have sexual fulfilment without becoming sex offenders. Either people would have to engage in an inorganic form of consent, one that stripped their sexual relations of much of their potential value, or legal practice would have to part company with legal principle almost wholesale, by turning a blind eye to what would in these circumstances be a comprehensive failure to obtain the very consent that the law called for, so as to make the law's requirement of explicit consent largely nominal. Yet it seems to me that upon reflection this impression of deep disjunction is in fact too hasty. Counter-intuitive as it may seem, one can fail to obtain explicit consent without thereby denying its importance. In fact, one's conduct can be fruitfully shaped by the requirement of explicit consent without one ever undertaking that consent. That is a consequence that the law might quite sensibly seek to bring about.

To require explicit consent to sexual relations is highly artificial, for all the reasons set out earlier, but it may also be astute. People who pursue good sex of the spontaneous, improvisatory kind, no matter how clumsily, how inattentively, and thus how badly, will almost certainly fail to obtain explicit consent and so will always be at legal risk. The presence of that risk can be morally productive, for it means that people need to be particularly alert to the quality of their interaction, and to the perspective of their partner, lest the risk be realized and they face a criminal charge. If their partner genuinely feels that sex, or some portion of it, is something that is just happening to her (and it will almost always be her), the requirement of explicit consent means that the conduct element of rape has been committed. That is a powerful resource for those who are vulnerable to sexual exploitation, and a powerful incentive for both parties to pursue sex in a way that is, at a minimum, properly attentive, and at its best, ever more responsive to each partner and to the good that can be realized through genuinely enlightened negotiation of sexual relations between them. It is sound reason for the law to insist on explicit consent and for those who engage in sexual relations to respect that law fully.

The one caveat to this is that one should not conclude from a legal requirement of explicit consent to sexual relations that sex is wrong if explicit consent is not present, so that quite apart from what the law requires we are under a moral obligation to obtain explicit consent. That would be to make the mistake of conflating legal reality and moral reality, the mistake of assuming that the law has simply lent the backing of its authority to a moral requirement that existed quite independently of it. The law has more good to offer us and less power to demand of us. Common as the mistake is and tempting as it may be, therefore, it is one that needs to be guarded against if a legal requirement of explicit consent is to be reconciled with the value of active engagement in sexual relations.

The alternative is that the law be satisfied by implicit consent, and that it find implicit consent in what is in fact negotiated interaction, so that from the legal point of view good sex would become standardly and implicitly consensual, whatever a moral philosopher might think. The problems that this would give rise to are the problems of all make-believe, of all mend and make do, of creating a legal morality that is not merely semi-independent of but at odds with moral reality. That is not fatal but it is fraught. It would mean a constant wrestling with the unaccommodating gap between legal reality and moral reality in this setting, a need to stipulate sources of implication and to reconcile them with the respect and dignity owed to women (something that is particularly difficult to do in the setting of private conduct, where there are no ready models to assess or emulate), an ongoing argument with those who for good reason believe that explicit consent should be required, so that yes can only be communicated by use of that very word, and most broadly, a struggle with the general fact that people are apt to treat the law as reflecting moral reality and so would be apt to treat good sex as relying on the conveying of consent by implication, with all the pernicious possibilities that would give rise to, rather more pernicious, surely, than the possibilities that arise from treating good sex as relying on explicit consent.

The choice here is ultimately between different values, and it is one that only a particular community can make and commit itself to. One course is more didactic than the other, one more trusting; one more principled, one more rough and ready; one more interventionist, one more laissez-faire; and so on. It is a choice for men and women everywhere to make in the articulation of the social circumstances of their genders and their sexual relations, in the setting of particular relationships, particular communities, and broader societies. My only purpose in this chapter has been to offer some illumination as to some of the aspects of what is at stake in their doing so.

At the outset of this chapter I bracketed the possibility that we are all under an illusion if we think that we can legitimately engage in sex without consent, or more precisely, if we think that the sex that we engage in without consent is legitimate. I justified the bracketing partly on the ground that it seemed implausible to think that our basic grasp of the goodness of sex was an illusion, but more fundamentally on the ground that acceptance of the claim would make an investigation of consent impossible. Nevertheless, I undertook to return to the issue later. Is there enough in what has been said in the course of this section to support the idea that our everyday sense, embedded in the practice of our lives, that good sex can take place without consent is a sound one? Others will have to be the judge, but the delineation of the possibilities of sexual interaction, and of the value to be found there, and of the dangers of passivity, and hence the dangers in the practice of consent that licenses engagement with one who is passive, suggest real grounds to believe that not only is good sex possible without consent but that by eschewing the practice of consent we gain access to many of the most important goods that sex has to offer, though of course it remains a further and crucial question whether and to what extent, on particular occasions and more broadly, we succeed in using that access as it should be used, that is, in ways that are genuinely fruitful for those involved.

2.5.2 The Place of Consent and Its Absence More Generally

2.5.2.1 The Particular and the General

This chapter has been consciously framed so as to focus on absence of consent rather than on consent itself, and to focus further on the particular setting of sexual relations rather than on the many other contexts in which consent currently plays a prominent role in our lives. Is there a basis in what has been said so far to be less focused at this point, and to look for more general lessons about the value and wisdom of consent? That depends on what absence can tell us about presence, and further, on just what the particular has to teach the general. These are the special lessons of engagement, and it is the possibility of those lessons that has guided the framing of this chapter. The thought behind it has been twofold. First and most simply, to look at consent from the perspective of its absence helps to bring out the cost of consent, for that is one of the chief reasons for its neglect and thus absence. That cost is something that tends to be neglected, even overlooked, so making consent seem more promising than it actually is. Second, to look at consent from the particular perspective of sexual relations, and so to look at it in light of all the fine-grained debates over its significance that have arisen there, in the course of which the possible implications of consent have been closely examined and concretely understood, helps to bring out the full measure of the worth of consent in ways that a more abstract and general enquiry could not. Let me expand on these thoughts briefly before moving on.

As we all know from our grasp of the significance of engagement and accumulated experience in the achievement of understanding, it is often the case that more can be learned about a practice and its value by looking closely at specific instances of the practice, particularly those instances in which long-standing and thorough reflection has brought out the full colouring of the practice and thus something like its complete meaning in that setting, than by stepping back to consider the practice in abstract terms that are necessarily austere about experience. Doing so may enable one to notice important things that would otherwise be overlooked. Most obviously, and to unite the two thoughts behind the framing of this chapter, the context of sexual relations highlights the potential significance of absence of consent, and the value that it might give rise to, in a way that other contexts for consent do not, just because the practice of consent to sexual relations, even when it is entirely enlightened, distinctively neglects that which governs it in principle. Consent rules there, but its rule is disregarded. That is quite unusual in the practice of consent. It could not be said, for example and by way of contrast, that as an everyday matter we do not normally consent to medical treatment, although it could certainly be said that we do not consent to it as often as we ought to. That being the case, we could not hope to learn much about the value of absence of consent from the setting of medical treatment, and further, could not hope to learn about that value from any analysis of consent that was sufficiently general as to include medical treatment.

The thought in response to this way of approaching the practice of consent, of course, is that lessons learned in specific settings, such as they may be, are as liable to be rooted and specific as they are to have general import, and so are not to be relied upon as a guide to the practice generally and its common value. It might well be a very great mistake, therefore, to think that different settings for consent are simply different instantiations of the same practice, from the examination of any one of which we can learn about the general practice, rather than quite distinct practices that merely have a family similarity, just as it might be a great mistake to think that race discrimination, sex discrimination, religious discrimination, age discrimination, and disability discrimination are no more than different intonations of the same phenomenon. If that is so, then one would need to be quite cautious, perhaps quite sceptical, of the possibility of deriving general conclusions from any particular setting. Is that the case here? Does reflection on the place of consent in the setting of sexual relations have anything valuable to teach us about the place of consent more generally? In particular, is there reason to be found in the analysis of the practice of consent to sexual relations, and its absence, for taking a more modest view of the practice of consent generally, one that embodies rather less faith in consent than we have accorded it in the modern era, rather less reliance on its supposed power? Is there reason to take more seriously than we do at present the possibility and the desirability of absence of consent more generally?

It seems to me that there is no way to avoid the uncertainties of derivation in either direction, and further, no way to detach the general from the particular or the particular from the general, so as to isolate one perspective and prefer it to the other. Lessons are there to be learned wherever one begins from, although they are, of course and quite unsurprisingly, always lessons that one must be careful not to make too much of, lessons that it will always be necessary to qualify and to mute. There is much that the place of consent in sexual relations, including its relative absence in practice, has to tell us about consent in general, and at the same time there is much that consent in that setting has to tell us about the special significance of sexual relations rather than about the significance of consent. Sexual relations have the significance they do in part because they are an unusually intense case of the possibilities of interaction, and thus a case in which the stakes of interaction are unusually high, with a great deal to gain and even more to lose for those who participate in them. What is more, sexual relations are typically played out in private, making oversight of them, through the scrutiny of consent, somewhat at odds with their proper vindication. The combination of these features, and others attendant upon them, has the effect of making the disabilities that attach to the practice of consent rather more troubling there than they might otherwise be. Counter-intuitive as it may seem, that means that there may be greater reason to eschew the practice of consent in the setting of sexual relations than in some other settings, and thus greater reason not to carry whatever scepticism one may feel about consent to sexual relations into settings that do not share these special, autonomy-sensitive features of sexual relations. At least that is a possibility.

Just what broader conclusions might one reasonably draw then? Speaking for myself, because it does not do, perhaps, to speak more generally when one is being somewhat speculative, what I take away from having thought about these questions for some time is that the role of consent is something that on the whole we should be seeking to contract rather than to expand, at least if and to the extent that we are committed, as we are and as there is very good reason for us to be, to a life of autonomy. Consent by its very nature hobbles the active and empowers the passive. It tempts us to its embrace by holding out the promise of moral and physical authority over our condition, while delivering neither. It asks us to be insular rather than engaged, fearful rather than confident, suspicious rather than trusting, unaccountable rather than responsible. Those are not good things to be.

They are not, however, in any sense other than the contributory, sound reasons to eschew the practice of consent altogether. On the contrary, at certain times and in certain special settings it is absolutely right, perhaps even essential, to be insular rather than engaged, suspicious rather than trusting, and so on. Consent is the necessary gatekeeper to realms that are crucial to the quality of our lives, as well as a guardian, however fragile in practice, against intrusions that would otherwise cause us great harm. Yet we need to scrutinize carefully, and always be prepared to challenge, the claim that there is good to be found in any particular case of consent, for there is far more bad than good to be found in passivity, however full, free, and informed one's consent to that passivity may have been. In particular, we need to liberate ourselves from the idea that something is good just because it has been consented to, that a practice is necessarily better if consensual than otherwise, that where a person's consent has been given our questioning should cease and our acceptance of that which has been consented to should follow.[16] To say, for example, as is so often said, that the legitimacy of government depends on the consent of the governed, is not merely to insist upon democracy, but implicitly to accept a picture of government as something that one is more less passive in the face of, as something that happens to one either with or without one's consent, rather than as something to be actively engaged in. That picture may well be a sound, sensible, even necessary one in certain special settings, but on the whole it is not to be welcomed by the autonomous.

How much more specific is it possible to be about these general concerns, so as to move beyond the suggestive and the speculative, and test in other settings the lessons learned from sexual relations? If sexual relations are, however counterintuitively, a setting in which, the requirements of the law aside, one ought to be particularly cautious about the giving of consent, are there domains in which consent is more intuitively and just as correctly suspect? Should we come to doubt the practice as a whole, special circumstances aside? Or are sexual relations the

---

[16] The criminal law of England and Wales for many years incorporated a distinction that sought to capture one particularly egregious species of the special wrong that can be embodied in consent. To have intercourse with a minor without their consent was ground for the offence of rape, just as it would be for any adult. To have intercourse with a minor with their consent, however, was a separate offence, one that carried exactly the same very severe maximum penalty as rape, but that constituted a distinct offence, the purpose of which was to pick out and punish the distinctive wrongfulness of having secured the minor's consent, so violating their mind and will as well as their body, with all the special, enduring damage that follows from that. Presumptions that minors are incapable of consent presume what is not necessarily the case, that consent is necessarily a good thing, and that a minor never genuinely consents to his or her own sexual exploitation. One of the special horrors of offences of this class of conduct is that both consent and children can be party to their commission.

exception? Are there domains in which consent is less problematic? After all, we regularly give consent in a great many domains and find value in our doing so. Does consent operate differently in the setting of these domains from the way it operates in the setting of sexual relations? Or are these too, as the general logic of consent would suggest, domains in which consent operates so as to license our passivity in the face of the action of another, domains that we accordingly have good reason to circumscribe as far as possible for the sake of our autonomy? For all our everyday acceptance of them, are these domains of consent in fact, as might be said with some force of domains in which men still have their way with women, even if with women's consent, and governments still have their way with their subjects, even if with the consent of those subjects, domains out of time, in which a pre-modern, pre-autonomous way of life, one in which people normally had and expected to have little effective say in the articulation and development of their circumstances, and correspondingly little concern for the value that having such a say could bring to their lives, is very roughly reconciled, as an interim measure or otherwise, with some minimum sense of what is called for by the value of autonomy, by ensuring that impotence and lack of involvement is something that one has at least agreed to?

Perhaps that is going too far. Perhaps it connects consent to the passive too closely, too incontrovertibly. When we consent, is it inevitably at the expense of playing an active role in whatever is being consented to? And if we so consent, is it always at the expense of our autonomy if not shown to be contributing to it? Or is our autonomy sufficiently robust, sufficiently secured in other respects, as to be relatively impervious to such concessions, so that even if unwise they are not worth our worrying about? Once again, my sense is that in response to such questions there is not much that one can say in general that would be helpful or illuminating. Nor is it feasible to enumerate the sites or interests in which consent might have a role to play so as to evaluate them one by one. Better perhaps to look at certain prominent cases, and the kinds of interests that are at stake there.

2.5.2.2 Consent to Medical Treatment

Let me begin with one that has been touched on already, that of consent to medical treatment. Medical treatment of a kind that one consents to involves a surrender of autonomy on two fronts at once, that of one's physical integrity and that of one's judgement. Both forms of surrender are valuable just as and when they make possible an intervention, of therapeutic skill and professional judgement, that one could not avail oneself of without the surrender, and that has a critical role to play either in the direct promotion of one's well-being and its capacity for autonomy (as, for example, when one is freed from a debilitating condition) or in one's very survival, on which, of course, any possibility of one's having a well-being, autonomous or otherwise, depends. When soundly based and properly circumscribed, these surrenders are temporary, targeted, and autonomy-promoting. Unlike the case of sexual relations, they are not intrinsically at odds with the good that they are supposed to serve.

That does not mean that they are not debilitating or demeaning, so that passivity is untroubling in this setting. On the contrary, patients often feel that they are being regarded as bare mechanisms rather than as complete persons, complete in the sense of possessing a physical integrity and capacity for judgement that is as worthy of respect as the institutional expectations and professional judgement that is being applied to them, and willing though they may be, and necessary as they may think it, indeed freely as they may have consented to it, find themselves diminished by the experience. These facts are entirely sound reasons to be sensibly guarded about the granting of consent even in this setting, on the face of it one of the most obvious and strongest contexts for the worth of consent. They are reasons to arm oneself with all possible knowledge, and to limit quite strictly what is done to one without one's active involvement.[17]

One needs to pay particular attention to just what it is that a doctor knows better than one knows oneself, and not to allow the very many considerations that bear upon the wisdom of a course of treatment that one is asked to submit to, such as the extent to which its outcome fosters an autonomous life, and to the contrary, the extent to which its effects or side effects diminish such a life, to be subsumed in the question of professional judgement, as to which doctor (here a shorthand for the balance of competent medical opinion) really does know best. Doctor resoundingly does not know best about many of the most important matters bearing on medical treatment that is consented to, and even if he or she did, they are questions that proper respect for one's autonomy demands that one answer for oneself. That is why even the most soundly based, most conscientious, most diffident case of medical treatment is also often fundamentally debilitating, not just mentally and physically, but altogether more profoundly, in terms of one's status as an agent.

2.5.2.3 The Consent of the Governed

In the setting of certain forms of medical treatment, one allows oneself to be governed by the judgement of another for a very particular purpose, about which it is possible to assemble most of the considerations that bear upon consent in advance of its granting. In certain other settings, most prominently that of one's role

---

[17] One prominent instance of the difficulties that can be involved in doing this is that of consent to treatment or its withdrawal in circumstances when one no longer has the capacity to exercise one's own judgement, and so to be in any way autonomous at that point, and yet where decisions as to just how one's life is to end commonly feed back into and so inform its overall character and value. The choice here is between what is sometimes called a living will, in which one attempts to specify in advance when to treat and when to withhold treatment, and a lasting power of attorney, in which one delegates the relevant power to decide to a person whom one trusts to act wisely and sympathetically on one's behalf. The former course is marred by one's limited capacity to foresee all circumstances and, no less important, to imaginatively invest oneself in them, the latter by the limited capacity of another person, however loving, however empathetic, to exercise autonomy on one's behalf, both of which limitations entail that the consents involved diminish one by their very grant.

as a citizen, one is asked, notionally at least, to consent to the authority of another on a menu of considerations that one has yet to read, indeed that has yet to be written. On the face of it, such a grant is at odds with the very idea of citizenship, which came into being as a way of personifying an active role in government, one in which each citizen contributed, by action and by interaction, to the government of each by all, while also accepting the correlative responsibility of governing himself or herself in the very many respects in which government by another is not so much inept as inapt, respects in which one is bound to exhibit, for worse as much as for better, that independence of mind and action that constitutes the core of one's autonomy.

One needs to remember not to think of self-government in exclusive terms, so as to vest it wholly either in the state or in one's own person. Each of us has many selves and takes part in as many schemes of governance, in all of which the authority of the superordinate must be reconciled with due respect for the autonomy of the subordinate. Nor should one think of the autonomy of the subordinate as inherently marginal or companionate. On the contrary, it is fundamental. As Joseph Raz has emphasized, in accepting the authority of law or indeed any other authority, it is vital not merely to ensure that the requirements of the normal justification of authority are satisfied, in all the ways that he and others have delineated, but also to ensure that the central claim of what Raz describes as the independence condition, namely, the claim that it must always be open to one to prefer the exercise of autonomy to acceptance of authority, even when that authority is the legitimate exercise of a legitimate institution, is something that one is ever alive to, protective of, and ready to respond to.[18] That has a number of demanding implications for us, each of which, it seems to me, tells against the case for the patient acceptance of government, and so tells against the soundness of any practice of consent to that attitude, notional or actual.

Start with what consent implicitly calls into question in terms of autonomy itself, before moving on to the specific problem of consent to government. The value of autonomy is not premised on the idea that an autonomous life is better than its alternatives, and so is not vulnerable to a claim that it is worse than those alternatives, in general or in some particular respect. That is why the legitimacy of an authority and what it calls for does nothing to diminish the call of autonomy. Like all other values, autonomy is in fact ultimately incommensurable with its alternatives. We pursue an autonomous life just because it is autonomous, not because it is the best life to pursue. The same is true, of course, of the pursuit of any other valid way of life, the authoritarian for example. That being the case, a life of

---

[18] For what has proved to be Raz's final treatment of this idea, see 'The Problem of Authority: Revisiting the Service Conception' in *Between Authority and Interpretation: On the Theory of Law and Practical Reason* (2009), 126 at 136–42. Earlier treatments of the service conception are to be found in *The Authority of Law* (1979) and *The Morality of Freedom* (1986).

autonomy is necessarily one that we pursue by continually committing ourselves to it, in general and in particular respects, by reason of its distinctive value, which we must identify and ensure, and by various acts of will to embrace that value and the reasons that support it in preference to others, even as we are also steered towards that life by the circumstances of an autonomous culture, if that is where we find ourselves, so as to make the life of autonomy one that is unchosen as much as chosen.

Nothing in that commitment to autonomy entails that the autonomous life be better than other ways of life in any terms other than those of autonomy itself, and the autonomy-sensitive values that attend and enhance autonomy. On the contrary, in pursuing autonomy, and for as long as we do so, we are bound to remain autonomous even when that renders us worse off in terms of other values, as it very often does. That is simply what it means to pursue autonomy. To do otherwise, and so to yield autonomy as and when it makes us worse off in terms of some other value, significantly so let us assume, is either to abandon autonomy as a way of life in favour of some other, which one can always do but must do wholesale, or to succumb to the idea that it is possible to pursue a better life as such, one in which the claims of autonomy could be rationally traded off against other considerations, which one cannot do because no such trade-off exists. There is no other avenue available to us, other perhaps than to do both those things at once, as when the former course masquerades as the latter. However tempting it might seem, it is not possible to be opportunistically autonomous, that is, to be autonomous just as long as all things considered it does not cost us anything important to do so in terms of other things that are good for us. That remains the case even when we rightly yield our autonomy to the claims of authority.

As Raz makes clear, the point of the normal justification of authority, as he explains and identifies it, a justification that seeks to reconcile authority and autonomy, is not to show what cannot be shown, that authority is better than autonomy in any particular setting, so that we may rationally prefer it, but rather to show that in that setting an autonomous path to some other value would be less effective in terms of that other value than submission to authority would be. When met, the justification shows that submission to authority is rationally permissible, but not that it is rationally required. The justification says nothing about the value of autonomy as such and what we might owe to it, which is why the separate presence of the independence condition is necessary to the full justification of authority. Having committed ourselves to a life of autonomy, we can always prefer something else either interstitially or supportively, but any such preference must be reconciled with our basic commitment to autonomy, unless it is to become a turning away from it.

To consent to government, on the other hand, and hence to accept the authority of another over the direction of one's life, is to accept, with whatever restrictions, something that will happen to one without one's involvement, and correspondingly to abandon, to that extent, one's autonomy. That is because consent implies passivity, at least if it is a genuine consent rather than something else that one has mistaken for consent. It follows that the very idea of consent to government is fundamentally incompatible with either autonomy or citizenship, both of which depend for their meaning and value upon active engagement.

That does not mean that the giving of consent is fundamentally mistaken. As I have emphasized, one does not have to be autonomous. One can lead a very good life otherwise. To take the most familiar illustration, as a child one is governed not by autonomy, but by the identification, by one's parent or guardian, of what are one's best interests. Different parents inevitably will have different ideas of just what that means. That is their decision and their responsibility. Many happy childhoods have followed, and when they have not it has not been from neglect of autonomy. The transition from childhood to adulthood, by contrast, is not only a transition to full rationality, or something like it, but also, and independently, and in the culture that we currently inhabit, a transition to autonomy. As an adult, one's interests, whatever they may be, take a back seat to one's identification of them. At that point, one's life becomes one's own to make a mess of, rather than something that is, in rational terms, one's own just as long as one does not make a mess of it. In the autonomous worlds that most of us live in, to refuse this responsibility is to refuse to grow up, and more important, in doing so to refuse what is essential to one's well-being, for we currently generally inhabit cultures in which there is little scope, because there are few if any supporting institutions and practices, for the paternalistic direction of adult life.

By much the same token, the transition to political maturity and to the practice of democracy is a transition to a condition in which the idea and practice of self-government is put before any idea of what is best for us. The practice of democracy is not, as some assume, anomalously worse than the alternative. In terms of that alternative, it is worse by design. To give priority to self-government is to prefer that ideal overall to any other concerns that would undermine it, even when those other concerns are highly significant to one and the undermining is the only way to serve them properly. It follows that in a culture of autonomy that is true to itself there can be no such thing as a right to rule, even in the demos, or duty to obey, whether or not those things have been legitimately consented to, notionally or actually. That is because both those things put something else, whatever it is that warrants the right to rule and the duty to obey, before autonomy. In an autonomous life, there can be only a readiness to play one's part, through action and interaction, a part that includes both enforcement and compliance, in due measure and with the involvement of each of us, but not rule or obedience.

It follows further that consent to government, and the passivity that consent implies, entails the abandonment of self-government, not just in the sense of yielding to the government, in part at least, the regulation of one's own life, which only an anarchist could object to in principle, but also in the sense of ceasing to play an active part in the governance by the state of oneself and one's fellows. That is something that one can certainly do, and perhaps with good reason, but it is not something that one can do autonomously or for any reason of autonomy. The conclusion that one is driven to is that the modern commitment to the ideal of government by consent, which came into being alongside and in support of a commitment to the pursuit of personal autonomy and collective self-government, grasped the necessity of rejecting deference to the will of another, but failed to grasp further that the practice of consent has the inescapable effect of rehabilitating that very deference, albeit now vested in a different object.

Yet how could this possibly be so? Are we not bound to yield our autonomy to the good of government, and so bound to seek a device, such as consent perhaps, that will enable us to license our governance by another as and when the other is legitimately constituted and the demands that it makes are actually good for us? Not at all. Reason makes no such claim upon us. If and when we commit ourselves to a life of autonomy, for the many good reasons that tell in favour of autonomy and for the goods that it will enable us to create and to savour, we thereby commit ourselves to an active part in our governance by the state. In granting the power of the state, we are bound to preserve the condition that enabled the grant. That is not as self-contradictory a commitment as it might at first seem to be. It is not a matter of being master and servant at once. Rather it is a matter of seeing governance in terms of interaction rather than imposition, of realizing and following through on the idea that each of us has a vital part to play in securing the goods that governance is capable of giving rise to, even though that part is not one that mirrors the part that others play in the governing of oneself.

As I have sought to explain elsewhere, governments and the laws that they make have no real capacity to secure any of the goods of a life in common, the life that makes any assemblage of persons governed rather than ungoverned, merely by the content of what they call for or even by the force that may be lent to that content.[19] Every government needs the practical engagement and personal identification of its subjects to complete its project. That being the case, our passivity in the face of government, and the accompanying perception of government as by definition an unwelcome intervention in our lives and an imposition on our will, makes the project of government ineffective and an autonomous citizenry rightly resentful.

---

[19] *Law and Life in Common* (2015).

No less than in the case of medical treatment, passive engagement with the operation of government has the effect of debilitating the body politic, by undermining its status as an agent, individually and collectively, a status that is entirely fundamental to the idea of self-government. In politics as in medicine, one should bend the knee from time to time, but only that one may stand the more upright as a consequence.

How so? By turning against many of the most common ways of thinking about politics today, so as to be more old-fashioned and more committed democratic citizens. We need to draw upon good information from good sources; to devote time to its appreciation; to distinguish the politically telling from the merely dramatic; to value genuine political discussion as well as the other kinds of discussion, of science or entertainment, that fill our lives; to cultivate a political culture that presents issues in terms that are accessible to those who want to be serious about them without becoming professionals, so as to create a language of citizenship; to look to the long term as well as the short, so as to embrace the goals and ambitions that our autonomy, individual and collective, as well as that of our successors, is structured in terms of; and to insist on all those things from one another and from the institutions that are in our service. We need to commit ourselves to the level of engagement that will enable us to be autonomous political beings, with all the learning and responsibility that entails, rather than what we are too often now, objects of another's will, a will that we are fundamentally alienated from, other than at election time, when we engage with it in the manner of shoppers in search of pretty possibilities. We need to vote for parties not merely so that they may hold power because somebody must, but so that they may bring certain convictions to life, convictions about the particular shape that autonomy is to take for us, and the ways in which it might be extended to all, or at least as many as possible, convictions that we have had the opportunity to examine carefully before embracing, convictions that will need to be as complex, multifaceted, and even contradictory, as is the autonomous population that they are to serve.

None of this is compatible with the practice of consent. Consent and its conscious neglect, and the passivity that both imply, lead us down very different political roads, ones in which we have little active involvement in our political direction, so that if aware we find ourselves resentful of a process and a set of institutions that we no longer recognize ourselves in, and if unaware we no longer grasp the full significance of what we are missing, so as to be tempted to the insouciance of declaring that we are not political, as if that was a position that one could possibly hold rather than submit to. This is not to say that we should not insist on the consent of the governed, in the manner of the United States Constitution. On the contrary, there may well be good democratic political capital in doing so, as long as the consent that is being referred to is not only notional but also rhetorical. As a matter of language rather than analysis, consent can mean something akin to agreement or assent, as it clearly does when a local council gives planning consent for an addition to one's house. If that is what it means when used as a political slogan, there can be no objection to it, as long as the ambiguity that it embodies is sufficiently politically beneficial as to justify both the intellectual confusion it is bound to give rise to and the uncertainty over consent that such confusion is liable to create in other domains in which the idea of consent figures. Whatever language we use, however, and whatever political slogans we may adopt, we should not allow a government to rule us in ways that do not actively involve us, or accept that we have any like duty to obey.

It seems to me further that this is not a special fact about democracy and the self-government that it calls for. On the contrary, the same pattern holds true for all other structures of authority, even such as that of employment. As I have suggested, we each have many selves and take part in many schemes of governance, so that the logic of our autonomous participation applies to them all. Every exercise of authority, fruitful as it may be, is something that one must engage with in the manner of an unbeliever, one who is ready to trust but never to have faith, always wary, always probing, never comfortable, never unthinkingly accepting. As a teenager, new to driving, with a tolerant father in the passenger seat, I found myself stopped on a country road by a police officer, who wanted to know where I was coming from and where I was going, both of which pieces of information I gave him, more or less automatically. After all, and to be fair, autonomy was new to me. As we drove away, my father said, 'You really shouldn't do that.' I protested that the information was trivial and that providing it had cost me nothing much as far as I could see. 'I know it's a lot easier', he responded, 'but you really shouldn't do it'. And, of course, as embarrassingly weak-willed as it made me seem, he was entirely right. One really shouldn't. Tiresome as it often is, and hugely demanding as it sometimes can be, we are bound by our commitment to autonomy to take the harder road that true authorship of one's life, however shared with others that may be, calls for from one, and so to question all claims of authority on the part of all those who pretend to it, not merely police officers and other officials, who claim authority in the name of the public good, but employers, managers, and others who claim authority as a private right, and even neighbours and other fellow citizens who claim the authority of tradition, or religion, or some newer form of correctness, on atavistic or conventionalist grounds.

So when an authority of whatever kind makes a demand of one, an autonomous response to that demand entails that one actively engage with the demand, partly by reflecting on its supporting reasons, including the institutional goods that the presence of an authority makes possible, of which coordination is the most obvious but which also include all the many other instances of what John Finnis has identified as *determinatio*, the place of decision in rendering the abstract and many-sided character of morality into a design for living for a certain population (some of which goods may require that the authority be exclusive), and partly and no less importantly by deciding whether to lend the force of one's will to what the authority has willed. This is not a charter for chaos or a recipe for anarchism. We pursue autonomy in the setting of social practices that autonomy requires us to support, and with a proper respect for the autonomy of others and for the place of authority in the promotion and extension of autonomy, any and all of which may call upon us to yield certain aspects of the autonomy in our hands for the sake of autonomy more generally (perhaps because it may well be possible to sacrifice certain elements of our autonomy without imperilling our condition as autonomous agents), as well as to be ever attentive to the distinction between our autonomy and our desire, that we may practise properly the morality of freedom, as Raz has termed it.

A final note on a possibly marginal case of consent, yet one that figures largely in the law. It is common to consent to the presence of certain risks in what one does, and so to waive by contract what would otherwise have been one's right to take certain legal actions should those risks be realized. Is this practice something more that we should not be undertaking? In considering the question, it seems to me that the idea of risk is something of a distraction here. In undertaking certain activities, perhaps most activities, unwelcome consequences are more or less likely to occur, sometimes almost certainly, at other times with a low degree of probability. Such consequences are standard features of action and interaction, in all the ways that I have canvassed already, and as such are matters that one can consent to only if and when one adopts a passive stance in relation to them. In consenting to the presence of a certain risk in what one does, therefore, whether wisely or unwisely, one agrees to be legally passive, at least as far as the terms of the consent provide, should the risk be realized. That is something that one should be very careful about doing, for all the reasons to be wary of passivity, and that one should be ready to challenge at all times, by challenging the institutions and social practices that make consent seem necessary or inevitable in that setting. One's legal rights are an important aspect of one's autonomy, and their surrender may well do more to injure that autonomy than the subsequent taking of the risk in question contributes to it (a risk that social practice has dictated one can take only by consent to the full acceptance of the consequences of its realization).

That said, all this type of consent does is to foreclose one particular line of objection, that of legal reproach, and perhaps only one species of legal reproach at that. Whether the foreclosure takes place in the context of extreme sports, or surgery, or any other one of the very many settings in which it commonly arises, nothing in the consent that authorizes it is in any sense a warrant for the conduct of any other person who plays a part in realizing the risk in question or is otherwise morally responsible for it. Despite the consent, the person who injures one, directly or by contribution, remains morally responsible if the injury in question is wrong, or if the agreement to accept the risk is wrong, or both. One's consent to the presence of a legally salient risk does nothing to relieve the author of the risk of that moral burden.[20] That is precisely because in all respects other than that of a particular legal remedy one has retained one's full standing as an agent, and so has refused to take the moral wrong lying down.

---

[20] The discussion here, as in the rest of the chapter, focuses on legal consent, and so neglects the possibility that in certain circumstances consent may function morally as well as legally. In those circumstances, if agreement to accept a risk is not wrong the fact of consent may operate to foreclose any moral objection, by the consenter or by others, to the fact of the agreement. Consent cannot go further, so as to make wrongful conduct not wrongful, special cases aside (those in which the moral landscape is a product of the consenter's will).

3
The Goodness of Equality

3.1 Absence of Value and its Rewards

3.1.1 Neglected Lines of Thought

This chapter of the book reflects the long development of a line of thought about equality, in my own life as an academic, as it happens, but more important, in the intellectual and public cultures of which that life has been a part. It was inspired by my first encounters with Joseph Raz, as a graduate student some thirty-five years ago. Raz had just published *The Morality of Freedom* and, together with his other students, one of whom was John Gardner, I sought to absorb and come to terms with the many rich implications of that highly ambitious and densely rendered book. In our examinations in the summer of that year, we, the graduate jurisprudence students, were asked, inter alia, whether equality was an independent moral value. I realized that even to approach that question I would have to address head-on and at least temper, if not refute, what Raz himself had said to doubt the claim, in Chapter 9. The argument there was powerful, persuasive, and quite devastating to my existing, broadly egalitarian convictions. In asking me to meet that argument, on the same terms as its author, the highest of bars had been set for me, at the very earliest stage of my academic career. What is more, whatever conclusions I might manage to reach were liable to disturb beliefs that not only mattered greatly in my own life but that constituted vital connections to the public cultures within which I had become the person I was and out of the terms of which I had constructed most of my aspirations. I realized that I faced the prospect of becoming something of an enemy to my present self and hopes, as well as a stranger to my present companions and fellow travellers. My instinct was to see if there was any sound way to resist this, and that meant resisting in a way that not only faced up fully to the challenge that Raz had identified but also, as circumstances then had it, was capable of at least partly satisfying Joseph himself, as one of the examiners in jurisprudence.

The position advanced by Raz was not quite his alone, though the arguments in support of it certainly were. Similar positions had been taken previously by Peter Westen and would later be taken by Harry Frankfurt.[1] Various attempts had been made to rebut those positions, that of Westen in particular, without much success. At the time, the attempt that I (and my fellows) found most attractive, as well as most closely correlated to ordinary thinking on the subject (so perhaps explaining its attraction to us), was that offered by Michael Walzer in his *Spheres of Justice*. Yet there was something, perhaps several things, definitely not right about Walzer's

---

[1] Westen, *Speaking of Equality* (1990), expanding fruitfully on a line of thought that began in 'The Empty Idea of Equality' (1982) 95 Harv. L Rev. 537; Frankfurt, 'Equality as a Moral Ideal' in *The Importance of What We Care About* (1988) and 'Equality and Respect' in *Necessity, Volition and Love* (1998).

account. Could one do better than Walzer himself had done? One would need to take on board his general direction of thought while learning from his missteps, or to put it more constructively, one would need to draw upon those missteps as pointers to a rather stronger line of argument in favour of the worth of equality than the one that he had offered. One would need to find a different form of concession to the doubts of Raz, and others like Raz, doubts about the very idea of equality and its value, in place of the particular concession that Walzer had fastened upon, in distancing himself from what he labelled 'simple equality'. That would take time, and a good deal of living with and thinking about, to develop properly.

There is a melancholy pattern in much of intellectual life, in which debates fall from favour without having been in any sense pursued to their limit, let alone concluded. Participants in the debates and their successors simply move on after a while, to issues that seem more promising to them, or more in need of present consideration, given the temper of what are always changing times. Many signal achievements are forgotten, many promising lines of enquiry are neglected and obscured for lack of attention. My ongoing thoughts about equality gradually came to be somewhat idiosyncratic, a little out of time, as the egalitarian debate shifted focus, so that to rediscover their resonance it would be necessary to undertake a genuine journey, in something of the manner of the Wayback Machine. And yet, although this is undoubtedly, and often quite rewardingly, simply the way of the world, as new lives proceed in new directions with new objects in mind, such neglect matters, for it stands as a barrier to any prospect of cumulative understanding across intellectual generations, and the cultures of which they are an aspect. So, I held on to the project of investigating the value of equality, and to my sense of the worth of both, while many years and many other projects intervened, in my life and in those of my fellows.

Holding on meant that my response to the Razian challenge was more or less immediate and yet took the length of an academic career to develop. My immediate answer to the examiners, which provided me with some but not quite enough satisfaction, had a number of strands, the most important of which was the thought that equality is a species of community, or more precisely, one of the preconditions of any community. As David Miller once pointed out, people form communities through participation in shared practices, so that those who lack access to the shared practices, for whatever reason, are correspondingly and consequently closed off from participation in those communities.[2] It follows that the achievement of equality in access to shared practices makes participation in the relevant communities possible for all those in favour of whom that equality has been achieved. If the participation is a good thing, then so is the form of equality that enables it.

---

[2] David Miller, 'Arguments for Equality' (1982)7 Midwest Studies in Philosophy 73, and the argument from fraternity at 83–5 there. See further at n. 36 later.

The frailties of this answer as a response to doubts about the value of equality were plain on its face. Whether or not the two ideas inform one another in certain cases, community is simply not the same thing as equality, so that to explain the role (and value) of equality in the achievement of community is not to explain the value of equality. Many equalities engender no community and many communities involve no element of equality, at least, not in the familiarly progressive sense of equality that is a contemporary political ideal. More troublingly, it is at least a reasonable question whether the fact of community makes a practice better, rather than worse. Community might be susceptible to either rendering. In fact, it has always seemed to me, and indeed to a great many others, that the goodness of any association, like the goodness of other auxiliary and amplifying phenomena (such as the pleasure that may be derived from an activity, individual or collective) is a matter of extending the goodness or badness of the projects the association serves (or pleasure accompanies) from time to time. A farmer's co-op is capable of being better than the sum of its members' actions by virtue of its resonances, internal and external, even if those resonances have no impact on the constitutive projects of the cooperative; a gang assault is surely far worse than would be the same set of violations had they taken place separately. The same can be said of pleasure. Any pleasure taken in wrongdoing augments the wrongdoing rather than offsetting it. The argument in support of equality that I offered to the examiners, it seemed to me later, ultimately failed to capture either the distinctiveness of equality or its worth. And yet there was something promising in the idea of a connection between equality and community, as well as in the idea that the worth of equality is real despite the Razian fact, if fact it be, that equality is not an independent value.

The present project sets out to revive the fundamental question of the worth of equality and to offer a fresh way of coming to terms with that question. The hope is to make a genuine advance in our understanding of equality without claiming that the conclusions proposed are likely to be anything like the last word on the subject. The project has two main movements to that end. The first movement revisits Walzer's vision of equality in *Spheres of Justice*. The purpose of doing so is to develop a new and more constructive sense of what Walzer got wrong and, second and relatedly, to explore the possibility that the vulnerabilities in the idea of equality that Raz and others have identified are something to be embraced, as the resources for a sound understanding of equality and its worth, rather than avoided, as Walzer (and I, in my examination) sought to do. This movement will be focused on finding new possibilities in familiar lines of thought and criticism. There may be moments when it feels like a journey on the Wayback Machine, but in fact both the destinations and their possibilities are fresh ones.

There are two distinctive and revealing puzzles about equality that this part of the project seeks to highlight. The first puzzle is that the ideal of equality is oddly mercenary, detached from any deep commitment to the objects of its concern, whatever they may be. The second puzzle is that despite its long association with a progressive politics, equality in fact functions oppressively, to enforce a disregard, within the domain of its operation, for a range of circumstances that there may be good reason to pay attention to there, including the good reasons that derive from a proper concern for the particular people that equality is being called upon to serve.

The second movement covers less familiar territory. I will not attempt to anticipate the argument in its detail by offering a précis of it here. Nevertheless, it is possible and perhaps helpful to say, by way of introduction, that I will seek to develop a distinction between goodness and value, one of the features of which is that goodness is an artefact of existence, where existence is understood as participation in value. As an artefact, goodness operates to enlarge the implications of value in ways that value does not entail or anticipate, and in certain cases, by dint of feedback, may even operate to enlarge the realm of value itself. This means that equality can have real worth as an artefact of existence despite the fact that it is not a value. What is more, the fact that equality is not itself a value, and further, and more tellingly and characteristically, lacks a native commitment to any value in particular, is an essential ingredient in its possible worth. A vessel that has the capacity to carry cargo of any kind at all, without being committed by either its design or usage to any cargo in particular, is open to all cargoes, available to offer its structure and support, its shelter and mode of conveyance, to them all. Just which cargo is simply a function of our present politics, their ambitions and their consequences. It is from that politics, accordingly, that the worth of equality derives. Those two features are at once a very real limitation of the pursuit of equality as an ideal, and the source of its suppleness, relevance, and strength. So, the fundamental challenge raised by Raz, Frankfurt, and others is to be yielded to, yet there is more to the story.

Second and relatedly, equality functions as an aspect of culture, and further, as something of a culture in its own right, a mode of solidarity and belonging, the character of which is supplied by the domain of equality that is pursued and enforced in any given time and place. One could say that it is *equalities* that matter, not equality. Other than derivatively, equalities do not operate directly on our lives, so as to improve particular circumstances, individual or collective. Rather they serve as cultural resources for the possible enrichment of the lives they affect, resources that acquire particular resonance when partnered with framing cultures of certain kinds, most obviously, and relevantly today, when partnered with the dynamic, fluid, and relatively unstable circumstances of liberal political and social orders, orders in which the autonomous direction of lives individual and collective is central to their social practices.

If all this is right and illuminating, then it offers a form of backstory to the accounts of equality that have occupied academic research in the many years since the expression of doubt by Raz and others. It describes a terrain that is logically prior to currently prevailing accounts of equality, rather than being in competition with them.

3.1.2 The Betrayal of Equality

'Equality literally understood,' Michael Walzer once memorably wrote, all the more memorably because he spoke as a true friend of equality, 'is an ideal ripe for betrayal.'[3] Our commitment to it cannot survive, as he puts it, the first moment of our engagement with other people, in all the rich variety of rewarding activities that give our lives (and theirs) their meaning and value, and the very many ways in which that engagement brings out the best and the worst in each of us, not to mention the middling. Each of us is good at some things and not others, and that fundamental and inescapable fact[4] makes every one of us, just in those particular respects although not globally, better and worse than our fellows. There is simply no way of avoiding that fact without avoiding both value and our fellows, and so leading lives that, were they in any way actually possible, would be as empty as they were lonely. To the extent that we attempt to respond to the values present in the world, in all their richness and variety, as we are bound to do by our necessary commitment as rational creatures to the successful pursuit of lives worth living (taking into account all the differences of form and conviction that the ambition of a worthy life implies), and to the extent to which each one of us is properly sensitive to his or her more or less distinctive set of capacities (as best as he or she can develop, discover, and give effect to them), we distinguish ourselves in ways that, as Walzer expresses it, make us 'something more [and also less] than the equals of [our] comrades'.[5] To accept this fact, as it appears we must, is to reject the claims of 'simple equality', as Walzer describes it, that is, the claims of equality as and when it is literally understood and comprehensively pursued.

Like many others before and since him, including myself, Walzer is committed to rescuing the ideal of equality from a predicament that could, as it would seem and indeed as he sees it, consume it. He seeks to do this by proposing an understanding of equality that is fully at ease with our distributive instincts at their soundest. The equality that justice calls for, he suggests, is complex rather than simple. Simple equality both invites and deserves its own betrayal. Complex equality, by contrast, recognizes and accepts that differences both in the nature of value and in the character of human beings will yield outcomes in any given sphere of activity that betray simple equality, equality literally understood. Yet those outcomes do not amount to betrayals of complex equality as long as people who achieve pre-eminence in one sphere of activity cannot convert that achievement into pre-eminence in some other sphere of activity, thereby establishing a position of social dominance for themselves, and a corresponding condition of subordination for their fellows. It is

---

[3] Walzer, *Spheres of Justice: A Defense of Pluralism and Equality* (1985), xi.
[4] Inescapable both because the human condition is finite, and in the individual case quite radically so, so that we cannot be all things, and because it is in the nature of value that to be good in terms of certain values (many of them central to our lives) is by very reason of that fact to be bad in terms of others.
[5] Walzer (n. 3).

complex equality that we should care about, Walzer maintains, rather than simple equality. 'The aim of political egalitarianism,' he writes, 'is a society free from domination ... It is not a hope for the elimination of differences.'[6]

Walzer's account is a particularly elegant, sophisticated, and humane version of a line of thought that has been pursued by many, in the hope of identifying and sequestering a domain of equality that is both true to the egalitarian impulse and insulated from the arid outcomes that unfettered pursuit of that impulse would give rise to, or from what is almost as bad, the widespread hypocrisies that so commonly attend and sustain lip service to equality, coupled with commitment to the differences that betray it. For example, and to call upon certain deeply familiar and widely held cases, it has been often, indeed almost everywhere, said that we should seek treatment as equals rather than equal treatment, substantive equality rather than formal equality, and so on. Debate over these possibilities has been prolonged and in many ways unproductive. The answers that it has yielded seem to provoke anew the very questions that inspired them. It remains ever possible, of course, that a persuasive account along these lines is simply waiting to be discovered, just around the corner. That is not a corner, however, that I will be seeking to turn. It seems to me that there are foundational difficulties in all such positions, stemming from their attempt to isolate an ideal of equality that does not entail what equality entails, that at once capitalizes on the very real attractions of equality and yet seeks to avoid their correlative and conceptual downsides. These difficulties are present in even Walzer's account, for all its subtlety and finesse. Rather than try to negotiate them anew, the possibility that I would like to pursue here is that there might be real reward to be found in a very different approach, one that, among other things, faced up to and at least partially embraced what Walzer describes as the tendency to betrayal. What makes equality suspect is also, perhaps, what makes it good.

To begin to lay the foundations for that possibility, it might be helpful to look more closely at Walzer's idea of complex equality, the idea that equality forbids the conversion of success in one sphere into success in another. On this view, there is nothing wrong with succeeding in two spheres of value; what is wrong is succeeding in one sphere merely by virtue of the fact that one has succeeded in another. Is this true? Clearly a person can legitimately succeed in more than one sphere, provided that he or she lives up to the requirements of success in each. Might it further be the case that success in one sphere is sometimes, and perhaps commonly, among the ingredients of legitimate success in some other sphere, or less directly, that success in one sphere sometimes, or commonly, makes legitimate success in another sphere more likely, enough so as to give rise in certain circumstances to reason to offer those who are successful in one sphere special

---

[6] Ibid, xiii.

opportunities to succeed in the other sphere, opportunities that would make the achievement of success there that much the more likely? Were this indeed the case, practices of conversion would be open to justification.

On the other hand, were this not the case (so that conversions were inherently illegitimate) it would seem that there would be nothing for complex equality to forbid; all that would need to be said is that in securing justice one is bound to ensure that the grounds of justice are genuinely met in every case (as they would not be in cases of conversion, given their inherent illegitimacy). On that view of affairs, there would be no egalitarian story to tell. Walzer's account would be nothing other than an account of justice (as its title implies), driven in its particulars by a distinctive attentiveness to the plurality of value, and by a related though not entailed commitment to human autonomy, and the concomitant liberation of the human condition from structures that deny autonomy, in practice or by design, in patterns that Walzer describes in terms of dominance and subordination. The people whose well-being he has at heart would in fact be unfree rather than unequal.

Walzer's story is surely, among many other things, an egalitarian story. Yet it seems to me that it is so just because the conversions that Walzer speaks of are in truth sometimes legitimate and sometimes not, so that a scheme that entirely ruled them out, and thus ignored the different reasons they give rise to, would be a scheme of simple equality, however circumscribed. That being the case, it would be *pro tanto* (and leaving aside for the moment the justification of its circumscription) just as vulnerable to betrayal of the kind that concerns Walzer as is any other scheme of simple equality.[7] And if that is indeed so, one is bound to ask why a simple egalitarian should not object just as strongly to the monopolies that Walzer would permit as to the dominance that he would forbid. Do not both those practices involve subordination, and is that subordination not sometimes warranted, in the case of each practice by genuine differences in the ground on which the

---

[7] A few words on simple equality. The idea of equality is notoriously slippery, most obviously because it can be applied with like facility both to the consistent application of standards and to the application of certain standards in particular, namely those that currently attract the description of egalitarian (most notably, those involving a progressive view of distributive justice), either of which can be framed in terms of the idea of equality without any loss to their import, yet the application of both of which may well yield contradictory conclusions. This elusiveness makes it extremely difficult to consider the idea in a way that avoids committing oneself in advance to understanding equality in terms of any domain in particular, as a non-tendentious investigation typically requires, and yet is just as precise and rigorous as a successful and helpful analysis demands. One is all too apt to find oneself speaking in ways that are inherently equivocal, or that shift from one meaning to another as the discussion shifts settings. At this stage, what I am in search of is a relatively accommodating placeholder, one that closes as few doors of enquiry as possible. I have used the label simple equality to describe this placeholder, because it seems to me that Walzer's term comes as close as any to capturing the sort of idea I have in mind. It is the idea of putting people in the same position as one another for the sake of that sameness, without yet committing oneself to just what sort of position (in terms of kind and degree) that should be. It is an idea of equality as a kind of circumstance that, if good, is a good distinct from, if not independent of, whatever good arises from the non-relational circumstance in that respect of each of the people in question. This understanding of equality is designed to bracket the question of the value of equality, and more particularly and more importantly, the tendency to answer that question in ways that feed back into the idea of equality itself. The aim of this placeholder understanding is to permit the largest possible view

relevant distribution is based, and unwarranted otherwise? If there is good reason to forbid either practice in every case, as Walzer, no less than any other egalitarian, maintains, it is a reason that must be looked for in the idea of simple equality, a reason that must be reconciled with what Walzer describes as the tendency to its betrayal. Indeed, one is soon tempted to wonder whether it is possible to conceive of equality in anything other than simple terms, and by the same token, whether it is not in that very simplicity that its goodness is to be looked for and its badness faced up to by all those who are in any way attracted by its possibilities. To search for complexity is to betray lack of belief in the value of simple equality. There might be greater promise, richer possibilities perhaps, in pursuing one's belief in (simple) equality, rather than in embracing such compromise.

The intuition that inspires Walzer and animates his account is that those people who succeed in achieving dominance as he understands it, just because they succeed in converting success in one sphere into success in another, are not overall superior as people, though they are often regarded as such by themselves and by the social orders that foster and validate them. What is sound in this intuition, it seems to me, is that the people in question are indeed not overall superior and inferior to one another, even when one of them is, natively and without any reliance upon conversion, superior to the other in all the spheres in which they both operate. It does not follow, however, that they are equal. They may simply be different overall, and hence incommensurable overall, for the straightforward reason that their differences, as and when fully and accurately comprehended, are not susceptible to being captured on any scale in terms of which they could be understood as better, worse, or equal. By the same token, it also does not follow that we are morally bound to bar such conversions just because they would generate the inequality of people overall. Yet the possibility remains that we might have reason to insist upon this and other cases of (simple) equality, not because the *inequalities* that they would forbid are illegitimate, but because the particular *equalities* that they would give rise to may, in the special circumstances that prompted the insistence, be good, or more precisely, be capable of contributing to what is good.

3.1.3 The Need to Temper the Claims of Equality

Before going any further, there is another issue, closely related to the first, that is raised by Walzer's account, and by the distinction it seeks to draw between simple

---

of the idea of equality and its evaluative implications. In doing so, it should not be understood to be embracing a sceptical outlook. Rather it assumes that the concept of equality, like nearly all other concepts, is susceptible to being and becoming the bearer of different values and disvalues. See further on that point, Macklem, 'Ideas of Easy Virtue', first published in John Keown and Robert P. George (eds), *Reason, Morality, and Law: The Philosophy of John Finnis* (2012), 346, and reproduced, in elaborated form, in *Law and Life in Common* (2015).

equality and complex equality. There is something more comprehensive involved in the idea of complex equality than its purported freedom from the betrayals that simple equality invites, and its correlative protection of social practices that recognize and give effect to certain differences between people, namely, those differences that populate the spheres of justice that Walzer identifies and defends. Walzer speaks very largely in terms of the betrayal of equality, as is natural when addressing an audience whose primary concern is with living up to the ideal of equality, but in fact the logic of the betrayal that he draws attention to runs in both directions, as he himself recognizes in referring to the strictly egalitarian state (based on simple equality) as a Procrustean bed (whereon, it might be thought, difference is betrayed by the pull of equality), and as his ideal of complex equality, and the consequent architecture of his spheres of justice, recognize in protecting the content of those spheres (what he calls monopoly) against the claims of equality, no less than in securing their structures against the claims of difference (that is, claims that would tell in favour of the conversions that the integrity of the spheres forbids in order to prevent dominance). Walzer cares as much about betrayals of other values (for Walzer, justice in particular) at the hands of equality as about betrayals of equality at the hands of other values.

In every case of equality, be it complex or simple, so as to track Walzerian justice or to ignore it, to be equal is necessarily also to be different. That is part of the idea of equality, and what distinguishes it from identity.[8] As Walzer himself emphasizes, equality as a moral and political ideal exists to secure certain commonalities in the human condition, while acknowledging and giving effect to the correlative differences that otherwise exist between people, differences upon which much of the value of their lives trades, and with which any genuine commitment to their equality must be reconciled. It is in recognition of that fact that Walzer observes that it is the goal of equality to end domination, not difference.[9] Equality, in its nature and its ambitions, is only ever a companion to other ideals in our lives, all of which operate to trade upon, give effect to, and in certain cases even alter and enlarge the significance of differences in the human condition.

It follows that there is a necessary tension between the pursuit of equality and the recognition of difference, and consequently an equilibrium to be looked for in their relationship; if we are to pursue equality and difference together, each needs to be protected in some way from the claims of the other. Their mutual flourishing is dependent upon the successful articulation of a principle that limits both. Yet there is on the face of it no natural, logical equilibrium between the pursuit of equality and the recognition of difference. The idea of equality does not

---

[8] For an extended, helpful, and very illuminating consideration of these points and some of their implications, see Peter Westen, *Speaking of Equality* (1990).
[9] In speaking of equality here I am, following Walzer, speaking of a historic political movement. This movement is soundly based if and to the extent that equality is rightly animated by the goal of ending inequality, as I have doubted.

incorporate any instinct to Walzerian justice; on the contrary, the ideal of justice has either to be set against that of equality or to be incorporated by stipulation as part of the understanding of a particular conception of equality. Conversely, the recognition of difference, even when that is just, does not incorporate any instinct to equality, a fact that the contemporary world offers us rather more unhappy reminders of than most of us would like.[10]

Of course, like most other modern egalitarians, all of whom seek to transcend the shortcomings of what he calls simple equality, Walzer would present his own account of (complex) equality as a refutation of this claim. Yet if the answer suggested by that account to the need for equilibrium is that there are principled limits to complex equality, namely those described by the architecture of his spheres (albeit no such limits to simple equality), surely the response to that answer is that there are in fact no significant relevant limits to the spheres of distributive justice. Those spheres are a function of the relationship between the values existing in the world and the capacity and inclination of people, in all their variety, to pursue those values in the advancement of human well-being, the combination of which is comprehensive of human experience as we know it at any given moment. To limit the number of spheres in any way one must invoke a conception of justice rather than of equality. What is more, if the idea of complex equality is at bottom an idea of simple equality, as I have suggested, so that the scope of complex equality is driven by a conception of justice (these equalities and no more) and its operation is driven by (simple) equality, then the problem becomes all the more pressing. The problem here is not just the bare fact of betrayal, in other words, but that of its scope.

The idea of simple equality as a value in its own right is insatiable and self-defeating. It does not contain within itself any capacity to tie its claims to its worth, however worth may be understood. It could yield valuable lives only if there were functional identity of both people and values. So the pursuit of simple equality, even if good, needs limits, not limits that deny the virtue of its simplicity, not limits that seek to avoid its betrayal, but limits that check its scope while respecting its nature, limits that have to be looked for in the context in which it is called upon to operate rather than in the understanding of equality itself. That simply follows from the fact that the pursuit of equality is not by its nature self-limiting and cannot be made so by any recognizable development of that nature.

In short, while it is important to face up to and accept them, one can no more wholly embrace the betrayals that simple equality invites than one can avoid them. Walzer is quite right to look for limits to the claims of equality, if not right to look

---

[10] The consistent recognition of any difference, of course, generates equality in the dimension that describes the difference in question. Speaking more precisely then, what I mean here is that the recognition of difference has no tendency to accommodate equalities other than that which arises from the proper recognition of the difference in question.

for them in the idea of equality itself. He may also be quite right to believe that the pursuit of equality, in the modern world at least, is closely allied to questions of distributive justice, and further and more profoundly, to believe that the relationship of equality and justice in any given society is definitively shaped by the social forms and practices present there. These are issues that I will take up at a later stage. Before turning to them, further consideration needs to be given, first, to the meaning of equality, and then to its value. I will address the meaning of equality and its nuances in the next section of this chapter, and then try to identify and draw out the two main puzzles of its value in the next sub-chapter.

3.1.4 Equality and the Accommodation of Difference

There is quite widespread resistance, both popular and academic, to the idea that equality can only be conceived of in simple terms. Walzer is far from alone in this: many other scholars, and surely most ordinary people as well, believe that such a vision of equality not merely invites but deserves betrayal. In their view, this vision of equality is at best a misunderstanding, at worst a misrepresentation, one typically promoted by the enemies of equality and one that consequently ought to be roundly rejected by its friends. Properly understood, they maintain, equality in fact notices and serves those differences that make our lives better, and it does this by insisting that as a society we attend, sensitively and appropriately, to the particular qualities of character and predicament that, taken separately and together, genuinely distinguish people from one another, so as to capture accurately and thereby render in all its proper detail a sound understanding of particular human needs (to take but one example), and the ways in which those needs ought to be responded to if we are to ensure that each one of us lives well, or more precisely, as well as possible and no less well than any of our fellows.

From the opposite perspective, on this view equality calls upon us to discard the many presuppositions that stand in the way of a sound appreciation of the qualities that genuinely distinguish people from one another, qualities in terms of which (equal) respect for those persons must be couched. So understood, equality and difference are said not to be in any way at odds with one another; on the contrary, the pursuit of equality specifically calls upon us to register, as accurately as possible, the differences that give our lives true substance, differences that in all too many settings we have long and shamefully neglected. It follows that we could not hope to achieve equality by setting out to serve it literally, and so allocating the same portion of good or ill to every person. Rather we achieve equality by responding in the spirit of equality to the distinctive substance of each person's concern for a good life. This is a vision of equality as an end, not as a means, a vision of a society in which people become equal just by being treated as equals (whether by virtue of their common humanity or otherwise), and where they would be treated equally, in the literal sense, only as and when doing so would bring about the equality of their condition, in terms of the substance of a good life.

Is this really a different view of equality, or does it just trade on a sleight of hand? Suppose, for example, that the custodian of an orchard has the welfare of his or her workers in mind, as a good in its own right as well as an aspect of a professional concern to ensure that the apples are harvested as successfully as possible, and so to have a workforce that is well fed and properly motivated. Knowing better than to take equality literally (or formally, as it is more often put), the custodian rejects the idea that each worker should receive the same quantity of food and drink for lunch. Rather each should receive in accordance with his or her needs (which might vary depending on how large a person was, or how well fed otherwise), or his or her desert (some workers may have been more assiduous than others in the morning's harvest), or some other legitimate ground, just which one depending on one's view of just what respect, or concern, or justice entails. Suppose that as a result one worker received half as much again as another worker. What would make this distribution an equal one? How would the custodian, or the workers, or anyone else in a position to evaluate the distribution, know that equality had or had not been achieved?

The answer seems at once obvious and inescapable: the distribution is equal if and to the extent that the ratio of the allocation is the same as the ratio of its ground. The workers in question will have been treated as equals if the need (or desert) of one is half as much again as the need (or desert) of the other. Notwithstanding its description and self-understanding, it is a straightforward case of simple equality, no different in what makes it equal than the case of giving all workers the same portion. All that has happened is that there has been an unacknowledged shift in the ground of distribution. This is not a shift to a greater or truer equality.[11] The workers remain at once both equal and different, equal in terms of what the distribution is sensitive to and different otherwise, most obviously, different in terms of all that the ground of distribution is correlative to. To allocate the same portion to every worker is to enforce equality in the face of potential differences in all respects but that of the ground of (say) common humanity; to allocate different portions to different workers, as different instances of need (or desert), is to enforce equality in the face of potential differences in all respects but that of the chosen ground of need (or desert).[12] The locus of equality has changed, and with it the nature of the

---

[11] This is one of a number of reasons to question the helpfulness of the distinction between formal and substantive equality.

[12] I have simplified the picture here, in at least two ways. First, I have assumed that common humanity is the ground upon which allocation of the same portion would be based; in fact there might be other grounds of distribution in terms of which all workers would legitimately be allocated the same portion, including those of need and desert, should the workers in fact be just as needy as one another, or as deserving. Second, I have assumed that the workers differ in respects other than that which ties the ground of distribution to their treatment, when in fact they are bound also to be the same, whether relevantly so (in terms of common humanity for example) or not (if all are male or female).

case that will need to be made for the rationality and legitimacy of the distribution, but no greater or truer form of equality has been achieved just because people have been, as it is often put, treated as equals rather than equally treated. Equality tracks (and perhaps inspires) putative reasons in both cases; equality is achieved just as fully as the application of those reasons is consistent.

One could multiply examples but there would be no point. It is simply not possible to imagine a case of equality that does not operate in this manner, not because there is something biased or limited in the workings of my imagination, or the imagination of others, but rather because the very idea of equality is incompatible with the presence of difference in the particular dimension in which equality is secured. One cannot simultaneously be of equal status and different status, generally or in some particular respect; on the contrary, one status is a contradiction of the other. That is not to say, of course, that the question of status is necessarily an all-or-nothing matter, for that would not be true; as and when status is multifaceted, as it often, perhaps typically, is, one may well be of equal status in certain respects and yet of different status in others. It remains the case that in the respects in which one is of different status (whatever they may be and whatever their legitimacy), one self-evidently is not and cannot become also of equal status. In those respects, the existence of one status is secured precisely to the exclusion of the other.

Otherwise, as has been frequently acknowledged, equality is fully compatible with difference, in at least three ways. First, as I have noted, conditions that are equal in a particular respect are necessarily different in other respects; where that is not the case, the conditions in question are either comprehensively different or identical. Interestingly, it seems to me, cases of the latter two kinds are not simply vanishingly rare but surely non-existent in the human condition. We often say that people have nothing whatsoever in common, but in fact they are equally human, equally alive, and much more; we characteristically say, to the opposite effect, that certain twins are identical, but in fact they differ in a host of respects, from the moment of their births, to the narrative of their lives, to the circumstances of their decline and deaths, which inevitably part company to greater or lesser degree, if only because of their necessarily different loci. It seems to be the case that people are in fact always both equal and different, so that it falls to us to ascertain and give effect to whatever good and bad may come of that fact, or more fundamentally, to give effect to whatever good may come of the particular conditions and circumstances that are open to classification in terms of equality and difference, as well as to whatever good and bad may derive from the (relative) fact of that classification, as equal and different.

Second, though perhaps it need hardly be noted, the presence of some difference is the necessary trigger for any claim to equality; by its nature, however, the inherent purpose of the claim is to eliminate that difference. Finally, to notice that equality does not always allocate the same portion, be it of benefit or burden, to each person is simply to notice that the ground of a legitimate claim to equality need not always be universally possessed, and what is more to the point, be universally possessed without question of degree. Important as recognition of our common humanity and other universals, the grounds of which all people possess in like degree, undoubtedly is to the success of our lives, these are far from the only forms of commonality upon which the worth of human lives turns, and certainly not always the most telling. That sets limits to the equality of form, important though equalities of form are in identifying and securing the essential circumstances of respect. Our needs, our deserts, our aims, and our achievements, and so much else of what makes our lives matter, are more or less local, and are experienced by different people in different degree, thereby distinguishing some of us from others, those who share in the condition from those who do not. If equality has any role to play in the goodness and badness of our lives, it must bring its claims to bear on the local no less than on the universal, or to put it more recognizably, on experiences that are susceptible to variance among human beings as well as to those that are not. Hence the familiar concern for equalities of substance.

3.1.5 Paradigms of Equality and the Contestability of their Grounds

The only way in which this picture could in principle be altered, so as to eliminate the need to reconcile equality and difference (quite impossible though that would be in practice), would be either through the elimination of every meaningful difference between people, that is, through everything that distinguished one person from another apart from the fact of their separate existences, so that human beings would not merely become as twins from the moments of their births, bearers of (as far as we were able to tell or care about) the same properties, but would also live their lives as one, interacting with the world and with one another in exactly the same ways; or what amounts to the same thing, through the elimination of our engagement with any values that would register such human differences. This outcome would require, of course, that we all live in identical evaluative environments, make the same decisions, and experience the same fortune, good and bad. Not only is such a world inconceivable; it is surely deeply undesirable, for its realization would entail a radical reduction of the range of values that human beings were able to give effect to through their lives, albeit perhaps with a limited degree of concomitant deepening of our engagement with those values that survived in our experience, just as deep as the strength of engagement which that degree of human commonality made possible.

That is not to say that the picture in question cannot and should not be altered in certain limited respects, so as to help make certain people equal in those respects. The good to be derived from ensuring that people are treated in the same way as one another is a genuine one if and to the extent that people are in fact much the same as one another, and further, to the extent that prevailing social practices, whether grounded in ignorance, indifference, or malice, have conspired to deny that fact, in circumstances that, by chance or by design, have undermined the wellbeing of the people in question, or are likely to do so in the future. In such cases, the pursuit of equality might be thought (correctly or not) to give rise in principle to two possible goods: first, the dispelling of the misconceptions in question and, second, the encouragement of those people who have, either personally or in tradition, historically been marred by the distinction to live lives that are more like the lives of those who are in key respects no different from them, so as to avoid staking the worth of their lives to any significant degree upon a distinction that has so often and so damagingly been invoked against them or their like in the past. This might be done broadly, as and when people are broadly the same as one another, or more sensitively and tactically, in certain specific respects, as and when people are the same as one another in those specific respects.

Anti-discrimination law has long incorporated a mission of equality that might in principle be justified along those lines. The mission works by insisting that people both be and be treated as more like one another than the straightforward recognition of relevant differences would call for, that is, would call for in the terms in which we understand them, and in the range of values and related social practices with which they are engaged. Such a mission works much less well, if at all, to the extent that people are rightly and relevantly defined by their difference, so that their equality as persons turns in part on the recognition, accommodation, and valorization of that difference. And, of course, many, perhaps most, cases of distinction are profoundly mixed in this respect, so as to raise deep questions about the value to the people involved of the pursuit of equality, as with sexual orientation and certain forms of disability, to take but two prominent contemporary examples, or even with gender and, peripherally at most, race.[13]

These special cases aside, together with the special domain of the anti-discrimination principles to which they give rise, people are and must remain at once both different and equal, so that the inescapable question arises, in the setting of distributions for example, in which respects, if any, they ought to be treated as equals. Certain distributions may have a paradigmatic ground, embedded in social forms and practices, as when nourishment or health care are, in accepted principle if not in practice, distributed to those in need, so that food and drink are in principle if not in practice properly allocated to the most hungry and thirsty, just in proportion to their hunger and thirst, while medical remedies are in principle properly distributed to those who suffer illnesses of the particular kind that those

---

[13] For further and much fuller exploration of these thoughts in the context of the disadvantaging of women and its remedy, see Macklem, *Beyond Comparison: Sex and Discrimination* (2003). Notice that the anti-discrimination mission is based on the presence of damaging misconceptions, not on the value of equality.

remedies were designed to respond to, just in proportion to their suffering. It is in reliance upon such paradigms that claims to substantive equality rather than formal equality are standardly made.[14] Walzer for his part relies on certain such social paradigms as the basis for the definition of his spheres of justice and the ideal of complex equality that they are designed to serve. Yet as we all know, social paradigms may be mistaken, and even if sound, are not usually exclusive. The mistakes are all too familiar, perhaps, to need exemplification, but the lack of exclusivity is somewhat less straightforward. It comes in two kinds.

The first, and perhaps most obvious, variance in the social paradigm of equality is to be found in its underpinnings, which vary, not merely in what constitutes substance with respect to different goods, as one would expect and as Walzer's entire account is dedicated to delineating, but also in the foundational principle of distribution, which is as liable to be formal as it is to be substantive even for those entirely committed to substantive equality, to return to that distinction. So, for example, it is a commonplace, subscribed to unhesitatingly by those committed to the achievement of substantive equality, that every person is entitled to a vote, without any sense that there ought to be some sort of connection between the right to vote and questions of qualification to vote (at least once the age of majority has been attained, whatever that age might properly be said to be), in any sense that might permit a varying answer.[15] This is a vision of formal equality, as it is often put, one that is typically accompanied by similar commitments to other formal consequences of citizenship or of residence, such as access to public education, or to health care that is free at the point of provision, or to a basic state pension. (To say that these are questions of capacity but that everyone has them in like degree is to either to define the substantive in terms of the formal in ways that are not helpful to the understanding of the distinction between the two, or to make a factual claim that would seem to run counter to the evidence.)

The other form of variance in the social paradigm of equality is to be found in the ground of distribution in a particular domain of equality, which is as liable to be contested in certain settings as it is to be mistaken in others. The means of physical nourishment, food and drink that is, are properly distributed according to need, so that they go first to those who are the most hungry and thirsty, until the point at which those people are no more hungry and thirsty than the next most in need, who are then to be included in the distribution, and so on until the point at

---

[14] I will use the terminology of formal and substantive equality in the paragraphs that follow, not because I regard those terms as illuminating (they aren't, as suggested in the text at n. 11 and in the paragraphs that follow this note), but for the sake of convenience, as a placeholder that will sufficiently stabilize the analysis to bring out the broader points that I am trying to make here.

[15] There are certain well-known marginal cases, such as the electoral rights of prisoners. Yet even here the issue continues to be addressed in binary terms, so that prisoners are or are not denied political citizenship as an aspect of their punishment, that is, are or are not regarded as falling outside the reach of formal political citizenship, without assessment of their qualification to vote, as a matter of degree, in the way that substantive equality might be thought to call for.

which all people's needs in terms of food and drink have been equally met, to the extent that the resources that are available permit. Few would dispute this view of distributive justice in respect of food and drink, far as we fall short of honouring it in practice, where people often go hungry while their fellows grow fat, where many face shortage while food is discarded by the lorry load.

And yet distributions of food and drink in certain circumstances, most notoriously those involving a shared experience of extreme need, very often flout this principle, and adhere instead to the principle of formal equality, so often indeed that to do so might even be regarded as paradigmatic in such settings. On the Scott expedition to the Antarctic, for example, the last four men, those making the ultimate journey to the pole and back, shared what little food they had equally, that is to say, by allocating the same portion to each man, despite the fact that their relative sizes and thus their relative needs differed significantly. Those whose needs were less well met as a result of this formally equal distribution suffered accordingly. Nevertheless, while that ground of distribution may well have been misguided in that particular setting (given that all perished), it does not strike most people as either perverted or unjust. On the contrary, in many circumstances of destitution and privation food and drink are allocated in accordance with the principle of formal equality, so that ship's biscuits and water are often divided evenly among those stranded in a lifeboat.

The thought seems to be that in extreme circumstances of privation, where solidarity is no less important to survival than is proper nourishment, formal equality may be regarded as an appropriate basis of distribution. Putting to one side for the moment any potentially contentious question of its legitimacy as a response to special cases of privation, what might this conclusion tell us about the goodness to be derived from the circumstances of equality, to the extent that it captures something at all sound, in certain settings at least? If the social paradigms of distribution cannot be looked to, not simply because they are subject to error, error of the kind that we might be expected, on appropriate reflection, to recognize and negotiate, but because their grounds are fundamentally contestable, not because anything goes in terms of justification, but rather because several things might do so in any particular case, albeit none of them in a way that is capable of wholly defeating the others, then just what can we look to for guidance? Is it possible, as in so many cases, that the answer is multivalent, so that we will need to look to several domains of concern at once in order to arrive at it? Or, to take the next step, might the answer be that the grounds of equality are just not derivable from the idea of equality, whether directly or in conjunction with due consideration of circumstances, but are always matters for cultural direction, in need of political stipulation?

3.2 Two Troubling Puzzles

What good might there be in putting people in the same position, apart from the value to each of them of the position in question?[16] If the position in question is a good one, just what additional good might equality with another person in respect of it be thought to contribute to it? On the other hand, if the position is a bad one, what if anything might its equality do to offset that fact?

One possible line of response would be to look to the resonances that can arise from shared experience, of which, as in the example of the pickers in the apple orchard, equality can certainly be an instance. The meaning of certain predicaments, for good or ill, may undoubtedly be altered, again for good or ill, by the sharing of those predicaments. Yet many of the respects in which equality between people exists and is thought to matter involve no interaction and so cannot be explained or justified in terms of a shared experience. The ultimate value of equality will have to be sought elsewhere. Another no less ready line of response might be that, properly understood, equality is in fact the name, not of something that is a value in its own right, but rather of a mixed value. A mixed value is a value that is in fact the proper name given to a cluster of values that are pursued, in the setting of any particular culture, as a socially determined package, the specific composition and admixture of which is consistent with value but not determined by value, and the all-things-considered worth of which is derivative of the worth of its several constituents.[17] If equality were a mixed value, then the practice of equality in any particular setting would be valuable if and to the extent that at least one of its constituents there was both valuable and successfully realized in the social practice that bore its name. This understanding of equality would avoid the challenge of showing that equality was a value in its own right, but at a price, for it would mean that the value of equality was entirely derivative of the value of its constituents and thus was unrelated to the idea of equality itself. Yet the question of its price aside, the practice of equality seems to lack the character of a mixed value, for a mixed value is by definition a value and yet the idea of bad equalities is not only fully intelligible (as the many cases of pernicious equalities attest) but necessarily applies, presumptively at least, to all those species of equality (simple, formal, and the like) that are rejected by the proponents of rival, incompatible forms of equality (complex, substantive,

---

[16] If access to the latter was all that was at stake, then one should properly speak of that access in terms of due recognition of the presence of its ground, and consequently, of ending any denials of that due recognition, so that women were enabled to become engineers or surgeons (for example) just because it is or ought to be clear that they possess (whether with or without modifications to their education and role models) the relevant capacities, rather than in terms of equality, which would, if framed in terms of capacity and opportunity, focus on the relative rather than the absolute capacities, and consequent opportunities, of women and men.

[17] I take the idea of a mixed value from Joseph Raz, *The Practice of Value* (2003).

and the like) as being unworthy of the name rather than as being strangers to it. It remains the case, therefore, that we are in need of a proper answer to the question of whether equality is a value, or somewhat more accommodatingly perhaps, of whether and in what way it constitutes a worthy ideal.

3.2.1 The Levelling Down Objection

Derek Parfit has posed the question in the following dramatic manner, to which he has given the name of the Levelling Down Objection: how can an experience be better for anyone when it is bad for some (those who are denied the goods that would otherwise give rise to an inequality) and better for no one (all those whose position is unaltered in any respect other than that of its equality)?[18] To put it in everyday terms, the situation Parfit has in mind is the simple case of making people equal by taking away from one person rather than giving to the other. If children are going to argue endlessly over who is to have the ball, then take it away from both. This strikes me, and to be fair, Parfit as well, as an inconclusive way of presenting the issue: arresting as it may be as a way to frame an objection, it does not take us very far, for the question that it poses is the very question that was in need of an answer in the first place. Parfit's particular taxonomic project may not require that he personally provide such an answer, but any other project in which the worth of equality is what is at stake certainly does.

Plainly the experience involved in levelling down is not better in terms of the underlying value in terms of which the people involved are being compared (or by reason of its sharing). The possibility remains, however, that it might be better by reason of its equality, albeit that it would not necessarily be so. How is that possibility to be properly assessed? The question raised here can be approached from within a commitment to equality as well as from outside it: Larry Temkin is no less assertive than Parfit, but in the opposite direction. Temkin suggests that a circumstance in which everyone is blind, rather than some being blind and some not, would in one way (if no other) be a better circumstance than its alternative, just because it would be a circumstance of equality.[19] Yet exactly what kind of better

---

[18] 'Equality or Priority?' in Matthew Clayton and Andrew Williams (eds), *The Ideal of Equality* (2002), 81 at 98, 115. Put the other way round, given that the experience is plainly not better for anyone, what improvement in the human condition can equality claim to have secured? The thrust of Parfit's challenge is this: given the brute logic of the levelling down objection (which I have rhetorically framed here as a question rather than as a premise) and given that equality can be achieved as fully by levelling down as by levelling up, how can it be claimed that equality makes lives better, as it would be bound to do if it were an independent value? Dramatic as it is, levelling down is not simply a thought experiment; as most anti-discrimination lawyers and campaigners are all too aware, legal benefits are routinely stripped from men (rather than extended to women) in order to secure the equality of women. One of the most common justifications for doing so in the judicial setting is that courts are said to have the power to reduce but not to extend a scheme of public expenditure.
[19] Temkin, *Inequality* (1993), 282.

does Temkin have in mind, particularly once shared experience has been removed as a possibility? On the face of it, both these analyses seem only to postpone the problem. In the first case, one is pointing to something as empty of value without explaining why it should be regarded as so; in the second case, one is pointing to something as valuable, again without explaining why.

One possible answer is that the worth of equality is simply not susceptible to the kind of analysis that would trace that worth to the worth of some set of its constituent elements. If, for example, one were to seek an explanation of the worth of kindness, or of courage, the only answer that one could find or be offered would be a kind of pointing, of the kind that is engaged in by Parfit and Temkin. Yet the worth of equality does not seem, on any recognizable account of it, to be worth of that kind. We already know, in the Aristotelian manner, that kindness and courage are good things, though we cannot explain just why, other than by further forms of pointing, and it would be foolish of us to try to do so. Our grasp of the value of kindness and courage is immanent in our experience of them and simply has to be left at that. In the case of those qualities, and of others like them, the search for explanation might be said, colloquially, to be a question of why worthy rather than whether worthy. The inherent immunity of their worth to analysis rather than to experience and intuition is a good answer to a 'why' question of that kind.

In the case of equality, however, the question might more accurately be said, again colloquially, to be not so much one of why worthy as one of whether and in what way worthy. That sort of question is not and could not be immune to analysis. In other words, the question of the value of equality cannot be answered by regarding the value of equality as a brute fact, for it is simply not so. Defenders of equality no less than its critics accept that equality is a special case of the issue of worth, one in which the fact of value cannot be straightforwardly apprehended from experience. Some kind of explanation of the worth of equality is called for.

It should not be assumed that such an explanation must yield an account of equality as an independent value in order to be successful. Indeed it might be thought that the critics of equality have raised the sort of doubts about the value of equality that the defenders of equality ought perhaps to be prepared to accept, as basically unthreatening to their egalitarian project, and so ought to be as ready to avoid as to answer. Surely it need not matter to friends of equality that equality is not an independent value, if that were indeed to prove to be the case. Rather it should be enough for them that equality might have an auxiliary, albeit something more than instrumental, role to play in the worth of human lives, one that is neither exhausted by the goodness of what it is in aid of, so as to be functionally indistinguishable from its companion values, nor detachable from what it is in aid of, so as to be indifferent to the goodness or badness of its now putative companion values. On such a view, equality would not be an independent moral value, yet might, in certain circumstances, have a key contribution to make to both goodness and badness. To unpack that thought, and to make any kind of a case for it, one would have to be able to distinguish the realm of value and disvalue from that of goodness and badness, a possibility that I will take up in the next sub-chapter.

3.2.2 Levelling Down and Value Pluralism

Joseph Raz has pointed out that the levelling down objection is not a decisive objection to equality. If equality were a value in its own right, its claims would routinely be set against the claims of rival values, values that differed from equality in kind, and in any cases in which the claims of equality were preferred, as reason would permit though not require, that preference would involve a sacrifice of the claims of some other value, a sacrifice of just the kind that the levelling down objection notices. Yet far from being a special fact about equality, this kind of sacrifice is a standard feature of the operation of values that differ from one another in kind as well as in the degree of their instantiation. Not only do all value pluralists necessarily take this view; all believers in equality are necessarily value pluralists, because belief in the value of equality entails belief in at least one other value that the value of equality allegedly rightly regulates the allocation of.[20]

Raz is interested in the fact that the objection fails rather than in what else it might tell us, as of course is entirely reasonable, given that his project is to show that a different objection succeeds. Yet there is also reason to be interested in what the objection might teach us about equality, even if that is not that equality is not an independent value. If equality is indeed not a value, as Raz seeks to show, then the answer to the levelling down objection cannot simply be that when values clash, and one must be preferred to the other, then something like levelling down

---

[20] Joseph Raz, 'On the Value of Distributional Equality', University of Oxford Legal Research Paper Series 41/2008, SSRN 1288545, reprinted in Stephen de Wijze, Matthew Kramer, and Ian Carter (eds), *Hillel Steiner and the Anatomy of Justice* (2009). It seems questionable, however, whether an egalitarian can indeed be a value pluralist, since a political commitment to egalitarianism normally requires that one be able to compare and rank different predicaments, which is possible only if the various features of those predicaments can be reduced to a common scale of better and worse, that is, can be fully captured in terms of a single value. In a monistic universe, equality could both operate on that calculation, in the same way as does a commitment to more good rather than less, and ultimately figure in it, as contributing to more rather than less. So if one is a monist who believes that happiness is the one and only good, one would also believe in the existence of a controlling maxim, say, the greatest happiness of the greatest number, and if one is an egalitarian monist one might then believe in equality both as a further controlling maxim, and as a contributor to happiness, called into play by the maxim of the greatest happiness of the greatest number. If on the other hand one is a value pluralist, then it is difficult to see why one should think that there are only two values in the world (a monistic value and the value of equality) so as to be a two-value pluralist, for once a second value is admitted why not more, or to see how one could possibly reconcile a commitment to equality that is based on ending inequalities with a commitment to the recognition of human diversity in the manner that value pluralism calls for. If values are plural, equality cannot look into the different lives of different people as they are, so as to rank them as equal (though a commitment to equality in certain respects can make people equal in those respects, by changing them). In short, visions of equality as a response to inequality depend on value monism, although a vision of equality as a special, limited form of goodness does not.

is bound to take place, because if equality is not a value then it cannot warrant the levelling down of value that is undertaken in its name. In that case, one must decide what to make of claims to equality. Either they are deeply misconceived, so that it is always wrong to level down for the sake of equality (and no less wrong to level up for its sake, unless doing so is independently called for by the value in question), or something else supports the egalitarian intuition, in certain cases at least. As Raz himself reminds us, deeply held and long-standing ideals very often have something to tell us even when they are quite mistaken, for the nature of the mistake may simply be that people have arrived at the wrong explanation of a moral impulse that is, in at least certain respects, sound, so that in committing themselves to the impulse people are in effect on to something good, even if it is not the good that they think it is.

Sound as I take it to be, therefore, Raz's response to the problem needs probing to uncover just what it tells us. The putative value of equality is not quite like the other values that regularly come into operative conflict with one another, and that in doing so require us to sacrifice the claims of one in favour of the claims of another. If equality is a value at all, it is a value of a special kind, for its role in the achievement of value is intrinsically auxiliary. If on the other hand equality is not a value, then something other than the claim of value is needed to explain the auxiliary role that equality is taken to play in the management from time to time of the pursuit of value. It seems to me that what in fact the levelling down objection exposes is but the most dramatic and apparently paradoxical of three features of the auxiliary character of equality which, taken together, constitute the first troubling puzzle about its contribution to value.

3.2.3 The Puzzle of Detachment

First, to be auxiliary to the achievement of value is necessarily to lack any independent relation to value. It makes no more sense to think that there is value in being equal *simpliciter* than to think there is value in terms of being better *simpliciter* rather than worse. It is better to be better at something valuable, worse to be worse at something valuable; it is better to be worse at something disvaluable, worse to be better at something disvaluable. If equality has any kind of positive contribution to make to value it must be in the same way. The language of better and worse by and large makes the fact of this dependency clear, because it has a natural tendency to import an awareness of the necessary and appropriate accompaniment of value; the language of equality, being neutral between better and worse, lends itself to masking the essentially supportive nature of the role that equality is bound to play in the realization of value. In fact, however, whatever language may tempt us to believe, if equality has any contribution to make to value, then it is good to be equal in terms of something valuable, bad to be equal in terms of something disvaluable, and meaningless to be equal in terms of something it is impossible to imagine discovering value or disvalue in.[21]

Second, what the levelling down objection further reveals is that the auxiliary character of equality is deeply equivocal, precisely in that it does not care about better or worse, as indeed one should perhaps expect, given that commitment to the circumstance that it is (neither better nor worse) is just what distinguishes equality from better and worse. From the perspective of equality, if from no other, it matters not whether people are doing well or badly, because doing well or badly, as such, is not its business. What matters is that they are experiencing just whatever it is (whether doing well or badly) equally, which in turn means not so much experiencing it together (though that may also be so) as in the same way. If there is any good in equality, it is a good that is not only detached from but indifferent to the goodness of what it is in aid of.

Third, and as Peter Westen most famously pointed out (though a great many have followed in his footsteps), a surprising feature of the auxiliary character of equality is its pseudo-mercenary quality, its willingness to come to the aid of any cause, of whatever kind, be it even good or bad.[22] This feature goes beyond the levelling down objection, which focuses on the character of the commitment that equality displays to whatever cause it is invoked in aid of. What is at issue here is the fact that there is nothing in the idea of equality that would predispose it to one commitment rather than another, powerful as is the tendency of contemporary egalitarians to identify equality with a commitment to progressive politics, that is, to the politics of concern for the socially disadvantaged. Equality lacks any capacity to direct its enterprise to one end rather than another, to progress rather than to reaction, to the good of the many rather than of the few, to welfare rather than to opportunity, and so on. The politics of egalitarianism in its current incarnation, in which equality is associated with a particular species of progressive politics, is a contingent social fact rather than a moral fact, one that is compatible with the idea of equality but that is not entailed by it.

Here then is the first fundamental puzzle, at least as I see it. The ideal of equality is by its nature at once attached to value and detached from value. It is attached to the pursuit of value (at least when rationally engaged in) but not to any of the

---

[21] I do not mean to pre-empt here the possibility that there may be some good to be found in certain cases of being equally badly off, such as the one that Larry Temkin imagined, of blinding the sighted to make them equal in condition to the blind. In fact, however, my own sense is that Temkin's premise is wrong, just because, as I see it, the pursuit of equality is not in fact the pursuit of what is intrinsically valuable, but rather is a practice of goodness that may under certain conditions, including the condition of being equal in terms of what is disvaluable (as Temkin assumes blindness is), be constitutive of what is valuable, as a function of the forms of goodness that the practice of equality gives rise to in that setting, other goodness, however, not the goodness of its own existence, as Temkin would have it.

[22] Westen, *Speaking of Equality*, which drew upon and developed ideas first put forward in a series of articles in the Harvard Law Review, the most notorious of which was entitled 'The Empty Idea of Equality' (see n. 1), to Westen's later regret.

means or outcomes of that pursuit. It is concerned with value, at least in the shape of the particular value or values that it is from time to time attached to, but it has no deep, engaged concern, even derivatively, with anything that those values themselves are concerned with. It is this fundamental lack of concern (of which levelling down is but a prominent aspect) that is deeply puzzling in the nature of equality, all the more so perhaps given that equality is a moral and political commitment that, for most of its adherents, is the very apotheosis of a true concern for human well-being. The point should not be misunderstood: equality is as consistent with concern as with lack of concern. Yet the concern that equality displays is the concern of a chameleon, or of a careerist, taking on the colour of its moral surroundings without ever being committed to them.

It is possible, of course, that the commitment to equality is simply a profound mistake, one that, as it happens, characterizes the modern era in something the same way that other moral and political errors have characterized other eras. It is no less possible that as a matter of the history of ideas, this mistake is one we have been largely led into by a Christian cultural legacy, the legacy of a moral ethos that was not circumscribed by accountability to a secular understanding of human well-being, with mortal limits, and so perhaps was more open than most today would approve of to ideas of human well-being that were detached from the lived experience of value (though this view of history would discount the roots of Christian equality in other earlier egalitarian traditions, and the many subsequent borrowings that have yielded the practice of equality as we experience it today). It is no less possible, however, that commitment to equality is a poorly understood, imperfectly articulated commitment to something that, in some way that we have yet to grasp properly, in fact contributes to the worth of human lives as they are lived, or at least that is capable of doing so, if not (as far as we can presently tell) as a value, be that independent or auxiliary. It is possible, to lapse into suggestiveness for a moment, that the direction of influence in the relations between equality and a well-being that is based on the realization of value may run from lives to value rather than from value to lives.

3.2.4 The Puzzle of Suppression

The second puzzle can be more briefly stated perhaps, because it might be thought to derive in certain ways from the first. As long and as closely as equality has historically been associated with liberal cultures, it in fact gives every appearance of being not merely uncommitted to a liberal culture, just because it is uncommitted to any given culture by reason of the fact that it is uncommitted to any given value or set of values (other than provisionally), but more profoundly, of being committed, in the mode of its operation and in whatever contribution to value that operation is capable of making, to what is fundamentally illiberal. Equality operates by overriding the claims that certain differences would otherwise make upon us in our collective pursuit of value, differences that it is the paradigmatic business of liberal cultures to notice and give effect to just as and when doing so is apt to advance the role of autonomy in the achievement of human well-being. The puzzle that this gives rise to is not that it is in any way puzzling to be illiberal; rather it is that the pursuit of equality, at least when operating under that description, despite the fact that it has been closely associated, to the point of near-identification, with a project of human liberation (as Walzer has emphasized in speaking of equality in terms of a politics that is committed to the ending of dominance), in fact seems to have no natural affinity with that project. On the contrary, equality seems not only to be quite as at home with the practice of dominance as with its ending but, more profoundly, to depend on the practice of a distinctive form of dominance all its own for whatever good that it is capable of giving rise to.

So we are regularly reminded, and quite rightly so, that there is what is described as rising inequality in the world today, meaning that the incomes of the rich are rising more rapidly than the incomes of the poor, so that the gap between them is ever greater. We are no less often reminded, again quite rightly, that this plays out not only at large, across whole societies, but also in particular workplace settings, where the incomes of the best paid are now many more multiples of the incomes of the lowest paid than was once the case, even relatively recently, and where it must be the goal of equality, or so it is said, to reduce the number of those multiples, so that the best paid decile will earn no more than five times (let us suppose) the income of the lowest paid decile. These gaps in income are indisputably alienating, albeit that there is obviously room for argument as to the point at which alienation is likely to arise, and further, the point at which such alienation is likely to have an impact on human well-being. As David Miller once pointed out, people who do not more or less share income levels cannot share the distinctive experiences that particular income levels make possible, so that the wider the distance in income between rich and poor in any given society, the wider the distance between their ways of life, indeed the wider the distance between their understandings of the world, because the wider the difference in their incomes the fewer the facets of their experience they will have in common.[23]

---

[23] See n. 2. Although the thrust of the argument offered here is such that it is not necessary to pursue these matters, it will be clear that in order to isolate the role that equality plays and its possible value (instrumental or intrinsic) one must, first, isolate issues of relative deprivation from those of absolute deprivation, so as to compare people whose incomes, for example, are unequal (that is, neither equal nor roughly equal) without either of them suffering absolute deprivation and, second, isolate the fact of inequality (which does not admit of degree) from the fact of difference (which may do so). Although we typically speak in a manner that suggests otherwise, there is no such thing as a lesser or a greater inequality (other than rhetorically). An income that is five times larger than another is just as unequal as an income ten times larger. What there can be, of course, is greater or lesser difference, as in the case of five and ten. There may well be reasons to reduce the scale of such differences (which would turn on the import of the differences, not on the numbers attached to them, which might or might not have import), but they are not reasons of equality.

All this is true and in many ways to be regretted. It is also true, however, of every other form of distance that exists between the lives of people, distances that it is on the whole the goal of liberal cultures to foster, not because it is good to be distant from other people and their other ways of life, but because it is good (although not exclusively so) to foster a culture, together with its attendant and constituent social forms and practices, that supports a wide range of ways of life, a range wide enough to permit the realization of as many different ways of life as are necessary to the well-being of the population there. These liberal distances give rise to many reasons to regret, as we all know from our broad experience of the partings of the ways that regularly take place in liberal cultures, and that most of us have undergone in one way or another, as family members, friends, neighbours, and indeed we ourselves, have regularly moved on to new lives, leaving unfillable holes behind us. These distances, and the reasons to regret that they give rise to, are distances not simply in the fabric of our emotional attachments, but also and rather more woundingly perhaps, in the projects of our lives, that is, and more precisely, in the future prospects of the ways of being that we had committed our lives to at some point, the existence of which reflects both backwards, on the worth of our lives as we have lived them, and forwards, on the dimensions of the particular form of civilization that our lives would otherwise have contributed to the continuation of, had we not moved on as we did.[24] These distances, and the reasons to regret them, have no more or less a claim upon us, of course, than do the liberal reasons to the opposite effect; in many settings, liberal distances are constitutive elements in the achievement of a diverse, pluralistic, socially liberal order of the kind that characterizes life as it is pursued in contemporary Western societies. That does not make them any the less worthy of response.

If the reasons to regret liberal distances have any special claim upon us, however, ensuring equality of income would at best be but one of many ways of responding to them in a way that ended at least the most telling of the distances that they draw attention to. So if we are concerned by the social distance between rich and poor and the alienation that such distance gives rise to (as distinct from and in addition to our proper concern for real poverty of circumstance and prospects as a disabling condition in its own right), as we have good reason to be, we ought to be no less concerned with every other form of social distance, and the other people affected by them, and so ought to be as correspondingly committed to the ending of the differences that constitute those other forms of social distance as to the ending (or at least the narrowing) of the gap in incomes between rich and poor. If it is the function of equality to end the differences that divide us, or the most telling of them, then that function is an illiberal one by the very mode of its operation, despite appearances to the contrary. It is only the prevailing conflation of the project

---

[24] See the films of Molly Dineen for resonant expression of this.

of equality with a progressive agenda, an agenda that in fact it has no deep attachment to, that is apt to beguile us into thinking otherwise.

Part of the reason for this puzzle, it will be seen at once, lies in the fact that equality is ready to ally itself to any good. Yet the answer to the puzzle cannot be looked for in the careful monitoring of the alliances between equality and other ideals. Rather we are bound to recognize and face up to the fact that at a deeper level it is the role and function of equality to suppress relevant differences for the sake of whatever good its pursuit gives rise to. The pursuit of equality cannot be rendered in liberal terms all the way down, just because even when paired with a given liberal commitment, the role of equality is to ensure the dominance of that particular commitment in the face of the claims of any rival commitment, notwithstanding the fact, if fact it be (as it often is), that the claims of the rival are no less rational, and no less relevant to the community in question, than are the claims of whatever equality has been coupled with in that setting. (Indeed, if the claims of the rival were irrational one could, and probably should, respond to them on that ground rather than on the ground of equality.) This, it would seem, is the truth behind the tired old bogey, one that has been regularly invoked against various forms of socialism, that the pursuit of equality is inherently oppressive and life-denying or, as it is sometimes put, the enemy of freedom. The fact of the matter seems to be that if and to the extent that equality affirms a way of life, as it is necessarily part of its project to do (a way of life that admittedly is as apt to be liberal as it is apt to be anything else), it unavoidably affirms that way of life through the suppression of other, rival, rationally sound ways of life, ways of life that it is otherwise the business of liberal cultures to foster.[25] Put another way, the only thing that equality is indissolubly committed to is the mode of its operation, which is to override the claims of what it would otherwise be rational to give effect to, thereby denying the liberal possibilities of whatever distinction equality is secured in terms of. This, of course, is nothing other than the corollary of the fact that equality cannot by its nature recognize and give effect to difference in the very dimension that it is vindicated in. The more equalities we are committed to realizing, the more differences we are correspondingly committed to ignoring.

These strike me as the two most troubling puzzles about equality, those that are in greatest need of explanation and proper response. Can there really be a value the nature of which is such that it can neither be a self-sustaining value in its own right (because it is fundamentally auxiliary) nor be committed to any other value

---

[25] Something of this kind is true, of course, of the application of any principle. What is distinctive in the case of equality is that the good of its pursuit is the alleged good of applying a principle for the sake of its character as a principle rather than for the sake of whatever it is a principle of. That is like applying a rule on the basis that it is good to be rule-bound rather than on the basis that it is good to be bound by good rules (proper allowance having been made for the fact that good rules may up to a point depend for their goodness on acceptance of the bindingness of bad rules).

or set of values (because it has no capacity to discriminate among the values that it may be auxiliary to)? What would be the enduring character of its goodness? Can the ending of domination (which implies some kind of release and liberty for those who have been defined in terms of the distinction that domination turned on and that the project of equality has been called upon to override) be sought through the realization of an ideal that can only operate through dominance? Perhaps, but it may be worth contemplating another possibility, one both more recognizable and more fruitful.

The thought here is that there is some hidden room in the worth of human (and other) lives, one that lies between the facts of our lives and the realm of value, between what we do in response to the claims of value and what is expected of us, room for dialogue and exchange, a room that taken as a whole constitutes the realm of goods and goodness. This is a realm that is created by valuers in and through their grounded engagement with values, a realm that the practice of equality, when rationally guided, may sometimes, though not always, help to contribute to, by securing the circumstances that make certain forms of goodness possible, and in doing so becoming itself partly constitutive of those forms of goodness. It is a realm that might in many ways be thought to be central to our understanding and pursuit of the modern era, or more precisely, of the possibilities for well-being and value that have come to be characteristic of that era, as a consequence of their invention or their particular pre-eminence there.

3.3 (Mortal) Goods and Goodness

3.3.1 The Interdependence of Value and Valuers

Assume that it is the case, as Joseph Raz has persuasively suggested, that value is for valuers, not in the self-serving sense that the content of value is just what valuers would have it be, but rather in the conceptual sense, that the idea of value is dependent upon the idea of there being valuers to appreciate it and to engage with it. Without valuers there would still be such a thing as value, so that if all valuers were to disappear from the world value would endure, as indeed it would be present and endure if valuers had never come to be part of the world as, of course and in the event, they did. However, without the conceptual possibility of valuers there never would or could have been such a thing as value. Value is there to be valued, just as flavour is there to be tasted.[26]

Yet what exactly do valuers bring to the encounter, especially in its details? We know from deep experience that engagement with value may sometimes give rise to new values, not by unearthing them from some hiding place, but rather through a process of creative participation in existing values that, in certain particular and relatively stable settings, yields, sometimes fortuitously and sometimes by design (although never merely by force of will), an implication that is fresh and at least to some extent unexpected, one that is sufficiently novel and sufficiently distinct to count as a new value, and to be recognizable as such by reason of its genealogical connections to the structure, pattern, and character of existing values. Many rich and profound legacies of human civilization have observed this pattern and so have entered the realm of value.[27] Is that kind of outcome an aberration, or but a particularly deep consequence of a standard feature of the engagement with value? Do valuers merely sup at the table of value as diners at a buffet, selecting dishes, appreciating them properly (so responding to the quality of their ingredients and the skill that has been put into their combination), cultivating particular palates (so as to focus on a particular cuisine or be open to a wide range of cuisines and flavours), reflecting on their experiences (so as to become better responders), sharing those experiences with others (so as to contribute to a particular culture

---

[26] Raz, *The Practice of Value* (2003). See in particular the first lecture, 'Social Dependence without Relativism'. The picture that I am trying to present in this section has many affinities with that offered by Raz, mostly as the result of influence, but also as the result of a congeniality of outlooks that underpins what are slightly different concerns. Whereas *The Practice of Value* is primarily concerned with the social dependence of value, I am here primarily concerned with the dependence of value on life. These might be regarded as different perspectives on the same facts, although, of course, I have no real idea whether Raz himself would see things that way. It has now, since my writing this, become too late to ask him.

[27] For the time being I am presenting the standard view of the recognition of new values. For an alternative view, based on analogy rather than genealogy, see Raz, 'Can Basic Moral Principles Change?' in *The Roots of Normativity* (2022), 94.

of value, or set of values, and of practiced responses to value, one that is capable of complexity, scope, and history)? Or is that an inadequate interpretation even of a buffet supper? Is the engagement of valuers with value just a matter of responding to value along these lines, a matter of how well we as valuers respect and live up to the demands of value, or is it also a matter of creation and contribution, of what we have to bring to value, so as to enlarge its implications? From the human point of view, might it be thought that there is anything special that we have to offer to the fact of value, other than our distinctive ability to respond to certain values, and our just as distinctive inability to respond to others? Are there ways in which it might matter that it is we as human beings who are doing the responding, where the reference to we as human beings is a reference to living creatures of a specific kind?

Perhaps the answer is that valuers bring nothing very important to value, that is, apart from the capacity to respect and respond to it. If that is indeed the case, then the realm of value must be the sole and complete guide to the goodness and worth of our lives, and the soundness of equality as a moral ideal will thus turn on the question of whether the place of equality in the realization of value is either instrumental (as it seems to be in certain settings) or intrinsic (as it seems not to be). Something like that picture is what might be described as the standard view.

The thought to the opposite effect, however, is that at least as far as we are able to comprehend it, the very idea of a valuer imports not only the idea of social dependency, as Raz emphasizes and as I will return to, but more fundamentally, the idea of life itself, and of the various dynamics that life embodies, most notably that of creation. In engaging with value we inescapably do so as living creatures, and so inescapably bring the possibilities of value to life in that sense, thereby embedding them transiently in all the complex apparatus of a living world, while at the same time and by the same token subjecting them to the contingencies of life, contingencies that are fully comprehensible in terms of value without being logically derived from value, from the fine-grained dimensions of the ordinary, everyday fact of temporality and the challenge of living well from moment to moment and over time, to the governing fact of mortality. We and all other living things bring value to life, and so also to death: to the life and death of each one of us, of everything we do or give rise to, of our ways of life, and ultimately, of the very fact of life itself and the living world that it constitutes.

In introducing this thought by means of an example a few paragraphs ago, I sought to draw a contrast between responding to value, as at a buffet I supposed, and engaging with value, but in fact, of course and as the above proposal assumes, there is no real depth to this distinction, just because both responding and engaging are functions of the exchange between value and life, so that when we take part in the buffet that I imagined we do not in fact simply respect and consume what is on offer, and thereby honour and absorb its value, but rather participate in an occasion that, no less than any other, constitutes an engagement with value, both active and passive, in all the variety that value happens to present in that setting, from the range of dishes on offer there, to the quality of our possible appreciation of them, to the various dimensions and implications of the social setting that a buffet is an aspect of, both immediately and in the longer term. That is a lived experience of value, one in which life impresses its character on the engagement with value that it gives rise to. My considered instinct is that it is simply not possible for us to contemplate value in any other terms, helpful though I hope the distinction that I have drawn between responding to value and engaging in value is in bringing out that fact, despite its superficial character.

Perhaps that is just because that is the way that value is, just because the experience of value is necessarily a lived experience, so that it is not inherently conclusory on our part to speak of the experience of value as experience, where the idea of experience itself necessarily imports the idea of life and of living. It is in accordance with that possibility that I suggested above that, at least as far as we are able to comprehend it, the very idea of a valuer imports the idea of life. Perhaps, however, that is not in fact the way that value itself is; rather it is but a function of our distinctive fate as the living inhabitants of a living world, so that things would be rather different in other possible worlds, those without life as we know it and are capable of understanding it, whether those worlds now exist, have ever existed, or indeed could possibly exist in any dimension that we could contemplate and imagine value in terms of. If such worlds exist, perhaps they offer different modes of engagement with value, with the kind of meanings and consequences that, positioned as we are, we cannot even begin to contemplate, because we lack the resources, intellectual as well as experiential, that we would need to call upon to distinguish such a potentially alien reality from mysticism.

No matter. In the only world that we can comprehend, value is something to be lived, and the issue that this raises is the particular consequences of the condition of living for the engagement with value. To the extent that value is a feature of the living world, so as to be embedded in the structures of life, it necessarily participates in all the various consequences of life, from the detailed features of the fabric of life to the fundamental facts of birth and death. The experience of value in our lives is by definition a mortal experience, one that comes into being and goes out of being just as we do, most obviously in company with our births and deaths as living creatures, but also in the more detailed, metaphorical births and deaths of all that we do in the course of our existence, much of which is of even briefer and more fragile compass than are our natural lives, some of which endures a little longer. The vital corollary to this fact of mortal experience, it seems to me, is that all the artefacts of our successful engagement with value, from the various goods that we produce to the forms of goodness that we practise, from the narratives of our lives as individuals to the broader narratives of our cultures, or still more broadly, of our existence as a species, or most broadly of all, of life on earth, are mortal. By very reason of that fact, they do not enter the realm of value, for the realm of value is a realm that is by its nature distinct from the record even of our successful engagement with it.

One aspect of that distinction is that the realm of value endures and is in principle immortal, because its continued existence is conditional upon the possibility of there being valuers rather than upon the actuality of life. The other complementary aspect of the distinction is that the realm of goodness is as mortal as the lives that give rise to it. If we and other living creatures were to disappear forever as actualities, value and all it promises would remain, but whatever goods and goodness had flowed from all those actual lives would die with them and without succession, albeit that the fact of their former existence would endure. As long as life itself continues, then as and to the extent that each of us, and all that we do, disappears with the fact of our many, detailed deaths, both great and small, the goods and goodness that are dependent on the existence of our particular lives die with us, albeit that the facts of their existence, like the facts of our existence, endure. People like us, and goods like the ones that our lives have given rise to, may well succeed us, so that the forms of goodness that are constituted by our lives appear to achieve a kind of immortality. In fact, however, what takes place as and when this happens is a kind of rebirth, one in which the interaction of value and life gives rise to familiar consequences, in much the same way that sabre-tooth cats, at least as I understand it, have become extinct and then have re-emerged several times in history, without thereby being either immortal, or what would appear to be but a variation of the same idea, reincarnated. It is true to say that the value that underpins such goods is reincarnated in new goods (given that to be incarnate is to be alive), but that does not alter the fact that the successor good that the value is subsequently brought to life through is a new one, albeit that it may look very much like one that existed in the past.

The pattern of dependency runs in both directions. Inescapable as it may be, it is engagement with life that makes value something to be experienced, though of course the capacity for such engagement is inherent in the very idea of value, at least to the extent that we are able to comprehend fully. Without the fact of life, and the more particular fact of human life, value would, in general and in the particulars of its engagement with human experience, be inert rather than active, potential rather than actual, static rather than dynamic, fixed rather than evolving. The contribution that life makes to value is thus vital to the significance of both life and value, though that does not give life any ultimate authority over the enterprise of value, whether by power or by veto. Living creatures can neither make value nor prevent it from arising, straightforwardly and by act of will, and what is more, can give rise to goodness rather than to badness only as and to the extent that the circumstances of their living meet the enduring demands of value, or live up to them, as it is commonly put. We find our meaning and purpose in the realm of value, and it comes to life through us.

There might be thought to be something of an echo of this idea of a symbiotic relationship between value and life in the core image of the Christian tradition, the image by means of which that tradition at least partly distinguishes an immortal god from the mortality of his son, and in the extent to which the tradition conceives of the son's mortality in terms of a vision of goodness that places him and his works in two worlds at once, thereby fusing the claims of value (as personified in the idea of God) and the facts of life (as personified in the earthly existence of the son), thus endowing life with the significance of value, thereby imbuing it with meaning and purpose, while correspondingly making the lived experience of value, to which non-believers would give the name of goodness, as fragile and as transient as life itself. The crucial difference between the Christian world and the secular world, of course, is that in the latter there is no such thing as transubstantiation (in the broad sense): value cannot remain value and also live and die, cannot be both immortal and mortal, and by the same token neither can we. We enter the realm of value just as value enters the realm of life, through the mediation of what I have labelled at the outset of this section as mortal goods.

To label these goods mortal is, on the one hand, to speak tautologically of what I am maintaining is (at least in any world that we can grasp) a necessary truth about their nature; on the other hand, it is to emphasize the significance of a fact (if fact it be) that it is all too easy to overlook. After all, the fact that something is analytically true does not mean that it is also obvious, in no need of being pointed out, in no need of being refined. The implications of mortality need to be drawn out explicitly in part because they need to be rendered precisely, lest their significance be misunderstood. Aquinas regarded mortal goods as those goods, such as air, that are essential functions of our mortality and hence essential conditions of life itself. In the setting of the present discussion, the reference to mortal goods is a much wider reference, to the fact that all goods are, by their very nature as goods, just as mortal as we are. Their existence is dependent on our existence, their life on our lives, and indeed and more particularly, on the lives that we lead within our lifespans, that is, the several subordinate lives that each of us lives in the course of our natural life, sometimes concurrently, sometimes successively, and usually distinctively, yet always in common. Air and sunshine are mortal goods just because their appreciation and consumption by living things is good for those living things as living things, good for them in the same sense as is engagement with any value through the medium of any other good, be it an artefact or a practice, namely, that it participates in value and exhibits value. Their goodness, like any other goodness, is mortal.

It is sometimes observed that certain values are time-locked, so that values that were readily accessible in the Middle Ages, for example, are quite inaccessible to us today, or may be so. Yet this is not a special fact that flows from the nature of time. Space and distance are just as apt to lock value into their contours as is time. It is a familiar fact that many values are culturally bound, so that humour, for example, often does not travel well. These are both instances of what Raz has called the social dependence of value. That idea needs careful delineation however. It is access to value rather than value itself that is socially dependent, which is why Raz is at pains to distinguish his social dependence thesis from social relativism. In the terminology that I am offering here, access to value is embodied in the grounded artefacts of goods and goodness. It is this grounding that life, and human life in particular, has to bring to value. Subjectivism and social relativism might perhaps be best understood and explained as exaggerations of the very real contribution that human existence makes to the significance of value. Human lives are inescapably interwoven with the life of value, so as to make each of us, within the limits of our particular existences, in some respects the authors of both. Yet it in no sense follows that in doing so we become the authors of value, other than as value itself recognizes and allows, let alone that authorship of such a kind is merely a function of our wills. On the contrary, we depend upon the fundamental distinction between our lives and the values that they are capable of exhibiting for our vital ability to draw upon value and its relative independence from our lives, so that we may have a guide to our endeavours, a measure of their worth, and a sense of purpose to the narrative of our lives, individually and collectively. As they say, there is a moral to the tale, but only because morals and tales are mutually supporting rather than one being servant to the other.

3.3.2 The Interdependence of Goodness and Value

It seems to me that there are three significant implications to this picture. The first is that the various forms of goods and goodness that our lives give rise to, as and when those lives go well, display value but are not, strictly speaking, themselves values or aspects of value, convenient as it may be to think and speak of them as such. We speak of acts of kindness or of courage as valuable, and intrinsically so, yet it seems to me that it would be more accurate of us to say that the virtues of kindness and courage, in respect of which they are rightly regarded as moral ideals, are intrinsically valuable, but that the actions and characters that from time to time succeed in displaying kindness or courage do so as distinct species of goodness, where goodness is understood as the name we give to successful engagement with, in this case intrinsic value, rather than as the name we give to a case of intrinsic value itself. Acts of kindness to a stranger, or acts of courage on that person's behalf, are good things, and what is more, are good things just because they exemplify value (the value of kindness), but they are not by reason of that fact values themselves. In all cases of goodness, service to value is more than happenstance yet not profound enough to give rise to a value, other than in certain exceptional cases. Goodness is the display of value in living form (albeit not living in the living and breathing sense, of course, other than by virtue of dependency). Goods are but the artefacts of goodness. A good person is a valuable person in the sense of being a creator of goods and of goodness and open to evaluation as such.

Even if true, in what way might this matter? The distinction here may seem somewhat strained, particularly in the case of key virtues such as kindness and courage; how much more straightforward, one might reasonably think, to regard the practice of kindness or of courage as inherently valuable, in the sense of being an instantiation of an intrinsic value.[28] Indeed there is much to be said for being straightforward in this sense, not only because it is often convenient to do so but also because in many settings a certain bluntness of grasp may make the practice of the values in question more effective. The distinction seems rather less strained, however, and the consequences of overlooking it less promising, when what is at stake is something, such as the pursuit of equality perhaps, that cannot be straightforwardly read back as a value without doing a disservice both to value and to the possible good in question, convenient as that kind of reading may otherwise be.

The very fact of goodness has different implications in different settings, implications that are overlooked, at what may well be a significant cost, if and to the extent that the distinction between the presence of goodness and the instantiation of value is neglected. We need to notice the fact of goodness and its implications in order to capture and give proper rational attention to the worth and significance of matters that are not values themselves yet may have valuable, perhaps vital, contributions to make to the success of our lives. In particular, if practices of goodness are contingent guides to the presence of value, the strength of the contingency varying with context, so that their pursuit is generally (let us suppose) but not necessarily valuable, we have good reason to pursue those practices on the basis of their potential value, have further good reason in doing so to remain always alive to the fact that their value is no more than contingent, and have good reason finally to find a way to reconcile, as best we can, our attention to both of the first two good reasons, so as to avoid the debilitating consequences, both for value and for rationality, of treating either as having priority over the other.

3.3.3 The Interdependence of Value and Social Practices

The second implication of this picture, as Raz has clarified, is the crucial fact of dependency. One can speak of this broadly, as Raz does, in terms of social

---

[28] It is difficult to use the word valuable without suggesting, as ordinary usage of the word assumes, that whatever is being described as valuable is so because it makes a direct and positive contribution to the value of our lives, and more generally, to the presence of value in the world. Ordinary usage, I am bound to grant, is not particularly friendly to the picture that I am trying to present, and to the distinction it seeks to draw between value and goodness. As I see it, the forms and practices of goodness are subject to evaluation, and so may be rightly described as valuable as a consequence of that evaluation. Yet they are valuable because they answer correctly to the demands of value, not because they are themselves instantiations of value.

dependency, and learn much by doing so. Yet not only is the idea of social dependency as fine-grained as is the idea of society but the practice of value may involve certain commonalities of outlook that exhibit interdependence, whether consciously or unconsciously, that are rightly understood as social without, however, amounting to societies. The question that the dependency of value on practice raises is what dependency looks like in any particular setting, and the answer to that question is to be looked for and taken account of not only in general terms but also in the particular facts in and through which the dependency arises, so as to probe and be responsive to the specific character of what is broadly and accurately described as social dependency.

In pursuing goodness, separately and together, we generate social forms and practices (including the social practice of individuality), very often unavoidably, but also as means to ends. Sometimes we do so self-consciously, as when we engage in knowing structures of collaboration, so as to operate by design to develop, elaborate, respect, and conserve social vehicles that are thought to serve the realization of value in our lives, by making that realization richer and more accessible. At other times we do this unselfconsciously, as when we unwittingly engage in social patterns of awareness and orientation, or perhaps experience a convergence of like minds on like situations, so as to find ourselves surprised and perhaps a little pained to discover, once again, that the paths we are pursuing or have taken are not quite as special to us as we had thought, but rather are instances of emerging trends in our particular culture, ones that we participated in before recognizing. The processes by which social forms and practices come into being are thus bound up with the creation and pursuit of everyday goods in our lives, some close to universal, others more or less local, all of them with local dimension and interpretation. The consequence is that in any given culture there is a ready, and in most cases a sound, identification between the pursuit of everyday goods there and engagement in the distinctive commitments, institutional and ideological, that in any given culture function as goods in their own right, while also functioning as necessary vehicles for our engagement with all the other everyday goods that we are pursuing, and thus for our participation in the various underlying values that those everyday goods exhibit and bring to life.[29]

---

[29] The distinction drawn here between what I have described as institutional and ideological goods and the ordinary everyday goods that they provide the structural setting for the pursuit of is largely one of degree rather than of kind. In fact, by virtue of their status as goods, institutional goods are contingent in all the same ways as are ordinary everyday goods, though by virtue of their framing role they tend to be significantly less transient. The distinction between the two kinds of goods is designed only to capture the fact that ordinary everyday goods depend upon institutional goods for their structural settings in ways that are not fully reciprocated. In fact, and to be more precise, there is a chain of contextual dependency that runs from the fine-grained to the coarse-grained, so that practices of goodness come to function structurally as and when other such practices depend upon them as institutional settings. It follows that institutional goods may depend upon one another in this way, as may ordinary everyday goods. The distinction between the two becomes telling as and when the stability of one good (that labelled institutional) exceeds the lifespan of another (that labelled ordinary and everyday) that depends on it.

So certain, guiding social forms and practices come to be pursued in part for their own sake, that is, if and to the extent that they are believed to be constitutive vehicles for the realization of goodness in that setting, some of which will be known and pursued as such, while some of which is be yet to be discovered or created (to the achievement of either of which the forms and practices in question may be either essential or contributory to some species of distinctiveness). Those guiding social forms and practices also come to be pursued in part for the sake of what they bring about, so that we typically pursue certain forms of commonality of outlook either in their own right and for their own sake, or inescapably in the course of pursuing everyday goodness in the setting of one or more such commonalities. We may undertake the preparation of a particular style of pasta because it is (let us say) the Pugliese style and we have some independent reason to be engaged in the appreciation of Pugliese cuisine, or we may ourselves come from Puglia and so may find ourselves preparing pasta in the Pugliese style just because it is the necessarily grounded, locally accessible way to prepare pasta in Puglia, a way that has over time become embedded in our being, together with all the other relics of our commitments. To put the point in general terms, one may live one's life (at least in part) to be oneself or to be true to oneself (with whatever identifications and commitments might be thought to be entailed by the idea of being oneself), or one may be oneself because in pursuing a good life one is necessarily bound to do so as oneself, just because one can do no other, or at least, can do other only at great cost.

In both these ways, the inhabitants of various societies find themselves participating in their specific cultures and sub-cultures both as means to goodness and as goods in themselves. It follows that specific forms of goodness and the vehicles for its realization may not only be definitive of particular cultures; they may also be in many ways the gatekeepers to value there, so that one can gain access to many, perhaps most, values in those cultures only by negotiating their culturally specific gates successfully. It further follows that there is a necessary congruence between the pursuit of certain recurring, general forms of good and the specific vehicles through which those goods and other related goods may be pursued in any given culture. By and large, we can only pursue the goods that a supporting culture fosters or permits the pursuit of. In the pursuit of value, and in the creation and development of goods to that end, one is bound to work with the forms and practices that are to hand, together with any that may be compatible with them.

In rooted, atavistic cultures the local and the native will be key, so that many values will be accessible there only to those who are both willing and able to align or commit themselves to the local and the native, so as to become as rooted there as grasp of and access to the forms and practices of the cultures requires (to the extent that the cultures permit or are able to permit without self-contradiction). In modern, fluid cultures congruence between the pursuit of value and available goods is no less necessary, despite the fact that it looks very different, given that the cultures in question lack localism, nativism, or much that can be relied on in the way of stability. Many values and their mediating goods are accessible in those cultures only in modern, fluid form, and so are available only to those who are willing and able to commit themselves to such forms and practices of modernity and fluidity. If a plausible account of equality is that it should be regarded as a good for contemporary cultures, just because the commonalities that it is capable of embodying are compatible with the successful pursuit of an autonomous life to a degree that other pre-modern forms of commonality are not, the account will be persuasive just because and to the extent that the picture of equality that it presents is one that is capable of satisfying those conditions of contemporary access. If sound, that particular narrative of dependency might go some way towards navigating successfully, although not dissolving, the challenges inherent in the pursuit of equality, as evidenced in the two puzzles of its possible value.

3.3.4 The Fallibility of Goods and Goodness

I have spoken so far only of goods and goodness, but the third and final implication of this picture is that the forms and practices that help to constitute goods and goodness also help to constitute bads and badness. In pursuing what we believe to be goods and goodness, we impress our condition and circumstances upon our engagement with value, so as on the one hand to give value life, and on the other hand to circumscribe its possibilities, for better and for worse. Our pursuit of the project of goodness necessarily bears our imprint, individual and collective, so as to be not only as mortal as we are, and as socially dependent as we are, but also to be as predicated on the exercise of rational judgement as we are, and so to be as vulnerable as we are to mistakes of belief, and to the false convictions and commitments that such mistakes entail.

What exactly is the connection between mortality and fallibility? Is it simply that living creatures, and human beings in particular, are, as it happens, both mortal and fallible? Or is there something more than mere happenstance at stake? The thought in response is a simple one, namely that the latter is a function of the former: fallibility is an aspect of mortality. It is only in and through living that we are in a position to make mistakes or avoid them. Were it otherwise, goodness would wear the enduring aspect of value. One can, of course, intelligibly speak of eternal life, and by extension, of eternal goods, but in terms of any experience that we can comprehend those are oxymorons, for life and the goodness that it gives rise to subsist just as and when something is mortal, not eternal. It is an essential function of mortality, and of the contingencies that mortality embodies and to which it is subject, to be lived badly or well, and in doing so to yield the practices and artefacts of badness as readily as those of goodness, rather than have its condition as one or the other established analytically. To put it succinctly, life is morally dynamic. That, as much as any physical fact of breathing and blood circulation, is what makes it life. One cannot live other than by responding to reasons. When a capacity to respond is absent, what is left is something less than life, albeit that it may yet be worthy of a certain respect.[30]

So rather than being quintessentially good, practices of goodness are actually practices that, analysed more closely, are animated by a belief in their goodness rather than by the fact of their goodness. This has two notable consequences. The first consequence flows from the different varieties of goodness to which a practice may be directed and that it may succeed in displaying (bearing in mind that the variety that a practice succeeds in displaying may be either greater or lesser than the variety that it was directed to). The second consequence flows from the rational vulnerability of our thoughts and actions, which makes us correspondingly vulnerable to mistakes of both direction and execution. These two consequences may operate so as to reinforce one another. When we make mistakes in one respect, we may still get things right in some other respect, albeit not the things that we sought to get right. On the other hand, even when we avoid mistakes, what is good in terms of one value may very well be bad in terms of some other value, indeed is likely to be so, so that we get things wrong even as we get them right. It follows that the realm of goodness is, in all those respects that derive from either human frailty or the plurality of value, a realm also of badness.

If the pursuit of equality is rightly understood as the pursuit of goodness, we should expect that the pursuit (like the pursuit of any other good) to be just as apt for the bad, and so to be as open to miscarriage, as its pursuers are vulnerable to rational error, not only in general but in respect of the pursuit of equality in particular. After all, it is in the nature of certain goods to be distinctively susceptible, not only to rational error of a general kind but also to the generation of the distinctive rational errors that flow from their character (perhaps because pursuit of the good in question is typically hot-blooded rather than considered), and so place them at risk of a corresponding degree or kind of misapprehension. Of course, the converse is no less true: certain goods are by their nature unusually proof against such errors (perhaps because pursuit of them is typically considered rather than hot-blooded). The point that unites these cases is that as far as matters that fall within the realm of goodness are concerned, the possibility of badness is as present in their pursuit as is the possibility of goodness.

If equality were intrinsically valuable, there would be at least that value to be found in its every instance, and so at least some value to be found, for example, in

---

[30] In identifying life with the capacity to respond to reasons, I have the lives of valuers in mind, not those other forms of life, such as that of plants, to which reasons apply but whose capacities preclude them from responding to reasons themselves and so preclude them from being valuers. If this is true, then plants are mortal but not fallible. We may fail them but they cannot fail themselves. Of course, this may not be true. I may be wrong about the responsibility of plants. It may be that plants are fallible but that their fallibility is biologically determined. For a fuller analysis, see Macklem and Gardner, 'Human Disability' (2014) 24 KLJ 60 at 76–7.

blinding all the sighted, as Temkin maintains, the same egalitarian value as there would be in giving eyesight to all the blind, as appalling an idea as it would in every other respect be to take eyesight away from people, and as good an idea as it would be in every other respect to give eyesight to the blind. If, however, equality is part of the realm of goodness rather than the realm of value, we should expect to be entirely familiar with instances of its badness, as indeed we seem to be, in all the ways that the levelling down objection sought to capture and analyse. We should further expect the goodness and badness of equality to be distinct from other forms of goodness and badness, and thus in any given case to be unlikely to map straightforwardly onto the other forms of goodness and badness that are present there. Were it otherwise, equality would have no independent contribution to make to goodness and badness. It does not follow from the potential badness of equality, therefore, that there would be no good to be found in blinding all the sighted, although it does follow that any such good could not be thought to proceed *ipso facto* from the fact of equality.

To join those several implications together, as they are inevitably joined together in the course of living, suppose that a person, the settled denizen of a settled culture let us further suppose, passes the day in much the same way as might any reader of this chapter, which is to say, in much the same way as its author. The day begins, as a matter of fact, with a run several times around the park, is then occupied with writing and reflection, and ends with a visit to my mother, in hospital with a broken femur. Clearly there is good to be found in each of running, writing, and visiting. Yet all of that good is mixed rather than unalloyed, successful in different ways and only in part. None of it can be aptly described as constituting value, though all of it is inspired by value, shaped by value, and subject to the judgement of value for its meaning and significance. What is more, and more to the present point, all of it is guided in its realization, for bad as well as for good, and yet more particularly, for certain specific ways of being bad and good rather than others, by the presence of prevailing social forms and practices that operate upon and thus govern the local pursuit of goodness in ways that simultaneously both empower and restrict.

Running around a London park is a special kind of running, quite different from that which takes place in Coral Gables or Naoshima, not only in the particulars of the geography and climate there (though those things matter too) but in terms of the particular culture of participation in the physical environment that exists there. Writing and reflection are occupations that, as it happens, I engage in and am bound to engage in as a legal and moral philosopher in a British academic setting, with all the specificity of ambition and audience that those several contexts give rise to, separately and in combination. Visiting my mother is a filial responsibility that, as it also so happened, I undertook in the setting of a hospital across the river from Westminster, a hospital that is part of a particular approach to health-care provision, an approach that has an impact both on the condition and circumstances of a patient and on the experience and thus the filial role of her visitor. Necessary as these settings, or others more or less similar to them, are to the realization of physical well-being, mental well-being, and emotional well-being in any given physical and cultural context, none of them are instantiations of value, not simply because their contributions to value are likely to be flawed, indeed are almost bound to be so in certain respects, but also when those contributions are wholly valuable.

As I see it, these are the salient patterns of practices of goodness: projects that are worthy in their own right without being values in their own right; projects directed to value that are valuable in different ways and only in part; projects that depend for their success on the support of sustaining, framework social forms and practices that are themselves only contingently valuable, so that we are bound to look to those practices for value while remaining aware that the value in question is itself only contingent, albeit that we must generally take account of and indeed rely upon its ongoing presence in our lives as if its value were not contingent. The present question that this gives rise to is whether the pursuit of equality, suitably confined and animated by the goal of fostering the pursuit of other goods (in the same way as must be the pursuit of any other sustaining, framework good) for the sake of the values that those other goods give rise to or are capable of giving rise to, is a practice of goodness of that sustaining kind.[31]

---

[31] In this discussion I have spoken largely of goodness, drawing attention to badness without entering into consideration of it. There are two reasons for this. First, the possibilities of badness, in principle and as a function of human frailty, are open-ended (there seem to be few limits to our capacity for wrongdoing), and so a good life can only be fitfully informed, rather than inspired and made virtuous, by strategies of avoidance. Second, and more to the point, there is little to be discovered in attempting to delineate this propensity. What matters in the fact that we all must find our flourishing in a fallen world, is that we must constantly negotiate accommodations with that world. That is a creative project, and so embodies all the moral possibilities of creativity I have tried to highlight.

3.4 Commonality in the Modern Era

The possibility that I would like to investigate in some detail here, so as to pull together the several threads of the previous sub-chapters, is that equality is a species of commonality which, in the world that we now live in, is able to provide solidarity and hence structure to the projects of our lives, in the face of the powerfully centrifugal, dissolving forces that constitute the circumstances of the modern era, circumstances in which other older solidarities are vulnerable or absent. The value of the several contemporary forms of equality, as we practise and pursue them, is not the value of equality as such, for there is no such value (or so this project is assuming), but rather is the value that may be generated, when things go well, by the particular species of commonality that the equalities of the modern era happen to constitute and describe, from setting to setting and from time to time, and the special resonances that those species of commonality can add to the particular distinctions that they describe. That value is in turn a product of the soundness, and lack of soundness, of the particular politics that contemporary equalities support, and of the contributions that such politics are capable of making, in sympathetic circumstances, to the proper flourishing of modern life projects, and to the wider worlds, human and environmental, of which those projects are an integral part. (In speaking loosely, in terms of ordinary language, of the value of equality here I am, of course, speaking broadly of what I have suggested is more accurately understood as goodness.)

Begin with the idea of social forms and practices, and the context they offer to the pursuit of value by all those who have access to them. Our lives are guided and shaped, not only by the demands of value (to be generous, say, or kind), demands that fall upon all valuers without distinction or favour, but also by the presence of the framing forms of goodness that I sought to draw attention to in the previous sub-chapter (particular vehicles for being generous, say), some large in scope, others limited, some relatively transient, others relatively enduring, all of which exist more or less precisely just in order to distinguish and to favour, and that because they exist just so as to bring out value all the better, by offering sympathetic settings in which it can be richly, readily, and creatively realized. These are forms of goodness whose role it is, in part at least, to structure and shelter the pursuit of a range of other goods, as well as to shelter one another, thereby making the realization of those other goods that much the more possible (and that much the more resonant), albeit at a price. In short, these forms of goodness come, over time and from place to place, to constitute cultures, with their attendant cultural rewards and costs.

The price of social forms and practices, the cultural distinctiveness they are apt to embody, and the context they provide to the pursuit of value, stems from the fact that the support they offer is by its nature not in any sense disinterested, and so is not merely instrumental. On the contrary, these forms of goodness perform their function by virtue of their distinctive (if derivative) character and commitment, and of the capacity of that character and commitment, when properly attended to by those who have access to it, to enhance the prospects of those projects of goodness that are consonant with it, while correspondingly diminishing the prospects of those that are not. In doing these things, they inescapably impress their character, sometimes unwittingly and sometimes by design, upon the goods that they shelter and support, and thereby become partially constitutive of the distinctive form in which those particular goods are realized (and other goods are neglected). They are correspondingly facilitative of the distinctive set of values that each of those forms of goods serves and fails to serve, be those forms of good the projects of a society, the goals of a person, or the shared projects and purposes of a range of intermediate entities, some self-conscious and self-referential, others not.

Consider as an obvious case in point the culture and sub-cultures of a contemporary state, one that embraces a range of ways of life and of ethnicities, so as to be more state-nation than nation-state. Those who are inhabitants of that state are bound to work within the commonalities that it establishes and supports, formally and informally, in order to gain access to most of the goods that are present and accessible there, and are no less bound to avoid the pursuit of goods that lack the protection and support of such commonalities, so as to be alien at best, antithetical at worst. To pursue the example offered above, just as I am bound to seek and secure access to certain ingredients of my physical, mental, and emotional well-being in British ways in British settings, as the only locally viable forms of the more universal goods the value of which gives the projects of my life their meaning and worth, so other inhabitants of British culture gain access to the other goods that each of them happens to have fastened upon in the course of constituting their goals in life, as central ingredients in the achievement of their particular physical, mental, and emotional well-beings, walking down British streets to British jobs, taking British exercise and enjoying British entertainment, taking part in British public goods and conducting their personal relations in a way that bears a British stamp.[32]

The dependence of one's life for its character and success upon participation in a set of social forms and practices that one has no real say about participating in and very little say in the shaping of may be welcome or unwelcome. To borrow a metaphor that is all too common in academic life (perhaps damagingly common), in pursuing any element of one's well-being, in response to the value that is to be

---

[32] In speaking here of Britishness, I am speaking only of social practices that are more less distinctive to at least some inhabitants of this island, so as not to be Japanese or Brazilian for example. I am not assuming that the various forms of what I have called Britishness map onto one another, or are in any significant sense coextensive with residence in the British Isles. Many forms of Britishness have been exported, including certain forms that are now extinct in their homeland; many social forms and practices common in Britain have foreign origins and may retain their description as such; many social forms and practices that are distinctively British are not recognized or pursued as such.

discovered there, one inescapably joins an ongoing conversation. The participants in that conversation are kinds of neighbours, though they need not dwell nearby, today less than ever. The commonality displayed in the conversation, in its choice of topics, its direction, and its tone, constitutes a culture in itself (as well as being an aspect of a larger culture within which it is nested), one that tends to be recognized after the fact, and then sometimes to be honoured and sometimes to be resisted. One may or may not like or admire the tenor of the conversation, but one has to take it on board lest one's life become a non-sequitur. One cannot either simply ignore it or take part in it as if it was something other than it is.

More tellingly perhaps, in many cases one's participation must be committed rather than detached in order to secure full access to whatever a social form or practice has to offer. Many goods in many cultures are fully accessible only to the committed, so that there may be a trade-off between preservation of one's autonomy, in a range of what may be key respects of one's well-being, and full achievement of that well-being. This is not to say that we are completely enmeshed in the toils of social forms and practices, nor to suggest that there is not a great deal more to the story of the presence of value in our lives than the prevailing commonalities that we are bound to respect, observe, and take part in. Our engagement in prevailing social forms and practices, like the pursuit of some aspects of our autonomy, is patchy and incomplete, although the degree to which it is so, or is permitted to be so, is itself a function of prevailing social forms and practices. As matters now stand in a state such as Britain and the many others like it, one has a good deal of scope for personal autonomy, out of which one can build a life the particular virtues of which are both more and less comprehensive than would be called for by the forms and practices of the prevailing culture. That does not alter the fact that we are also bound to commit ourselves to certain local ways of being in order to live well, even autonomously.

Just as important as conditions of access, and more relevant to the possible case for equality, are the underlying preconditions for the existence of these cultures and their constitutive social forms and practices, and hence of the distinctive goods that they make possible. There must be a reasonable degree of congruence between a distinctive way of life and the structural context in which it is pursued. That congruence is often uncertain, contested, a matter of more or less, and in need of development, but it is no less necessary and real. The British culture I have been speaking of, for example, like so many others today, is a culture in significant tension between its atavistic and its liberal instincts. More broadly, the world in which we currently live and pursue goodness is a world in which Enlightenment and post-Enlightenment forces of rationality and mobility have achieved a degree of influence and status sufficiently profound as to render vulnerable a whole range of what one might describe as un-Enlightened social forms and practices, some of which contemporary culture is a nominal companion to and so would claim to draw succour from (typically, those forms and practices that are described as multicultural), others of which the weight of contemporary culture is in conscious opposition to, or is perceived to be so (most recognizably, the forms and practices of authoritarian societies, be they religious, or tribal, or otherwise ideological in character). At a minimum, this gives rise to problems of transition, for it means that the prevailing ways of life in most Western societies, the goods that they embody, and the values that they seek to give effect to, are at odds with many of the framework goods that we have inherited and that we continue to rely on, indeed seek to update, as structures and as shelters for the pursuit of the other goods in our lives. From the opposite point of view, the liberal structures of Western societies make the pursuit of traditional ways of life problematic in those societies, whether the traditions in question are local or imported.

The deeper point here, however, is not so much the obvious one that atavistic and liberal instincts are in tension with one another. Rather it is that liberal instincts, no less than their atavistic counterparts, depend for their full realization on the presence of framing structural goods, goods the character of which must be consonant with the pursuit of autonomy if they are to perform their structuring and sheltering functions successfully. Quite apart from the problems of inheritance and of comity that this inevitably gives rise to, there is something of a practical paradox at work here, for the very idea of structural goods implies a set of qualities that by virtue of their nature as structural are liable to be in tension with significant aspects of the claims of autonomy. Structural goods limit our options in ways that may well deny autonomy, just because it is difficult for a structural good to be sufficiently defined as to do its work well, and yet be sufficiently capacious as to accommodate the many different species of autonomy that it is liable to be called upon to shelter and support, the more particularly, one would expect, in fluid and porous societies, many of whose members will not have been raised and shaped in terms of the prevailing structural goods that they now find themselves bound to live in terms of.

The consequence is that the post-Enlightenment cultures of the modern era are predisposed to neglect the structural foundations that they are more or less bound to rely upon for their successful realization. One might say, in a metaphorical spirit, that the pursuit of liberty is liable to take on something of the character of an autoimmune condition, although it is not in any sense compelled to do so, let alone to do so to a damaging degree. The present question, therefore, is whether the practice of equality, if suitably contextualized, could function as a sound response to the paradoxical character of the relationship between the pursuit of autonomy and the structural goods on which autonomy depends for its full realization. Is the ideal of equality, if circumscribed, capable of serving as a structural good that is peculiarly apt for the modern era? What might be its strengths and weaknesses as a candidate for that task? Might its elusiveness, its slipperiness, fit it well for such a role? Might its natural capacity to dominate other goods without conviction be valuable in this setting? Does the paradox that it embodies match fruitfully the paradox that it may be called upon to serve?

In considering this possibility, one needs to bear in mind the key features of equality, the most basic of which is the fact that it is not possible to pursue equality *simpliciter*. Problems of coherence aside, there could be no value in doing so. The role of equality is inherently auxiliary, so that to gain any kind of purchase on value equality needs to be tethered to the pursuit of some other good, or set of such goods. In a post-Enlightenment social order, the forms and practices that equality is tethered to not only have at a minimum to be compatible with that social order but, more plausibly for committed participants, have to be fully intelligible as vehicles for (let us say) a project of autonomy, to the point at which, as in all other cases, their pursuit becomes identified with that project. The presence and influence of this condition on the part that equality might be asked to play in structuring the pursuit of autonomous lives could go some way to explaining the extent to which the idea of equality is today commonly identified with a commitment to progressive politics. What is doing the leading in establishing and articulating that commitment, however, is actually the practice of progressive politics, not the idea of equality, which is just as at home with one politics as another, and so is at home with reaction as much as with reform. It is a certain politics that may require the support of equality, not equality that requires a certain politics. It is politics and political commitment that supplies equality with its direction and much of its value.

The particular forms of equality that we endorse and seek to give effect to today are those that we believe will offer the inspiration, support, and guidance that is required to sustain the particular ways of life that, as it happens, we are currently committed to, ways of life that taken as a whole express variety for the sake of the range of autonomies that it makes possible. The idea of equality itself, it will be remembered, has no capacity to articulate its own contours for this or any other end, and so must rely on the character of a given culture's political commitments for its significance and value. Equality thus derives its import on the one hand, from just whatever it is that we have committed ourselves to valorizing, and its value on the other hand, from the soundness of that valorization and the additional weight that equality may lend to that soundness. One consequence of this fact is that the forms of equality present in any culture remain contested just to the extent that the politics of that culture, and the values that underpin it, remain contested, so that we continue to find ourselves, for example, in protracted disputes about the respective merits of equality of opportunity and equality of welfare, to take a perhaps overly familiar division of opinion, or equality as non-discrimination and economic equality, just because and to the extent that we continue to disagree, either as to the soundness of the political outlooks that underpin those equalities, or as to the specific political and cultural commitment that makes them ours. The other consequence, of course, is that our political beliefs may be wrong-headed, indeed are bound to be so in many ways.³³ Admittedly, conflict and error are not altogether bad things, but their presence does make the guiding role of equality less certain and less morally reliable than one might have hoped. That is reason to have some reservations about its potential as a structural good. Can it actually do the structural work that it is called upon to do, or is its role by and large rhetorical?

It must not be forgotten that if equality is not a value, as seems to be the case and as this project is premised on not assuming to the contrary, it cannot be pursued as one, that is, cannot be pursued as if it was inherently valuable. Its instantiation in any given setting might or might not be a good thing. Nevertheless it seems to me that there is good reason to regard the particular equalities that we have fastened on in our politics and our mores as the key commonalities of the modern age, central to many of the goods that our era has succeeded in giving rise to, perhaps because the very vulnerabilities that infect equality as an ideal express and embody vulnerabilities that are inherent in the project of most lives in post-Enlightenment cultures. Nearly all of us want at once to be different and to belong, and in doing so to avail ourselves of social structures and ways of being that we are always free to depart from in manners small and large.³⁴ In this respect, we are by conviction something close to commitment-phobes, suspicious of what we tend to see as the conservative claims of the forms and practices that have traditionally been looked to as the frameworks for the pursuit of valuable lives in our societies. In our attempt to give effect to that conviction, and to secure its reconciliation with the successful pursuit of well-being, we are naturally attracted to a structural setting that is inescapably committed and uncommitted at once, a setting such as that which equality provides.

That does not mean that we are right to regard equality as a value, but it does allow for the possibility that in certain circumstances equality might rightly be looked to as constitutive of what is potentially valuable to us as the kind of people we are in the present moment, committed to the distinctively fluid projects of modern lives, projects that equality is able to serve by providing us with a sense of structure that is ultimately amenable to, and so apparently compatible with, the many and shifting forms of well-being that we might wish to pursue. In short, an ideal of equality might be capable of functioning as a good, one that lends certain endeavours the aspect of commonality, with all the goodness and badness that

---

³³ Bound to be so both by the pluralism of value (which entails that to display value of one kind is often to fail to display value of another kind and to display disvalue of yet another kind) and by the human propensity to rational error.

³⁴ I say 'nearly all' here because there are, of course, those among us who are fully committed to traditional social forms and practices, and so feel bound to honour those forms and practices even to the point of sacrifice of their own autonomy. However, my sense is that in Western societies the vast majority of people give primacy to their autonomy, and if forced to a choice are prepared to sacrifice to it traditions that they otherwise honour in their lives.

is liable to follow from such a contribution. All commonalities are equalities, but only some, such as those that characterize the modern era, may be pursued as such.

Consider the case of anti-discrimination principles, and the problem of explaining and justifying the selection of the distinctions that enjoy special protection and of the domains in which that protection runs. As far as equality is concerned, and so without reliance on the non-relational value of the ends that equality is fastened to in this setting, the point is not to search for reasons that are capable of picking out these distinctions, or these ways of shaping our response to them. Such reasons certainly exist, but they have no capacity to defeat a range of other reasons with no less a claim to have the distinctions that they identify included in the ambit of equality and the protection and support that it has to offer. In relational terms, the particular distinctions that we have fastened upon are simply what make us the people we are and that define the political and social worlds that we inhabit.[35] We are the people who have committed ourselves to structuring our well-being in

---

[35] In saying this I do not mean to suggest that the dimensions of equality that we or any other culture fastens upon are bound to be identified arbitrarily. On the other hand, I am committed to the view that there is nothing in the idea of equality itself upon which one could draw in fastening upon those domains, so as to identify some in preference to others. The truth of the matter seems to lie between the two extremes. Every society is, on the whole, and with notorious exceptions, committed to bettering itself, that is, committed to some notion of moral progress for its members, and consequently, to the identification of something like what Walzer might call spheres of justice to that end. That said, there is almost always a good number of sound ways in which this might be achieved, so that there is almost always room to fasten upon one scheme of justice and its spheres rather than upon another. That is the first variable. Once such spheres have been identified, certain distinctions become salient, as for example with race in the United States, language in Canada, and religion nearly everywhere. The distinctions become salient by virtue of the terms in which betterment is understood in those cultures (that of autonomy being the most prominent in the Western world) and of the ways in which cultural practices there have systematically excluded certain categories of people from full access to that particular form of betterment (on the basis of race, or religion, or sex, or disability, for example). Salient distinctions are shared across cultures to the extent that conceptions of betterment and patterns of exclusion are shared. Conversely, such sharing is as limited as the cultures are distinct from one another. American patterns of autonomy are not the same as European patterns, and neither are their patterns of exclusion, significant though the overlap clearly is in a number of respects. It is then open to the cultures in question to pursue equality in the face of such distinctions, for the sake of the solidarity and kinship that it may give rise to (see later), as one aspect of their mission of self-betterment, and to do so in the substantive terms in which they understand self-betterment, including the substance of certain formal equalities.

However moral progress, even in those dimensions, may be no less rationally sought by other means. That is the second variable. There are bad as well as good reasons to assimilate the conditions of different peoples, and conversely, good as well as bad reasons to attend to, and indeed to emphasize and to encourage, distinctiveness in terms of the relevant spheres of justice. International human rights instruments offer a list of what are widely regarded as universally applicable equalities, but the construction of the list, and its subsequent endorsement by any particular legal order, are political acts that are morally permissible (at least, so we believe) but not morally required, other than to the extent that what is being referred to is not in fact equality, but rather the ending of schemes and practices of inferiority that exclude certain people from access to well-being. Even that is something that is typically visited upon such people in different ways in different cultures, so that a familiar species of discrimination may take very different forms in different cultures, or even not be present at all in some. And as has been emphasized by many, the ending of practices of inferiority may require the recognition and accommodation of differences as well as equality.

So, to put it summarily, the equalities that characterize the modern world are not in any sense accidental products of the times. Rather they derive from and amplify the dominant political concerns of contemporary culture, very often to the point of being identified with those concerns, so that we

terms of the commonality of religions, of races and ethnicities, of women and men, and of the several other beneficiaries of our protection from discrimination, and to the harnessing of that commitment to the extension of opportunity or of welfare, of some awkward albeit well-meaning mix of the two, or of some other good. That is part of what it means for us to insist on the political primacy of these and other aspects of what we describe as human rights. In doing these things, we consciously undermine certain existing structures and prevent others from arising, in ways that are bound to be condemned by our descendants no less than by our forebears, sometimes wrongly of course, but sometimes rightly. We will almost certainly be condemned for having done both too much and too little, for having been morally wrong-headed and morally weak-kneed. None of this is to deny the possibility that there is real goodness to be found in much of what we have done. The verdict on our endeavours is likely to be mixed, as should not be surprising given that such mixed verdicts are characteristic of commitments to practices of goodness for the sake of the values that they may help to constitute when correctly deployed. Put shortly, our equalities are just as valuable as our politics are sound, in their ends and in their execution. Every domain of equality that we pursue and secure falls to be judged, as valuable or not valuable, in whole or in part. It is not valuable simply because it is equal. Nevertheless, its value is enhanced by its equality, or to be more precise, may be so enhanced, when things go right.

Yet there is a question being begged here, perhaps just because the answer is too natural to be noticed. Just what exactly does commonality of any kind, including that which arises from one's participation in an egalitarian setting, bring to the value of an endeavour that could be thought to enhance that value, not by the addition of anything independent that the commonality has to offer in terms of its own value, but somehow by the augmentation of the value of whatever it is that the several participants in the endeavour are engaged in? Clearly it must be a condition of such a contribution that participants understand themselves to be operating in terms of the commonality, in this case to be operating in terms of equality. Otherwise no value could arise from the fact of equality, given that equality has nothing of its own to offer (on the working assumption here) other than whatever value might arise from the realization of one or more other values in circumstances that are known to be equal (as they must be known given that the good of equality is relational in character, as it unquestionably is).

That means that equality is a value that must be self-consciously realized, for one cannot derive value from circumstances that depend on awareness without being aware of them. If members of the Scott expedition had been served equal

---

come to see both anti-discrimination movements and the impetus to reduce income disparities as matters of equality. Productive as this identification may be, the danger it gives rise to is real and runs in both directions. On the one hand, there is more to our current political concerns than equality and the solidarities that it gives rise to, and on the other hand, our society depends for its flourishing on forms of equality that do not necessarily turn on former and continuing disadvantage.

portions of food without knowing that they were equal, no value could have followed from the fact of that equality. The same is true, of course, of any other commonality that is pursued for its own sake, if and to the extent that the commonality has no independent contribution of its own to make to value, and so is not itself the name for something that is distinctively valuable. What then is it exactly that might make two pairs of hands work better than one, apart from the independent value that might be found in the separate direction of each pair of hands?

The answer is solidarity, and it is not something that I think I can do anything much more than point at. Fellow feeling adds a special resonance to what we do, quite apart from any power that may be derived from a form of association or other relationship that gives rise to it.[36] It is good, sometimes, simply to know that one is not alone, that other people are in just the same predicament, or one very much like it. That knowledge creates a feeling of kinship, a feeling upon which one can draw in the course of engaging in whatever it is that is the ground of commonality and solidarity. Is this feeling only psychological? Perhaps. Yet it seems to me that there is more, that solidarity enhances the sense of possibility in what one does, in the same way that the indifference of others, or more precisely, their lack of comprehension and identification, diminishes that sense of possibility, and so crucially for the presence of value, with it diminishes the possibility of value itself. One needs to believe in order to flourish, or put more negatively, needs not to not believe, lest one decline. Solidarity and kinship, like forms of empathy and compassion, make belief not only more plausible but more justified. They stand in the place of love in the lives of people who know of one another's existence and predicament, yet are in no position to share their lives or care for one another in any other more intimate, more productive, more demanding way.

---

[36] The position here may be compared to the argument from fraternity identified by David Miller in 'Arguments for Equality', referred to at the outset, see n. 2. The two positions plainly belong to the same tradition yet also exhibit significant differences. Fraternity involves a relationship of some kind, and so depends in part on the presence of circumstances that are capable of giving rise to such a relationship. Commonality, be it of condition or experience, does not necessarily do so. It is more akin to citizenship than to fraternity, or even more broadly and loosely, akin to those forms of belonging that characterize cultures and sub-cultures, whether based on territory, modes of life, sets of convictions, or one or more of all those things at once.

To put the point from the opposite perspective, commonality simply involves the like possession of characteristics, and what is more important for the discussion here, of characteristics that those who share in them may be aware of the like possession in others. Fraternity does not necessarily involve either of those things: it is entirely possible to have very little in common with one's brother. In the case of fraternity, it is fraternal status that leads; commonality in certain respects may or may not follow. For that reason, fraternity may be as much a burden as a blessing.

The fact and presence of commonalities exists as a resource that people may or may not draw upon and contribute to, and so as a resource that exists as potential, to become either resonant or inert in people's hands. It seems to me that what is characteristically at stake in the equalities of the modern era is commonality, so that we are now equal without having to be fraternal. Fraternity expresses the spirit and outlook of an earlier, more rooted age, one that has now largely become something that we typically think of as pre-modern, though obviously that is to make a bet on the shape of the future.

Nothing in this makes equality an intrinsic value, for the resonances that arise from commonality and solidarity are as apt to foster badness as to foster goodness. When that happens, as it often does, equality makes a bad thing worse. We find this difficult to see just to the extent that we identify equality with a progressive politics that we are ourselves committed to. Most obviously, it is difficult to see the bad in what one takes to be fundamentally good. What is more, however, to the extent that equality is an apt vehicle for progressive politics, and to the extent that it is good to be progressive, we are quite right to have such difficulty. Yet equality has in fact no morals of its own, and so is in no position to be able to be choosy about its bedfellows. In this, it is no different from a great number of other forms of commonality and solidarity, such as those that attend certain species of nationality and ethnicity, commonalities that equality may in some settings even become a working partner with. These other forms of commonality are no better than the ends to which they are arbitrarily directed, arbitrarily because these are commonalities that have no character other than that which derives from the ends to which they happen to be directed from time to time. The power to enable and augment, the only moral power that equality, or any other like form of commonality, can claim as its own, is a power to deepen wrongdoing as much as its opposite, the more so to the extent that the equality or other commonality in question is otherwise associated with valuable endeavours that it enables, either in tandem or in some other setting, which then help to provide cover for the wrongdoing that it is enabling here. Even when equality is paired with what is valuable, it often arrogates to itself full authorship and credit for the realization of the other values with which its presence is associated and that it may help to augment in that setting. That arrogation (or even arrogance, as it often is) may be a good thing, in the cases where the delusion is constructive, but it may also be confusing, distracting, and even destructive.

So equality may well help us lead better lives without itself being an intrinsic value. It may establish a crucial precondition for the pursuit of certain possibilities for goodness, of which it then becomes partially constitutive, and that the signal of its presence helps to express. Like a great many other elements in the fabric of life, it is morally inert unless and until it is acted upon by living creatures, creatures of a special, rationally self-conscious kind, in such a way as to constitute forms and practices of goodness and badness. Its contribution to the realm of value, for good or ill, is thus rather more than instrumental, yet rather less than intrinsic.

What then of the two troubling puzzles with which this project more or less began? Does the account offered here suggest how they might be successfully navigated, albeit not dissolved? Is there anything further that might be said by way of conclusion to support that possibility, beyond whatever has emerged from the preceding reflections? The first puzzle stemmed from the fact that equality is at once attached to value and yet detached from value, and so cannot be said to have any deep concern for value, or as I put it, has but the concern of a moral chameleon.

The second puzzle stemmed from the fact that although equality is commonly, perhaps characteristically, identified with a progressive politics, and so with the liberation of human beings from unwanted forms of domination, as Walzer emphasizes, its function is fundamentally illiberal, operating so as to suppress the recognition of differences that we otherwise have reason to notice and give effect to. Are these puzzles in any way diminished or defused by the account of equality suggested here, one that would see it as a mortal good for the modern era, or more precisely, as a good that is particularly fitting for that era?

Once again the answer is something that at this stage I cannot do much more than point at. Something of the answer has already been offered, while the balance is such that it cannot be articulated with any real degree of precision or specificity. The response to both puzzles, it seems to me, is the response that was proposed at the outset to the betrayals that simple equality invites, namely that one must face up to and embrace them, within certain limits, the limits that are set by one's responsibility to pursue whatever benefits that equality makes possible while taking all proper account of their rational contingency, by which I mean the contingency of their value, and the dependency of that value on the soundness of our politics, formal and informal. In the case of the first puzzle, this means recognizing and exploiting the moral latitude that equality embodies and permits, so as to make it partner to endeavours the value of which stems in many ways from their openness and their fluidity. In the case of the second puzzle, this means recognizing that even the most open and fluid of life projects, be they the projects of a person or of a community, depend upon the support and guidance of institutional and ideological structures for their successful realization, albeit, of course, structures that are in every deep and sincere sense compatible with the projects in question. In the case of the modern era that we still inhabit, it means that liberal life projects depend upon liberal housings, housings that restrict as well as empower. Autonomous lives depend for their meaning and significance on their consonance with value, and what is more, depend for their present import and their place in time on their consonance with the specific set of social forms and practices that correspondingly and simultaneously guide a host of neighbouring and mutually informing life projects, making them all kin to one another in the narrative of our particular, distinctively autonomous scheme of structured contributions to what goodness can mean in the world. Equality is a crucial partner, perhaps even something close to a necessary partner, to the value of our present freedoms, in our present hands.

The apparently modest pay-off here may seem a little disappointing to some, but only if one is prepared to discount or otherwise overlook the claims upon us of the powerful reasons to doubt the independent value of equality that have been advanced by Joseph Raz, Harry Frankfurt, and others. It is, of course, true that in everyday life some sort of discounting of that kind is a perfectly sensible approach to take to practical reasoning. After all, if one could act rationally upon one's convictions only if and to the extent that they had been determined to be philosophically sound, one would be cut off from much of the good that one is able to achieve in life, in particular from all that is done better by not thinking too much about it, or even thinking about it at all. Indeed, as we have all learned, one may even do good in certain settings by acting on the strength of what are in fact misguided convictions, given the particular character of the options that happen to lie before one. Yet to notice, not for the first time, the significant distance between deep reflection and its objects is simply to recognize that much of philosophical enquiry is at best orthogonal to any practical pay-off, while at least some elements of philosophical enquiry may actually be debilitating of that end. It is not to overlook, or otherwise discount, the elemental fact that depth of understanding may well be something good in itself. It is in that spirit of a suitable professional and personal modesty about the practical significance of my (or indeed anyone else's) considered reflections that I have tried to ascertain the worth of equality, to grasp what that worth might have to teach us about goodness in general, and finally, to offer some sense of what understanding both those things might do to help us comprehend the temper of our times, out of which we have all been formed.

4
The Ideal and the Everyday

4.1 Grounded Worlds and Ideal Worlds

4.1.1 The Problem of Moral Inspiration

Life, at least in the hands of human beings, and very probably in those of other creatures as well, is a notoriously difficult business. So far, so obvious, you[1] might say, yet it seems to me that there is rather more to the observation than might at first appear to be the case, given its familiarity, something at once significant and not particularly familiar. On the one hand, it is of course obvious to any of its participants that life is difficult: that fact is something we know perfectly well, so well as to make it seem banal.[2] On the other hand, and despite its obviousness, the fact remains mysterious, elusive, and what is more, something of an affront. We tend to think that in an ideal world it would not be this way, that our lives are as hard as they are as the result of misfortune, or injustice, or our own failings, physical or psychological, or more realistically, of all those factors operating together, reinforcing one another. In principle, we feel, things should not be this way. We strain daily to make them otherwise. Yet upon examination the difficulty that we experience seems in fact to be traceable to the very core of our existence as rational creatures, in which our condition as creatures is as significant as our rationality.

In even the most straightforward situations in our everyday lives, it is so often so very hard to know just what one ought to think and what one what ought to do, and the challenge, mysteriously and without rational failing, seems to lie, if only in part and yet inescapably, in the very acts of thinking and doing, so as to be as much a matter of the act of reflection as of what is reflected upon. True, some of the difficulty that we experience undoubtedly stems from conflicts of values in the options before us, the sorts of things that afterwards give rise in us to a tempered species of regret, as we seek to reconcile, as best we can, the returns from what we have committed ourselves to and the losses that are attendant upon it, always in full awareness that reconciliation is just as unavailable to us as the values are in conflict. Life as we know it is fraught partly because of reasons like that, reasons that are a function of what is reflected upon, whether before or after the fact. Yet there is more, and it runs to the architecture of decision-making itself, as to which we seem not only to be but always to have been ambivalent, and that because we are rationally rather than psychologically bound to be so. Just what is it that makes rational decision so troubling and so vulnerable? Just what makes it so hard? What makes it apt to go wrong? How might the process be enlightened?

---

[1] The 'you' doing the saying here was my great friend and frequent collaborator, John Gardner. Death sharpens the need to pay tribute.
[2] My impression over many years has been that if someone's life ever looks easy that is almost certainly because one doesn't know enough about it.

Sometimes our decision-making is liable to be flawed for reasons that we can anticipate or at least recognize after the fact. Perhaps we are overly emotional: in my youth, when I was a hot-metal typesetter, I used to walk very slowly away from a cranky piece of machinery, to the end of a long room, and then slowly back again, as slowly as was necessary for my frustration to subside. Perhaps we are overly focused on ourselves, or what is much the same thing, on values and interests that we have special experience in and affinity for. In such cases, we archetypically try to step back, detach ourselves from our commitments, put ourselves in the shoes of others, so as to see the world as others see it, or more precisely, as it would be seen by others as detached as we have sought to make ourselves. Most profoundly, however, even when reflecting on matters that concern only ourselves, and even when in full command of our emotions, we often continue to approach moral judgement in terms of abstraction, disengagement, and detachment. Distancing yields a clearer understanding, we tell ourselves. When we adopt this perspective, we treat the very fact of the particular as morally distracting, thus warranting the most radical and dramatic forms of disengagement from consideration of the everyday in our decision-making. In each of these three cases, a different species of detachment from the particular expresses a different view as to what constitutes moral distraction, against which moral judgement needs to be secured and insulated, ranging from the emotional, to the prudential, to the phenomenal. In all of them, moral judgement is regarded as characteristically vulnerable to the corruptions of the everyday. Our efforts become directed towards its corresponding purification.[3]

In an ideal world, none of these distractions would exist for us, or more precisely, for the fact of decision. Of course, we do not live in anything like an ideal world, and yet the tantalizing question, which assumptions about the ideal tend to pre-empt, is how far that is actually a bad thing, as the association of moral reflection and abstraction suggests, and how far a good; how far a falling away from what one ought to think and do, and in that sense a source of regret and reproach, and how far a source of value, or more plausibly perhaps, of both those things at once? Put at its most blunt, would an ideal world be entirely a better world? What kind of scope and existence would it offer to the moral? Granted that the everyday is morally vulnerable, is that vulnerability an inescapable function of the everyday, as our practices of detachment treat it, or a possible function? In short, is the everyday a sufficient condition of moral vulnerability or just a necessary one? Most provocatively, and to the opposite effect, might the everyday be a source of moral insight and, if so, is the moral insight a function of its moral vulnerability, and vice versa? Is what makes the everyday morally vulnerable an aspect of what makes it morally

---

[3] Here and in what follows I use the word moral to refer to what reason and value expect, not only of humans but of all that is capable of rational response, as to which of course there are many different accounts. What I seek to outline in this chapter is largely independent of the correctness of any one such account, although it will be clear that my own convictions are realist and pluralist.

worthwhile? Does it enable us to live better than we could live in Utopia, in certain respects at least, that is, not in the sense that the ideal can be improved upon, but in the sense that it can be enlarged and enriched?

Challenges to at least some of the practices of detached judgement are all too familiar, and in many cases more than a little tired. It is often alleged that the account of morality that such practices give rise to is not fit for humans, indissolubly grounded as humans are in various dimensions of their particularity, to which it is as often replied that it is not the role of morality to fit the human condition, but rather the role of the human condition to fit morality. Both the allegation and the response are silent as to the possibility that the moral might in part be constituted by the human, so as to make a degree of fit between the two inevitable without being necessary, present in some settings but not everywhere. That fit, as and when it arose, would simply be a reflection of the human contribution to the scope of the moral, a legacy of the origins of certain dimensions of morality, not a consequence of subsequent accommodation of those dimensions to the human predicament.

Yet questions like these underpin an almost entirely contrary but no less familiar approach to decision-making. Disengagement is not our only or even our most common method of reasoning about goodness and value, so as to know best what to think and how to act. More often perhaps, we get stuck in. In many settings it is taken for granted that depth of engagement is crucial to the grasp of value. Perhaps the most ready example is that of skilled labour. My brother once had a summer job cleaning floors at the printing bureau in what is now Gatineau.[4] His boss, M. Nault (Dr No to his subordinates) insisted that handling a wet mop properly, so as to clean a surface fluently and effectively, was a skill that took many years to perfect. Some, including my adolescent brother, would disagree on the amount of time needed in that particular case, yet all but the very young recognize that there are very few activities that it does not take years to learn to do well, and some, such as art, or music, or philosophy, or fine craftsmanship, that it takes most of a lifetime to begin to master. Modern employment implicitly recognizes this in the investment that it has made in forms of artificial intelligence (starting with the word processor) that have stripped the nuances from the work done by the living, so as to make it both more easily acquired and correspondingly less valuable, and so as much less expensive for the employer as expense correlates with ease of acquisition and value.

An equally familiar example is that of personal relationships, some intimate, others less so, some with human beings, others with other living creatures, in which not only is depth of engagement typically crucial to the delicacy that is in many cases necessary to successful interaction but emotion must often be to the fore in most aspects of one's dealings if the value of the relationship is to be

---

[4] What was then Hull, Quebec, a sister city to Ottawa, where my brother and I grew up.

properly registered, as it must be if it is to yield itself up in all its possible richness. So, one usually needs to know just whom one is dealing with and to feel the appropriate emotions towards them on the appropriate occasions in order to value them just as one should. Such knowledge can only be acquired through engagement, and often deep engagement at that. Hence the common complaint about impersonal workplaces. Many interactions founder because one is simply not in a position to know enough to see that they flourish in the special ways that the characters of the participants call for. Very often we simply do not know enough about one another's needs and aspirations to be able to respond to them with the sensitivity and dexterity they deserve, so that our lack of detailed knowledge gives rise to moral failing.

Dispassion is so commonly linked to soundness of judgement that many have come to regard the emotions as inherently rationally suspect. Yet this is clearly not so, even in what appear to be the most straightforward cases. It is plainly a good idea to walk slowly down a long room, away from a cranky piece of machinery, so as to allow one's frustration to subside, just to the extent that one's frustration is liable to be destructive of a solution to the problem at hand, or worse. As I was warned from my first day on the job, force in general and hammers in particular do not mix with cast iron equipment. Yet frustration is very frequently the trigger for inspiration. Without frustration we would be much less likely to be inventive, much more likely to keep on trying the same things. There is always a balance to be struck, I learned, between patient persistence and starting afresh from another perspective, and a suitable level of frustration is a vital part of that balance. The same is true for a wide range of other emotions. Decision-making often depends on emotional investment for its soundness.

Finally and most broadly, it is thought by some (most notoriously Aristotle) that moral understanding of nearly every kind characteristically requires time, experience, and appropriate attention to granularity to master, so that one learns with practice, from one's elders, and in detail, and philosophizes only with age. To invert the earlier proposition about detachment, in each of these cases a different species of engagement in the particular expresses a different view as to what constitutes moral comprehension, in terms of which moral judgement needs to be undertaken, ranging from the emotional, to the prudential, to the phenomenal.

One prominent and, for legal audiences, relevant case of this attention to engagement is the practice of law as it takes place in and through the hands of barristers and solicitors (as well as trial judges, who are in a similar position), whose task it is to acquire the accomplishment necessary to bring together law and fact in such a way, from setting to setting, as to serve best the needs of particular clients. I was once, long ago now, a government adviser on constitutional law, expected (predictably) to be expert in certain clauses of the constitution, but also (perhaps less predictably) to become highly versed, through close engagement in working partnerships, in the missions of certain government ministries, so as to be able to offer appropriate guidance as to the demands of the same constitutional provisions (such as the right to privacy) in very different policy settings (from housing, to transport, to health care). A good lawyer, I was taught, quite carefully and in close detail,[5] is one who not merely points out problems but goes on to provide solutions, and for a government lawyer such as myself that meant being able to grasp what privacy might call for in relation to a criminal search, for example, as opposed to an administrative inspection. My task as counsel was, of course, roughly to anticipate what an appellate court might call for, but within the scope that gave rise to (bearing in mind the open texture of the constitution and the predilections of the locally prevailing judicial culture) to do so in a way that was rather more accessible, sensitive, and nuanced than any court, particularly an appellate one, could hope to be (distanced as judges rightly are from many features of everyday political life), so as to realize a value for a government client that a judge would be liable to realize ineptly, or at least less well.

The standard challenge to such ways of implementing principle, and one that was regularly put to lawyers whose advice ran contrary to the democratic will, or stood in for it (the will that had called for a search that lawyers advised could not be undertaken in quite that way), was that these modes of settlement are corrupt by reason of their very lack of distance. Their received character led them to be regarded as the views of the establishment, insufficiently attentive to new ways of thinking, minority interests, and the politically unwelcome. Any good lawyer, we were told by left and right, should leave these questions to the courts, and the courts themselves should become more genuinely neutral in their composition, thought, and operations than their critics at the time took them to be. The perceived limits of such a project became limits to the perceived wisdom of constitutional entrenchment and the consequent power of the judiciary.

The underlying point here, one that has been made with varying degrees of purchase against committed moralists from Aristotle onwards, is that engagement appears to license self-approval, or at least to turn a blind eye to it, to the extent of the engagement, in that it lacks the essential distance that valid criticism is thought to require. On the face of it, of course, claims of that kind are frankly conclusory in their assumption that criticism requires distance. After all that assumption is just what the morally engaged dispute and implicitly put in issue by virtue of their practices, for those practices take themselves to be capable of self-examination. Is the assumption a sound one then? Should we regard it as the aspect of rationality, and legacy of enlightenment, that it presents itself as being? There seems to be good reason to doubt it. As I have just suggested, a good many forms of moral criticism gain proper traction by reason of their degree of embedding, just because and to

---

[5] Thanks to Carol Creighton.

the extent that it is only possible to be aware of certain dimensions of the moral from an engaged perspective. So skilled workers, or more precisely, those skilled in the comprehension of that work (such as experienced critics, those who are in a position to be connoisseurs of the workmanship whether or not they possess the relevant skill themselves), are best placed to evaluate the work in question. That is just what M. Nault (my brother's boss from a few paragraphs back) had in mind, or at least sought to trade upon, given that his judgement gave every appearance of also being self-serving. The fact that engagement yields corruption of judgement (and M. Nault was employed by the notorious Department of Public Works) does not undermine the fact that it also yields moral insight. Distance makes it impossible to perceive granularity, and granularity is essential to many aspects of moral evaluation.

And yet the opposite is also clearly true. Some things come into view only with distance, just because the shedding of detail is as often morally revealing as it is morally obscuring. Without equating the metaphysics of the material and the moral, think of a photograph that has been taken from a distance and what it does and does not tell us. Structure becomes visible, as do certain dynamics, even as detail is lost, so that we come to see form at the expense of feature. As it is often put colloquially, and with reference to the moral as much as the material, sometimes the closer we get, the less we can see. So, we appear to be in a quandary, not with respect to different values, for that would be fairly readily explicable, but with regard to the same values. Hence the ambivalence about how to approach decision-making that I referred to at the outset.

Here is the thought in response. Both sides have simply overstated their case. Neither impartiality nor partiality, the ideal nor the everyday, are either necessary constituents of value, or necessary conditions of access to value. Rather they are necessary constituents, or necessary conditions of access to, certain values only, those in which impartiality or partiality are part of the ground, as a conceptual matter in some cases, and as a matter of the genealogy of certain morals in others. (Think of the value of justice on the one hand, and that of parenting on the other, and their respective associations with impartiality and partiality.) They do not play that role in relation to value in general. Indeed, they may not even inevitably play that role in relation to values in which they are part of the ground, for the grounds of a value may themselves be mutable to some extent. That means, and in this lies the departure from what I spoke of as the fairly readily explicable, that in all cases other than those in which either partiality or impartiality forms part of the ground, values are susceptible to either impartial or partial rendering, which is the reason that both renderings possess what plausibility they possess as aspects of value in general. Evaluation is itself a practice that falls to be evaluated, one that yields different values when differently undertaken, rather than a function of the very idea of value, to be executed only correctly or incorrectly, better or worse. It can, of course, be done wrongly but there are many ways to do it well, each with its own

184 THE IDEAL AND THE EVERYDAY

reward. Some of those ways are ones that we can assume, take on as we think fit, others are embedded.

4.1.2 The Problem of the Murdered Testator

Certain legal cases acquire an especially luminous life after their decision, as touchstones for practices of subsequent reflection, sometimes legal, sometimes political, sometimes philosophical, just because there is something deeply resonant about their facts that fits them to turn into parables. I am grateful to Fred Schauer for pointing out to me recently that *Riggs v. Palmer*[6] is one such case, in that it was already famous in legal circles before Ronald Dworkin made it more famous still. As is the case with parables, the facts can be very succinctly recounted.

Francis Palmer, a prosperous farmer, left the bulk of his estate to his grandson Elmer, with a gift over to his two daughters (one of whom was Riggs) should Elmer predecease him without issue. Whether from impatience, or out of anxiety that the will might be altered, Elmer murdered his grandfather and then sought to claim his inheritance. The will had been properly executed, and there was nothing on the face of its terms, or in the terms of the relevant New York statute, to suggest that the murder of the testator was any bar to inheriting under his will. Nevertheless, and surely not very surprisingly, the court denied the inheritance. As the majority put it, Elmer was to be enjoined from using any of the personalty or real estate left for his benefit; the bequest was to be declared ineffective to pass title to him; by reason of the murder, he was to be deprived of any interest in the estate left by his victim; and the testator's two daughters were to be declared the true owners of that estate. The choice of verbs here is significant.

The majority offered two grounds for its decision. The first rested on an interpretation of the New York wills statute which, in accordance with accepted canons of statutory interpretation, was to be read in light of the intentions of the legislator, so as to expand or contract the bare language of the statute, as far as judicial tradition permitted, in order to secure the legislative intention in cases where a literal reading would frustrate it. To permit Elmer to inherit would be to frustrate the very order that the legislators of the wills statute had sought to secure. The majority described this as rational interpretation, and was at pains to point to the many legal precedents for it. The second, alternative ground for decision was that there was a

---

[6] 115 NY 506 (1889). The occasion for Fred's comment was a lecture given by him at the Surrey Centre for Law and Philosophy in May 2018. I should emphasize at once that, unlike Fred's interest, my present interest in Dworkin is meta-ethical rather than jurisprudential. I am simply using his work as an illustration of a meta-ethical outlook that I am attempting to present an alternative to. If I am correct in what I say, then there is something very wrong about Dworkin's project, but that pay-off is incidental to this chapter, not its point. Yet even that is perhaps to overstate the contrast. Each of these approaches illuminates the other, and that is why the structure of this chapter alternates between them.

maxim of the common law, nowhere superseded by statute, that no one should be permitted 'to profit by his own fraud, or to take advantage of his own wrong, or to found any claim upon his own iniquity, or to acquire property by his own crime'. The equitable character of this maxim is visibly reflected in the *in personam* tones of the court's decision.

Dworkin called upon *Riggs* in aid of his view of jurisprudence on two separate occasions. In 'The Model of Rules', he relied on the majority's second ground of decision to argue that the law contained principles that a rule of recognition, as proposed by Hart, was constitutionally incapable of capturing.[7] Yet it is a little difficult to see how *Riggs* can be read to support that claim. What the majority describes as a maxim of the common law is in fact a familiar equitable maxim (a variant of the clean hands doctrine), and it has always been the function of the law of equity to temper the rigour of the common law, not by contradicting the common law (so as to declare a will invalid that the law regards as valid, or alter its terms in ways not permitted by law) but by imposing personal obligations that prevent people from exploiting the law to inequitable effect. The principle that no one should be permitted to take advantage of his own wrong is by its nature a principle of decision, to be used by adjudicators, and authoritative adjudicators at that (I find it hard to discern any other role for the principle), and its place in the common law, as we now describe it following the fusion of the administration of law and equity, is as well sourced as that of any other law.

In *Law's Empire*,[8] Dworkin deepened his critique by drawing upon the majority's first ground of decision to argue that the true meaning of a statute was always to be determined not simply by reference to the bare language of the statute, as shaped by relevant canons of statutory interpretation, but by reference to what he described as a practice of constructive interpretation, in which a court asks, first, which principle or principles fit the law on the question at hand (law here being understood in a pre-interpretive sense) and, second, which of those principles that fit makes the law (here being understood in a post-interpretive sense) the best it can be. This practice he called law as integrity. All philosophers of law, he contended, were engaged in the project of determining the grounds of law, and his account of law as integrity was, when evaluated against the relevant benchmarks, consistently superior to Hart's account on that score.

Once again it is a little difficult to see how *Riggs* itself can be read to support that claim, at least without a good deal of *legerdemain*. It is simply not true to say that all philosophers of law are committed to the identification of the grounds of law, as Dworkin understood those. As far as Hart was concerned, identifying the grounds of law (in Dworkin's sense of intellectual inputs) was the task of lawmakers, be

---

[7] This now very famous paper first appeared in the University of Chicago Law Review in 1967 and was later included in *Taking Rights Seriously* (1977).
[8] 1986.

they the legislature or the judiciary. Hart's project, in his delineation of the rule of recognition, was to identify the sources of law, or more precisely, to identify the ways in which the sources of law are identified by legal officials, so as to identify the lawmakers whose task it is to consider grounds of law and reach decisions on the basis of them. In Hart's hands, sources, one might roughly put it, are institutional; grounds are inspirational.

There is no trace of dispute in *Riggs* over the content of the rule of recognition as Hart understood it, for all the rules in the case were recognized rules. Dworkin presents the case as a dispute of that kind by insisting on reading into the rule of recognition (as Hart understood it) a level of detail (how to interpret the outputs of a source; how to reconcile the outputs of different sources) that on the whole the rule of recognition could not offer an answer to without undermining its own significance. By this means he turns Hart's question (about the validity of law) into Dworkin's question (of what law should be). This is a sleight of hand that use of the equivocal term 'grounds of law' (which is roughly equivocal between institutional grounds and intellectual grounds) both conceals and enables. In Dworkin's hands, that is to say in Dworkin's presentation of Hart, the rule of recognition as Hart understood it is called upon to identify the full resources of decision in every case, and to show how those are to be reconciled. This erases the role that Hart intended the rule of recognition to play and leaves legal positivists no question of validity to answer. Every legal decision becomes a decision about the content of the rule of recognition.

The deeper and more telling question, however, is not whether Dworkin was fair to Hart, a question that Dworkin was not the sort of combatant to be deeply concerned with, but whether the idea of law as integrity possesses the resources needed to identify the grounds of law as Dworkin understood them. By his own admission, Dworkin loved a distinction (they were vessels for his remarkable intellectual ingenuity) but the distinction between fit and justification is a troubling one, in its operation and ordering. The dimension of fit is troubling just because it precedes and is independent of the question of justification, so presenting for justification principles that have been identified without justification in mind, all of which may be bad ones, in certain settings at least. This may indeed be integrity, but if so it makes clear what the lives of consistently bad people have so painfully shown, that to possess integrity is not necessarily to possess virtue. Less obviously perhaps, the dimension of justification is troubling, not simply because the options presented to it may well be unworthy ones, for that is not its fault, unless and until it succumbs to rationalizing, but because the process of justification, as Dworkin describes it, is not only backward-looking and self-referential but fundamentally idealizing. An idealizing morality is not capable of doing the good that much of our living calls for, at least, if we are truly to live well (that is, with as much emphasis on the living as on the well) and to be truly justified in our doing so.[9]

---

[9] The broader implications of this consideration of *Riggs* will become clear in sub-chapter 4.3.2. As an aside, and to avoid misunderstanding, in speaking here and elsewhere of a separation between fit

4.2 The Problem of Living Well

Joseph Raz, with characteristic power, has outlined reasons to believe in the possibility of moral change, by dismantling arguments, most notably that from subsumption, that would limit morality to what can be explained by reference to existing moral understanding.[10] The limitation expressed in subsumption seeks to preserve both realism about morality and what I have called idealism, standardly by taking existing moral understanding to a new and higher level of abstraction, a level that is sufficiently general in its account of value as to be capable of including a value that would otherwise appear to be novel. By this means, it is said, we can come to see that the cases of value that we are well versed in are in fact part of a more capacious category of value than we took them to be, a category that is capacious enough to embrace an apparent outlier. The underlying and even more basic problem being tackled here is that of the recognition of the moral, and Raz is very persuasive in his contention that there are sound ways to recognize the moral other than by subsumption, most notably by analogy.

Raz's project here, not for the first time, amounts to something of a liberation movement, opening our thought, that about moral realism in particular, to possibilities of diversity and change that standard practices of reflection would rule out. My present concern, which is at once sympathetic yet ancillary to his, is to pursue the question of what might be good about such a liberation. What possibilities for our thought and action does the reality of moral change (if that is what it is) give rise to, and in what ways, if any, do those possibilities make our moral lives fuller, or richer, or more recognizable, or all those things at once?

The standard move, towards idealism, abstraction, disengagement in our moral decision-making, is driven by the sense of what the moral has to offer to life, of what we and other valuers need to attend to in and learn from the moral, so as to live well and make our lives genuinely good ones. The less standard move in the opposite direction, one that is not accidentally engrained in many aspects of our daily life, is animated by something less familiar and perhaps less comfortable for a moral realist, a sense of what life has to offer to the moral, so as to bring the moral to life, so to speak, with all that implies in terms of dynamism and finitude. As I see it, each of these two moves, taken in isolation and in general, risks not only

---

and justification in Dworkin's account of law I am not suggesting that the operation of either of those processes is entirely isolated from the other. On the contrary, Dworkin clearly contemplates, particularly in *Law's Empire*, that constructive interpretation involves a movement from fit to justification and back again, until the best interpretation is arrived at. Yet it remains the case that this very process, however prolonged it may be, depends on the separateness of the enquiry as to fit from the enquiry as to justification.

[10] 'Can Moral Principles Change?' (2017) King's College London Law School Research Paper 2017-40; Oxford Legal Studies Research Paper 58/2017. SSRN: https://ssrn.com/abstract = 3024030 or http://dx.doi.org/10.2139/ssrn.3024030; now available in *The Roots of Normativity* (2022), 94.

incompleteness but inadequacy. The former is liable to be too bloodless, the latter too bloody.

To speak of bringing morality to life risks being both rhetorical and overwrought. On the one hand, morality plainly has a life of its own without need of assistance from the living, in the sense of the flesh and blood living that I have been pointing to. On the other hand, but by something of the same token, to speak of life without more is simply to prompt the question of just what sort of life one has in mind. What kind of life could valuers bring to morality that morality did not already possess? The answer, as I see it, is the kind of life that is implicit in the very idea of valuers and valuing; the life of specificity and finitude that the ideal does not partake of but that makes evaluation matter, indeed makes it conceivable; the life that requires us to think and to do one thing rather than another, and that leaves open-ended the possibilities in doing so; the life that contains the ideas of creation and creativity as its premise and its purpose; the life that makes the moral world one that is dynamic as well as static; the life in which the same things can be good and bad at once; the life the history of which could never be entirely foretold, and that as a result, when brought into being and pursued through its course, in small moments and in great, makes the moral universe rather larger than it would or could have been otherwise, for better and for worse.

That is still quite rhetorical so let me be more down to earth. As I see it, at the heart of the idea and the experience of life is a sense of span. We live for a while and within a certain compass. Those parameters are what give life its basic outline, its narrative structure, and less obviously perhaps, its moral imperative. We quite unavoidably, but for the most part quite willingly, proceed from moment to moment, predicament to predicament, in patterns derived from our thoughts and from our actions. Because each of us is one person rather than all persons, because we each exist at one moment rather than another, because we can never be in two places at once, we must decide (if only by way of response to what has happened to us in cases when we are passive) and the quality of our decision turns in part on our finitude and specificity, so that our moral worth, which we cannot control or escape, turns in part on matters that could not be known in advance or from a distance, because their character is a product and function of our particular, and very largely randomly established, mortality. All of this is very far from ideal, and that is one prominent source of its richness.

We do all these things not on our own but in concert with one another, and as a result our finitudes are multiplied, our moral prospects complicated and enriched, by practices of association. In this way, we collectively beget cultures and aspects of culture. To live well in and through these cultures and their aspects very often requires us to master the intricacies of their goodness and badness, intricacies that distance cultures in varying degrees from the ideal and from one another, in their moral successes as much as in their moral failures. So when we pursue a skill, physical or intellectual; have feelings about what we do and where we find ourselves;

develop personal relationships with other people, other animals, or even places; in general seek to live well, so as to have what we take to be a good life; we necessarily work within contingencies of time, space, and incident, few of which are entirely or exactly shared with other people at other times and places (disconcerting though it often is to realize just how far one's life is a type, so that matters that one took to be particular to oneself are revealed as cultural or generational). Far from being morally inert, these contingencies seem to shape deeply our sense of the worth of our lives, the more so the more embedded we become in them, through investment in roles, people, places, and much else, so as to detail, or flesh out as we often and revealingly put it, the contours of our engagement in and appreciation of the artefacts and practices that we share with our moral neighbours and companions, our fellow travellers in the appreciation of value.

To put it at its most trivial, there was a time when there was no wet mop, a time when there was no terrazzo flooring, a time when there was no question of the consequent skill that could be developed, mastered, and transmitted to others, and a time, therefore, when there was no question of the aspect of value that such a skill can give rise to, an aspect of value that in its shadings is not simply an arbitrary variant of a more general and abstract value of cleaning and cleanliness (or something like that), but rather the legacy of a particular moment and culture. Indeed, there is probably a sense in which the value (and disvalue) of the practices that my brother stepped into and briefly shared was local to Gatineau, to Public Works, and indeed to the company of M. Nault and his fellows.[11] These are the things that give life its flavour, and there seems no reason to deny and good reason to accept that they form a large part of its value, as they routinely appear to us to do.

The example here is deliberately trivial, just because so much of our lives and their worth are similarly trivial. The point that I am trying to make is one that could be rather more easily established, for this audience at least, by reference to more ambitious practices, such as those of art, music, fine craftsmanship, and intellectual enquiry. Yet that would surely be to slip into something like the habit of elevation and abstraction in our reflections about what to think and how to act that I have sought to call into question, at least far enough to temper somewhat our embrace of it. It isn't just that what are sometimes referred to as the finer things in life are apt to be self-referential in the hands of most philosophers. It is that they are too easily thought of as approaches to and imperfect instantiations of the ideal. That is not the only or the best way to understand even these finer things. For those who are as old as I am, or are of an historical turn of mind, and to return to an example that I have relied on elsewhere, there is a Bob Dylan song that seeks to deny that art attains greatness only as and when it partakes of the divine: 'But Mona Lisa must have had the highway blues, you can tell by the way she smiles.'[12] The highway

---

[11] Returning to the question of skilled labour raised in the text at n. 4.
[12] 'Visions of Johanna' (1966).

blues: how redolent of value that is, and how very particular in its time, place, and ultimate flavour. Even Bob Dylan would have passed on it a few years later, when Woody Guthrie meant less to him.

The emotions too are often no less local than skilled labour. It is a little difficult to be properly precise here, because to be adept in the emotions is to be deeply versed in their local expression, for a family, for a community, for a national culture, in something the same way as it is to be adept at humour, so that it is as difficult to speak accurately of foreign emotions as it is to speak accurately of a foreign sense of humour. Nevertheless, anyone with experience of different generations and the quintessentially different outlooks that they often have on significant aspects of life, at least in all but the most stable cultures, will be familiar with the fact that such people do similar things in what are often fundamentally different ways, so that the intergenerational unities are quite shallow while their divergences are profound. It is a small and possibly unreliable example, but I remember noticing when young that while my grandparents and parents distinguished as I did (and as we are all bound to) between their positive and negative states of mind, their vocabularies were very different from mine, and the difference in our vocabularies tracked a difference in the quality of our evaluations. My grandparents spoke of joy and sorrow, my parents of happiness and unhappiness, while I at the time tended to speak of being up or down. Different values are at stake here, and to a great extent they are not just culturally rooted but culturally inspired.

I have written elsewhere, in the context of considering the worth of equality, of the distinction that is to be drawn between value (and disvalue) and goodness (and badness). Goodness and badness are reflections of the way we live, of the artefacts that our lives give rise to, including the artefact of their very existence, but also the physical artefacts that we call goods and the cultural artefacts that we call practices, in short the artefacts of the ongoing exchange between life and value, value and life. It is life and its very many by-products that can be either good or bad, or both at once. So one could say that it is life that brings goodness and badness into the world, and in doing so generates possibilities for value, partly within the boundaries of existing values, but also by aberrations, in something the same way that genetic variation generates new lives and from time to time, and through what might otherwise have been abnormality, such very new ways of being as amount to new species.

That sounds grandiose, but it is also and no less meaningfully or importantly, entirely trivial. When we do what we do from day to day, some of it inventive, much of it repetitive, and when we are a little lucky, we lead good lives. The flavour of those lives, in all their minutiae, is trivially distinctive, and that is what gives us reason to value them as our own, while being properly modest about their significance. We matter even as we do not matter.[13]

---

[13] As an aside here, for the point does not arise in the narrative to follow, in a range of human predicaments this suggests reason to pursue compromise, for the sake of the special goodness that compromise

Often this is quite inarticulate. It is one of those puzzles whether the facts of our lives call for valuation or whether the value of our lives calls for facts. Do we need to have an idea of something in order to be able to reflect on its worth, or is an idea something that would be difficult, perhaps impossible, to comprehend without some sense of the value that it could give rise to, or as Finnis might put it, some sense of its point? A solution to the puzzle is not required. For what it's worth, my prejudice tends to run in favour of the precedence of value. There seem to be many things that we can feel and do entirely inarticulately, from simply lying in the sun, or sporting in the water, to actively engaging in complicated activities that depend for much of their value on spontaneity and improvisation. *Pace* advocates of mindfulness, it is often better not to think about things at all, and no less often better not to think about them too much. That, after all, is what other animals seem to do much of the time, and what even plants may do, as long as one is prepared, as I am, to think of plants as valuers whose valuations happen to be biologically determined, so as to lead them to turn towards the sun, for example, and in doing so to convert the value of sunlight into the goodness of a flower.[14]

And yet, of course, that is only prejudice on my part. It seems to be the case that human beings are fundamentally not only valuers but pretty conceptual creatures, so that the smallest of children are as keen on naming as they are on valuing and often more accomplished at it, although not always. 'See car', I am told that I said as a very small child, looking out the window. 'See truck.' 'See ment mixer.' Naming is running ahead of value here.

All of this goes to the practice of evaluation no less than to what falls to be evaluated. There is no underlying algorithm to specify the shape of evaluation, although there are many working practices of evaluation, each of which fits, with greater or lesser success, values and practices of different kinds, while at the same time helping to characterize the culture of which it is a product, and thereby helping to contribute to that culture's worth or lack of worth, or more precisely, to the distinctive quality of its worth or lack of worth. Some cultures place great weight on the fact of embedding, using social pressure to enforce conventions across a wide range of practices, great and small. To use a trivial example once again, there is a right way to make a sauce, one will be told in such cultures, and if one presses for

---

can give rise to, beyond what it salvages. This way of resolving a predicament is not merely or even less good than a refusal to compromise, as many assume. On the contrary, it can and often does give rise to a previously unanticipated good, perhaps less worthy in terms of the relevant ideal, yet potentially more worthy in terms of what it makes possible, be that a reflection of a familiar value or of one that is novel. As I quite vividly remember Bernard Williams once drily observing, in a seminar he was sharing with Ronald Dworkin, after Dworkin had been dismissive of a possibility on the ground that it was a mere *modus vivendi*, a *modus vivendi* is not to be sneezed at, when you consider the alternative. Williams may have had only salvage in mind, but his reference to a *modus vivendi* has special purchase, in its attention to the role that living can play in the achievement of goodness.

[14] Perhaps I should speak of the value in sunlight, or the goodness of sunlight. For the full development of this particular thought, see Macklem and Gardner, 'Human Disability' (2014) 25 KLJ 60.

a reason what one will be pointed to is a custom, which will be treated as if it were a reason. There is clearly both good and bad in this. The good is surely to be found in the cultural stability that is generated thereby, in the mutual recognition of the members of that culture, and in the attendant goods that stability and recognition can give rise to. The bad lies in the rigidity, the closure, the lack of questioning, and the further consequences for the good in terms of the several losses of cultural adaptability, social mobility, and accommodation of diversity, and from the opposite perspective, of repression and unfulfilled lives.

Other cultures, such as those that are globally dominant at the moment, place great weight on abstract ideals (such as equality, democracy, and human rights) that not only take the place of former embedded practices (such as tribalism, oligarchy, and cultural taboos) but also treat them as both unnecessary and irrational. Trivial examples are hard to come by in this setting, because the idealizing outlook is by its very nature dedicated to denying their significance in its operation. One must ask more generally about the ways in which our lives have been shaped by commitment to an outlook that all rational beings are currently expected to share as a universal, which it is in its moral status but which it need not be in its engagement. Once again, there is both good and bad in this. Our world is fluid (but then also uncertain and angst-ridden), adaptable (but shallow), open to all (but committed to no one in particular), inclusive of all (but without the benefits that exclusiveness can give rise to), comprehensible to all (but without the benefits that the arcane can give rise to), and so on.

The contrast that I have been trying to draw is merely illustrative of certain familiar instantiations of different approaches to evaluation. Once it is recognized that evaluation is in many respects a social practice, one that itself falls to be evaluated, it becomes necessary to confront, in some detail, the different values that different practices of evaluation give rise to. Sometimes this confrontation is liable to take place at the boundaries of a culture, most obviously so in the case of embedded cultures. In fluid, liberal cultures such as ours, however, the confrontation is bound to take place at the frontiers of our individual minds (for that is the framework of responsibility that those cultures have assigned to us, so as to bring our lives as close as possible to their model of rationality), and so is bound to take shape not only in the decisions that we each make about what to think and do but in the higher-level decisions that we make about how to decide and with what frame of reference to go about doing so, subject of course to the claims upon us of the very many social practices in which, for all our idealizing convictions, we remain necessarily embedded, including the framework of the law and of legal system, as those things are severally and distinctively constituted and practised in different cultures and jurisdictions.

So, to take a prominent contemporary example, the practice of seeking to punish sexual transgressions through a public shaming by crowd action, rather than through the intervention of the law, represents a commitment by the individuals in question to shift the framework of decision-making on this issue from the idealizing to the embedded. People do not pursue this path as a second-best to the operation of the law. Rather they pursue it because they regard it as superior, in its operations as much as in its outcome. The fact that they are the authors of the criteria of evaluation, in all its detail, authors of the process of evaluation, and ultimately authors of their own remedy, is central to their movement. To put it in Dworkinian terms, they are not in any way prepared to turn to Hercules for relief. Those who believe that there is at least something to regret in this approach need to engage in the arguments about its strengths and weaknesses as a mode of evaluation. They cannot simply rule it out of court. To do so would be not merely strategically inadequate but morally unsound. Or so I am proposing.

4.3 The Value in Difficulty and Decision

4.3.1 The Problems of Integrity and of Purpose

Observations such as these have something to offer to those of us who have engaged in the practice of law, or in reflection upon that practice, in two ways. First, law is a practice of decision-making, and our understanding of it as such is necessarily affected by the views that we hold about the appropriateness of different modes of decision-making. So different legal cultures can and, as we all know, do adopt different approaches to legal decision-making, legislative and judicial, approaches that have come over time to characterize their legal traditions, in the many ways with which scholars and practitioners, particularly those with experience of transnational and comparative law, are entirely familiar, traditions the appropriateness of which is open to evaluation in the several ways in which evaluation may legitimately take place, some of which will be regarded as alien and others as appropriate by the legal cultures in question. The appropriateness of an approach to evaluation is liable to be measured on two levels, in terms of its consonance with the local forms of legal practice, and in terms of its consonance with local practices of evaluation, some of which will in turn be distinctively legal. That consonance is possibly but not necessarily suspect. It will obscure some matters and illuminate others. So, for example, some legal cultures (indeed all legal cultures to some degree) will be embedded, so that the way that things are done around here (to adopt the common expression) is central to their operation; will regard that embeddedness as entirely appropriate; and may well further regard as appropriate embedded practices of evaluation, including those of legal evaluation. They will not necessarily be wrong in any of this, even though a good deal of it will inevitably be self-regarding, by very reason of its embeddedness. Indeed, one suspects that it is almost bound to be the case that they are likely to be right about much of it, for the embeddedness of a practice is almost bound to beget a need for correspondingly embedded approaches to its understanding and critical assessment, in some respects at least.

Second, and more to the present point, the practice of reflection on the law, the practice that in academic circles tends to claim for itself the name of jurisprudence, is itself and in turn affected by the same views. For someone like Dworkin, of course, these two perspectives merge into one, given his conviction that law is but jurisprudence writ small. The real strengths and weaknesses of Dworkin's account, which are to be found, on the one hand, in the idealizing picture it offers of law as something that is to be identified with its own aspiration, and on the other hand, in the gulf between that picture and the everyday reality of what aspiration means on the ground, thought by thought, action by action, are ultimately located in the idea of law as integrity which, both seductively and disconcertingly, is in many ways anything but.

Recall that Dworkin begins with a distinction that he regards as essential to the interpretation and development of not only the law but every cultural text, whether it be aesthetic or practical, namely, the distinction between the requirement of fit and the requirement of justification. That distinction is rather more odd than it treats itself as being, for in our everyday moral lives fit is rarely if ever separate from justification (we think that our clothes fit because that is part of what we think makes them look good; we speak more broadly of fit and proper reactions, in ways that make clear that those two elements are presented as going hand in hand because the role of each is in part to shape the other), while in those everyday lives justification is rarely if ever separate from fit, for tailoring is a fundamental part of the idea of justification as we practise it (we think that justification must be such as could be offered to the particular person or persons who are its subjects, so that we make sure, for example, to offer to victims justifications that take full account of their distinctive history and predicament). To seek to sever these everyday partnerships not as a thought experiment, but as the heart of a programme for the life of the law as it should be lived in practice, as a guide to the exercise of judicial citizenship at its most admirable, is, it seems to me, to seek to take from each of those elements the crucial overtone that commends it to us as moral beings. It is to take from fit that which makes fit capable of being something worthy, while taking from justification that which makes justification something that is capable of life, in all the ways that I have sought to explore earlier. Let me explain what I have in mind.

In Dworkin's hands, fit becomes a matter of searching for the principle or principles that best fit the law as it currently exists, at first very locally and then, as and when necessary, by stepping back to more general and more comprehensive views of the law, legal history, and political history. The quest is always for fit, so that one steps back not to find a better principle but to find a better fit, officially at least. This results in satisfactory principles if and to the extent that one's legal culture is satisfactory, in its detail (for that is where the quest for fit may well stop) as much as in its broad outlines. One would need not only to be idealistic but chauvinistically so to be at all optimistic about the outcomes of such a project, for laws are the product of our politics, explicitly so in the case of statutes, implicitly so in the case of the common law, and the history of our politics, like the history of so much of human endeavour, is something that even generous observers are bound to describe as flawed at best.

Fit is not my principal topic here, and much has been said about it elsewhere, so there is no need for me to pursue its difficulties. It seems to me that there is only one slightly rueful observation that might be worth developing a little further. In articulating his picture of the process of constructive interpretation, Dworkin had a choice to make in his treatment of fit. Grant for the moment and for the sake of argument his desire to approach the issues of fit and justification separately. He needed to arrive at a model of what he described as law as integrity, a model of what he took to be the proper interaction between fit and justification, justification and fit, that would be at once recognizable (so as to be plausible as a description of the fact of law as it presently exists in a particular setting which, for Dworkin, was that of the United States) and virtuous. He might have given priority to the virtuous, but he chose instead to give priority to the recognizable. One can see the large temptation in the immense capital for a progressive politics that he hoped to realize thereby, while still believing that it was a temptation that should have been resisted.

It is Dworkin's treatment of justification that is perhaps more interesting, however, because it is more revealing. The temptations that his account gives in to here are not the immediate ones of the potential gains to be made in terms of domestic judicial politics, but rather the broader and more insidious (because less visible) temptations of twentieth-century idealism, in which the everyday came to be archetypically regarded as politically suspect, in which the idea of modernity came to be thought of as in just opposition to ideas of custom and tradition, in a vision of moral progress. As Dworkin would have it, when more than one principle fits as a solution to the problem at hand, the task of a court, exemplified by his ideal judge, Hercules, is to ask which of those principles would make the law the best it can be, once again stepping back as far as is needed to be able to appraise accurately the principles on offer. That principle is the law.

There are three significant difficulties in this approach, only the last of which I will dwell on. First, the identification of a principle as the one that makes the law the best it can be is possible only if the principles in question are broadly commensurable. This makes Dworkin's account of constructive interpretation something of a non-starter for value pluralists, for whom decisions involve choices of kind as well as degree. Yet there is more. In Dworkin's project, it is essential that law be self-determining, because that fact is vital to the immediate political capital that he hoped to realize for a progressive politics. The obvious problem with this proposal, and the single right answer that it is said to yield, a problem that value pluralists are particularly sensitive to but that others also share, is that in the bulk of life as we know it decision appears to be necessary to the reaching of moral conclusions. The less obvious but perhaps even more telling difficulty, to which I will return, is that the role of decision in our lives is surely morally desirable in itself. The presence of a single right answer, were it actually the fact of the matter, would erase the significance of the decision-maker, and by extension would erase the significance of all the rich rational detail that makes it possible to distinguish the moral character and function of one decision-maker from another. Remember that Dworkin's picture of constructive interpretation is not a picture that is supposed to be peculiar to the law, but to the contrary, a picture of evaluative judgement more generally, one that explains just how the next chapter in a novel should be written, and by extension, the next chapter in a life. In both those cases, it matters not to constructive interpretation just who writes the chapter: its proper content is the same. What room here for the author? What room for the fact that my life is mine? Someone else would be just as good or better at writing the script, not in all cases but surely in many.

The second difficulty with Dworkin's account of justification lies in its implicit yet powerful conservative bent. The quest for the best principle is one that explicitly canvases the world as it is and as it has been. The next brushstroke that a painter should take is one that is to be determined by reference to every brushstroke that has ever been taken, not only as a matter of fit but as a matter of justification. The life of an artist as so envisioned would become a matter of finding new implications for existing aesthetic values, and life in general would become a matter of discovering new, yet morally merely arbitrary, instantiations of the value of life as it has always been lived. It is possible to think of certain parts of the law (such as bills of rights) this way, because it is possible to think that the value of those particular parts of the law is to be found, to some degree at least, in their capacity to conserve certain political goods, so as to delay the amendment of those goods, let alone their destruction. Yet it seems to me, and I doubt that I am unusual in this respect, that it is not at all plausible to think of life in general this way, and that it is close to impossible to think of art this way, for to do so is to strip out from each of those things the value of creativity and the significance of voice.

That brings to me to what I see as the final and most troubling difficulty in Dworkin's account of justification which, ironically, is the obverse of what I take to be its chief attraction for idealists. To approach life, even the life of the law, in terms of integrity, so as to engage in the justification that constructive interpretation calls for, is to enter into a relationship with the moral that takes the very life out of the moral. As I have sought to put it earlier, value comes to life only in the hands of valuers. That is just what the world has to offer to morality. It is our existence, and that of other valuers, that provides the occasion and the opportunity for morality to inhabit the world other than as a potentiality, and more than that but also consequently, that gives morality reason and opportunity to grow, develop, and evolve, through engagement with the facts of existence, large and small.

Decision is not an affliction, something that we would avoid if we could. It is the stuff of life. It is through our decisions, in the nuanced sense of decision that I have sought to describe previously, the sense that treats our reactions as among our actions, that we articulate our moral character, and so describe our moral life. Without decision we would lack a sense not only of authorship but of predicament, and without predicament it is hard to see how there could be any such thing as responsibility, if responsibility is, as I take it to be, the account that is to be given of our engagement with value. It is the exercise of this responsibility in our thoughts and in our actions, through the authorship of our destiny, individual and collective, that enables us to bring goodness into the world (as well as badness, when we exercise responsibility badly). We are all too familiar with the fact that our existences are very often, and for the pessimistic, characteristically, a falling away from value, but we are much less attentive to the corollary, that it is those same existences that give rise to the realization and enhancement of value. That is just what makes the world a beautiful place, to the extent that it is so. Otherwise, the beauty and the place would never be in a position to come together, and to know one another.

All this is as true for lawyers as it is for other human beings. To be an actor in a legal system is to play a role of some kind in the collective exercise of responsibility for a certain strand of social life, that of the recognition, maintenance, and development of a set of norms that is sufficiently distinct from other norms, in its origins and status, to enable it to serve purposes that would be served differently, perhaps less well, perhaps not at all, by rival sets of norms. In the exercise of this role, it is the quality of decision that makes legal norms good and bad, and that quality is a product of moral perceptiveness in decision-making, fine-grained and large. The balance that is struck between those two extremes of granularity (and everything in between them), from issue to issue, decision to decision, comes over time to characterize certain cultures and sub-cultures, social, political, and legal, and those institutions that contribute to their development, from legislatures to courts, from lower courts to higher ones, from legal actors to legal critics.

Without the role of decision there would be no American legal system for Dworkin to speak to and explain, or for the rest of us to compare and analogize to our own legal systems. That is what the aspect of fit, as Dworkin describes it, implicitly recognizes but explicitly misrepresents, by removing the question of fit, and responsibility for its exercise, from the question of justification (where in fact it performs the vital task of humanizing the moral and making it our own), and assigning it an independent and semi-isolated role that has the effect of valorizing culture without attending to the reasons for its value and disvalue. As Dworkin presents it, constructive interpretation, in law and in life, makes our moral world smaller and more self-regarding than it ought to be, while at the same time and by the same token making us passive rather than active participants in it. Surely Dworkin's own remarkably inventive and distinctive intellectual legacy, in and of itself, gives the lie to this view. Is it at all possible to believe that the various chapters of *Law's Empire*, for example, the ideas developed there, and the potent vision that sustained them, did not ultimately depend on the vitality, fluency, and creativity of Ronald Dworkin himself? Do we not have him to thank for them, both for better and for worse? Did Dworkin really believe, having granted equal competence, absence of agenda, and an unwillingness to act as his *amanuensis* (for anything else would not amount to constructive interpretation as Dworkin describes it), that John Finnis could have alternated with him in the writing of that book to much the same effect? Or more precisely and more fairly, that some other writer, a literary Hercules, could have rendered the ideas present there at least as well and probably better? And if this last is something that Dworkin could possibly agree to, as he might have done if he was prepared to think of his life as an approach to the ideal, should the rest of us concur, or should we think that there was something quite special about Ronald Dworkin, something that infused his work, and that would not have existed in quite the way that it did but for the various accidents of fortune that came to constitute his mind? What reason otherwise for relative strangers such as myself to mourn his passing?

A couple of concluding observations. I have consistently spoken of courts generally but this is to fail to give weight to the fact that Dworkin's focus is on appellate courts, which are institutionally something of an ambiguous case. The ambiguity makes appellate courts rather more plastic in the hands of their interpreters than are some institutions, and that may have suited Dworkin. It does not alter the fact that appellate courts, no less than trial courts, are attentive to questions of fit in the patterns of their justifications. Appellate courts derive the fine-grained aspects of their decisions from the legislature on the one hand and from trial courts on the other. Two things follow from this. First, while the public face of appellate courts emphasizes their distance from fine-grained factual determinations, as confirmation of their supervisory rather than competitive institutional role, the fine-grained remains present in their judgments, albeit derivatively so. One can see this in the care with which appellate courts grant leave to appeal (to the extent that they control their own dockets), so as to make sure that the large national issues that they are asked to determine are grounded on what the courts regard as good facts. Second, both the public face and the actual decision-making of appellate courts constitute a shifting frontier of attention to the significance of different approaches to decision-making, a frontier that is as contentious as is the political culture in a given society. One can see this in the debates that take place about the attention that is paid, or ought to be paid, by those courts to the law of other jurisdictions and to international law in the development of the constitutional cultures of their own jurisdictions. In Canada, this plays out in terms of the attention that ought to be paid to decisions taken under the American Bill of Rights; in the United States, it plays out in terms of the attention that ought to be paid to certain decisions that have been rendered by international courts. To notice this is part of what it means to notice, correctly, that the appellate courts are fundamentally political (albeit not party political), and locally so.

Second, while I have focused on Dworkin in my comments, because the architecture of his theory is so explicitly isolating and purifying, the points that I have been seeking to make are in no sense *ad hominem* ones. They are also an issue for legal positivism, where they gain their purchase in debates about the purpose of law. To assign a purpose to a practice, whether accurately or inaccurately, is to impose a requirement of fit on the practice, archetypically a more or less conservative fit, in which the practice is expected to be something that it has always been, rather than to recognize it as open-ended, as practices are in fact more or less bound to be in their inception, maintenance, and development, simply by reason of their mortality: new aspects of the practice, new occasions for value, and sometimes even new values being born in the shape of new or altered purposes for the practice, even as old aspects of the practice die by reason of their relative neglect, whether out of cultural restlessness, or a shifting sense of cultural relevance as other connected practices themselves alter, in mutually informing patterns, sometimes to be remembered and perhaps revived in one form or another, sometimes to be forgotten.[15]

It is a notable feature of Joseph Raz's treatment of law and legal system that he never suggests that the purpose of law is to serve as an authority. Instead, he explains the ways in which compliance with the law, the ways in which doing or refraining from doing something just because the law has told one to, may be rational, so that it may be rational to make laws and to observe laws for the sake of the value of the authority they provide. That is to take no official position upon, and so to leave open, the question of what values inspired the creation of legal practice (assuming that such a question could have any kind of determinate answer) and in turn the question of what values the practice might be capable of giving rise to, now or in the future. Those are questions to which answers can be given only ever provisionally, and only through the constantly shifting shape of our social lives.

4.3.2 The Problem of our Times

The currents of this debate, or something like it, seem to me to be particularly active at the moment, as much of the world veers between the enlightened and the atavistic, as proper frameworks for sound collective decision-making. Just where those currents might lead us is as yet quite unclear, and likely to remain so, for the small fragments of social history in which we are embedded, and in which we are reasonably well versed, are compatible with many different larger histories, a good number of which remain entirely plausible prospects at the moment, and are likely to do so until they are taken over by a new set of long-term uncertainties. That means that, contrary to the apparent spirit of much of this chapter, any decisions that we might currently make will be only contingently connected to those larger histories, and in ways that are likely to surprise and perhaps even dismay us.

I say contrary to the apparent spirit just because in truth one of the implications of due attention to the fine-grained is that larger histories ought to be accepted as matters of contingency. It is true that to attempt to speak to them directly would be to open up possibilities for error that those committed to the fine-grained seek to avoid. Nevertheless it is always a good idea even for the most locally minded of us to have one eye to the horizon, and it is part of the purpose of this chapter to suggest modest ways in which at least some aspects of the standardly accepted

---

[15] For more on the problem of purpose, or point, see my paper 'Ideas of Easy Virtue' in *Law and Life in Common* (2015). See that volume too for consideration of the difficulties present in other dimensions of Dworkin's account, most notably the problem of deriving any form of communal guidance from law when the question of what the law is on any given matter is always open to further interpretation, that is, not susceptible to authoritative determination, of the kind that sharing requires.

contrast between the claims of modernity and those of its atavistic critics, between the ideal and the everyday, might be illuminated and perhaps even constructively muted, in a manner that we all already recognize and have a decent working understanding of.

So, there are many good ways to approach a situation such as that which arose in *Riggs*, many attractive ways in which to apply the claims of the general principle that no one shall profit from his own wrong. That principle could not be brought to bear other than by attention to the nature of the profit in the case at hand, and the character of the wrong. Suppose the wrong was a mercy killing of one spouse by the other.[16] Suppose further that although well intentioned the mercy killing was unjustified. The ending of the life in such a case might have been driven by the same quality of tenderness for the welfare of the other that animated the victim's testamentary provision, notwithstanding its wrongfulness. Courts since *Riggs* have gone both ways on the issue, not because they took different views of the general principle, but rather because they took the view that the principle gained life through its application to the facts, to which it was bound to respond as part of its being. And yet none of the facts to which the principle was called upon to respond would have any purchase but for the presence of the general rule and the moral perception that it embodied. That is why (or at least part of why) decision is so difficult, and so deeply resistant to schematization (resistant because most schematization is arbitrary, albeit that it may quite possibly give rise to value after the fact), but it is also why the exercise of decision, and the consequences of that exercise, can be so valuable.[17]

---

[16] This particular factual scenario was suggested to me by John Gardner.

[17] I first approached the topics in this chapter as part of a consideration of the treatment of morality in law in the philosophy of law, as a contribution to John Tasioulas (ed.), *The Cambridge Companion to the Philosophy of Law* (2020). See there, Macklem, 'Law and Living Well', at 78–94.

Afterword: A Philosopher's Life and its Worth

Academic researchers occasionally muse, in the spirit of a parlour game, about the question of their intellectual pedigree: Who taught us how to do research, at doctoral level and beyond, and who were they taught by? What did we learn from those people? What lineage of character, style, and perhaps even conviction are we part of? In certain disciplines the chains of heritage and influence are long; in the philosophy of law and its excurses into moral and political philosophy, the lineage is relatively short. In my case, I was taught by Joseph Raz, who was taught by Herbert Hart, who in this sense taught himself. John Gardner was taught alongside me; others preceded us, others followed. Our intellectual outlooks and our intellectual creations, be those books and articles or other forms of sharing, are the recognizable consequence. I want to say something about this heritage and influence, partly in tribute, and partly to cast light upon a particular approach to philosophy, one that is embodied in this book, that might otherwise seem a little puzzling to some.

What follows is a set of observations that I made as an introduction to a conference on the work of Joseph Raz, a conference organized in his honour by the New York and London institutions at which he was then professor, and held with his approval and his guidance. Joseph was at the time a couple of years short of a conventional tribute at age 80 but also in worsening health. None of us wanted to take a chance on a future so fragile.

Joseph made it clear that he would like the participants in the conference to be young scholars, still at the most formative stage of their academic life. As ever, his concern was to foster intellectual possibility, and to be kind. It fell to me to set out the distinctive character and depth of the contribution that Joseph had made to the lives of his students. I wrote entirely for the occasion, or so I thought, and it was only much later that I realized, to my surprise, that the tribute that I had written fed fruitfully back into the substance of my own work, so as to be something of a charter for my own intellectual outlook, and thus something of a guide to the nature of the philosophical understanding that I have pursued over the course of my intellectual life, and have sought to articulate most completely in this book. It is a sense of mission that I have in mind, just because Joseph did, rather than a set of ideas. So my comments here are doing double duty, as a tribute to great teaching and learning, with all I take that project to imply, and some of the architecture of which I seek to trace below, and as a valedictory act of accountability on the part of one of its products.

My name is Timothy Macklem and, like most of the rest of you, I am one of Joseph's students. As an organiser of this conference it falls to me to say a few words about the project, that is, about Joseph Raz and what he has brought into the world through his scholarship. May I begin by expressing our common gratitude to Joseph, for making it all possible.

It is conventional on these occasions to say something about the achievements of the person whom one would like to pay tribute to, about the trajectory of their career, the work they have produced, the recognition they have received, the impact they have made. All too often, on listening to such recitations, one begins to have an uneasy feeling that one has begun to recognize the content of the honoree's web page. The ritual starts to feel a little empty. We know all these things already. Yet it seems to me that the issue is not simply one of over-familiarity. CVs have their place, and it is good to be reminded of their content from time to time. The worry is more with what they do not convey, and I would like to try to say a little something about that, something that ties in with the theme of this conference, something that speaks as much to your place here as to that of Joseph, something that addresses the distinctive value of the social practice in which all of us, separately and together, have come to play our interdependent parts. As exemplified in Joseph's life as a scholar, that practice has, at least it seems to me, three prominent and familiar aspects. I wouldn't want to be so unconventional as to suggest that there might be four, though I'm sure that minds rather bolder than my own could readily prolong the list.

The first, of course, is the legendary rigour of his thought, that which causes students to reel back, that which is said to have led Herbert Hart to wrap hot towels around his head, and that which gives pause to even seasoned professionals. I remember thinking, when I was a doctoral student, that I had been looking for a challenge but not this kind of challenge. Yet what other kind could there be in the academic setting? What other warrant could there be for the claims of one mind upon the attention of others than the quality of the thought to be conveyed? Given the ambitions of philosophy and the depth of its history, the demands of quality are inevitably severe and meeting them is almost always painful. We all not only bear the scars of this but renew them whenever we do, as we always aspire to do, something fresh, unfamiliar, as challenging to ourselves as to others.

Yet to say this much and no further is a bit pat, a bit too quick. There is rather more to it than that. I remember many years ago when I was a law clerk at the Supreme Court of Canada, in my early days in the role, thinking that something that I had produced 'would do', only to discover that it would not do at all. Cases reach that court because they are very difficult. Beware of underestimating them. Give them everything you have to give. That is a kind of rigour, and yet it exposes the fact that rigour is not simply a matter of degree. What was wrong in my memo preparation at the Court was not that I asked what 'would do', but that I gave the wrong, too easy, too self-preserving, answer to the question. In academic life it is the question that is wrong, not the answer that one gives to it. To recognize this is to begin to comprehend the underpinnings of Joseph's rigour.

In practical life, there are practical benchmarks for performance, and questions of what 'will do' are entirely appropriate. They are ways of asking what the benchmark looks like. What kind of chair is the buyer looking for? Something simple, or something refined? Would this one over here do? Academic life, however, is not a practical life in that sense. We did not enter upon scholarly careers to make sure that we earned at least a 3* in the REF and so satisfied our employers, although that is, of course, the entirely correct answer to what 'will do' in our case. In academic life, the quest is for understanding, and the claims of understanding have no limits in that setting, just because they are not in the service of any end other than the quality of the enquiry that they prompt and the quality of the answers that they give rise to. An understanding can frequently be 'good enough' for daily life, but it can never be 'good enough' for a scholar. When my father took his driving test as a teenager, he passed first time, but the examiner noted on his report, 'cuts corners'. The notation could have been applied more or less accurately to the conduct of much of my father's subsequent life. Yet there is nothing very wrong in that. Knowing just when to cut a corner can be a valuable trait. In the life of an academic, however, cutting a corner amounts to a betrayal of the academic mission. In the setting in which we work, rigour is a necessity, not an option. It is not that the standards are high ones, as at the Supreme Court. Rather it is that our goal is to make them ever higher, and that the mark of our achievement is that we have extended rather than met them. In that project, we all need to learn to be self-flagellating, to know that we will always fall short, by virtue of the very mission that inspires us, and one of the sterling things that Joseph has done for us is to teach us that lesson well by his own example.

The second striking aspect of Joseph's scholarship is its startling distinctiveness. Time and again one finds that familiar ways of thinking about things have been turned on their head. The effect is liberating. Suddenly, there are all kinds of new possibilities for one's thought, very often in relation to topics that seemed to be inescapably settled in their ways. This is not a matter of being original. It would be less distinctive if it were. Originality exists in contrast to what is familiar and expected. It is everywhere to be found and seldom very interesting in itself. Little, if any, academic work is not original, modestly so though it may be. Nor is it a matter of being iconoclastic, of toppling yesterday's statues. Both of those endeavours take their cues from the conventional. Joseph's distinctiveness, it seems to me, stems from the fact that he takes almost nothing for granted. In this, he is as unsparing of his own ideas as he is of the ideas of others. Everything is open to question.

As scholars, we are bound to look in two directions in the course of our reflections, backwards and forwards, to those to whom we are bound to attend and to those whom we hope will attend to us in the future. Each of us makes a choice in those respects, in our careers in general and in particular projects in those careers.

How little should we presume? How abstemious should we be? How much should we take as read? How engaged should we be? Each broad course, and the many forms of balance that can be struck between them, has value to offer and cost to exact. Much fine scholarship, and many an admirable career, has succeeded by embodying some such balance.

In communities of scholarship, these balances soon form patterns, patterns of abstention as much as of engagement. In observing those patterns, one has company as a scholar. Joseph's restlessness, scepticism, commitment to deep questioning, his considered independence of tradition or prospect, lead him to challenge such patterns as much as anything else. It is an intellectual course that is liable to be just as lonely as it is productive. Yet it has none of the vanity of isolationism, for solitude is its possible price, not its point. The contrast here is between the solitary's unwillingness to negotiate and the radical scholar's willingness to negotiate just about everything.

Some people set up shop on the high street, as a restaurant let us suppose, take note of their competitors, have a view as to what will engage hungry passers-by. Other people set up destination restaurants, almost certainly not on the high street, and try there to confront expectations, not for the sake of confounding them, but for the sake of probing them, challenging them, extending them, reshaping them. When this works well, those who are interested in good food bit by bit learn to find their way there, to share in the possibilities that independence of thought and practice has brought into being. In doing this, they themselves become elements in that practice, contributors to its development, participants in its flourishing and in its failures. It is a kind of liberation, sometimes for better, sometimes for worse.

So Joseph does not tell his students what to read, let alone what to address. He never seeks to replicate himself in his followers. Indeed, he never attempts to proselytize his ideas to anyone. It's a bit like a good parent, who knows enough to raise children and send them out into the world without expectations, without an agenda, without seeing them in any way as reflections of oneself. Here again Joseph teaches by example. If from time to time we his pupils seem rather Razian, and we all do, it is not because we think it appropriate to carry his message on, to be his disciples and missionaries. We have long since, and under his stern discipline, learned better. It is our burden to find our own sources, our own direction, our own voice, our own audience, without taking anything much for granted. This we have done, if I may say so, and without reference to myself, remarkably successfully. There is no finer scholarship out there than that of Joseph's students, except of course, that of Joseph himself, although some of his students some of the time have learned to give even him a run for his money. If we are Razian, it is only because and to the extent that, searching as we have been, we have not in that particular respect found a better source, a better direction, a better sense of audience. That is but the legacy of his achievement.

Rigour and distinctiveness. What is left? Something more evanescent, more interstitial, that I will call sharing. We his students are not an accidental or contingent feature of Joseph's intellectual life. On the contrary, we are central to it, and that fact tells us something about the very shape and significance of academic life, and the essential but qualified role of research and teaching there. As the title of this conference suggests, ambitious intellectual life, whether in or out of the academy, constitutes a social practice, many of the richest aspects of which typically go unrecorded, as is of course the way with social practices generally, and with all else that lives and dies. Yes, there are artefacts, and those may with time and fortune turn into a legacy: books and articles produced, a world better informed, more comprehending of itself than it would otherwise be, students readied for fruitful employment, not to speak of roofs put over heads, and food put on the table. Important as these are, however, their significance is always a function of the part they play in something that is larger and less concrete, an artefact that includes those artefacts as subsidiaries. The presence of a flourishing intellectual life, flourishing in all the ways that Joseph's scholarship has embodied and inspired, is a vital element in a certain species of cultural achievement, and its vitality is just that, vitality: a way of living and being the value of which arises in the round, is informed by the interdependency of its elements, and is not always or entirely susceptible to ready division, not liable to detachment.

I am not religious and in the course of my upbringing I don't suppose that I attended a church service more times than I have fingers on my hands, but I do remember a slightly cheesy hymn called something like 'God Sees the Little Sparrow Fall'. That is wrong, and not because there is no God. It is wrong because it represents something unremarkable as something to be remarked upon, as if value went hand in hand with the remarkable. If God knew his business, as I understand he does by definition, then he would not remark upon the fall of the sparrow, for he would know that the value of the sparrow's life, and the loss that came of its ending, turns only in part on what is susceptible to notice.

In our professional lives, no less than in our personal ones, we are all sparrows, and our flights, no less than our falls, matter in all kinds of ways that are not susceptible to being remarked upon, no less so than in the traces that they leave. It is the quality of our life, *qua* life, that matters, and nearly everything that we do contributes to that quality, though we tend, for reasons good and bad, to parse our existences, so as to emphasize, for example, what is most impressive, or most enduring, even when we know that it is not what is most important. So, when we are good academics we play our parts in a social practice that is shifting, evanescent, amorphous, always more than the sum of its parts, crucial though they are to its worth. So too, Joseph teaches in part with regard to outcomes, but in part too because of the intellectual culture that is brought into being thereby and that is worthy in itself, comes to workshops and events like this one in part for what he and others have to learn there, but in part for the very occasion, for the fact of being there. This is something that one can do only in collaboration, and only by being rather than making.

My mother has an odd way of putting things sometimes. A very brief illustration, to set up the story to follow. She said to me one day, speaking of herself: 'I'm tired of this face. I've been looking at it for a long time.' It was hard to think of a constructive way to respond. Now the story. My best friend as a child was killed in a car crash when he was 19. My memories of him remain vivid: the shape of his wet footprint on a wooden dock; the way the hairs on his forearm sprang up as they dried off after a swim, as we lay on hot rock to recover from cold water, heads on arms, nothing to look at but the arm next to one, nothing to register except water drying. I take those memories seriously. They hold his death at bay. I told my mother these things not long ago and when we met the next day she said, 'I couldn't sleep last night. I kept thinking of that poor boy, trapped inside someone's head.'

Trapped inside one's head. That is the fate of everything we are or can be, until we bring it out into the world and engage it with others and what they have brought out. In that engagement lies the worth of our lives, some of which, like my memories, has a semi-independent existence as an artefact in its own right, but much of which is to be appreciated as it happens, without notice. My mother was right. What mattered was not the memory but the having been there. It is a terrible fate, one to lose some sleep over, to be reduced to a repeating flicker in somebody's brain. We are not what is memorable about us; we are not our legacies.[1]

Academic achievement is something more than could ever be captured in a CV. It exists in moments like the present one, in all the spaces between ourselves, as we pursue and embody a certain kind of life of the mind. That is not a charter for saying that we are worthy even though we fail to produce anything worthy. It is simply to say that the value of what we produce is in service to the worth of the lives that produced it and to the worth of the lives of those who appreciate it. Just to have been at this conference is a good in itself, an artefact to be placed alongside the articles we write and the classes we give, assuming, of course, that all goes well. That sharing too is part of what Joseph has helped to bring into the world, and it is something that he could not have done without us, any more than we could have done it without him.

So, rigour, independence, and a climate of sharing. Subject to what others might add, that is the story that a CV can reflect but cannot speak of. In paying tribute to Joseph, as inadequately as I have, I want to be sure to speak of such things, even as I know that they are not entirely susceptible to being spoken of, for they are the bones of what he has given to us, around which we have built intellectual lives of our own, the bones of which will help in turn to structure yet further intellectual lives, at least if we are lucky.

---

[1] Cf. Leonard Woolf, *The Journey Not the Arrival Matters* (1969).

Index

For the benefit of digital users, indexed terms that span two pages (e.g., 52–53) may, on occasion, appear on only one of those pages.

absence
   consent. of *see* consent
   value, of *see* value
action *see* consent
agency, active mode of justice xiii–xiv
allocation
   charity and 7–8
   conflict and 26
   distributive justice, and 7–8
   equality and 139–40
   good, and the 22, 23–24, 26
   just allocations 21–28
   justice and 9–10, 15
   misallocation 16–17
   between persons 22–27
   primacy as to justice 22
   Scott's expedition to Antarctic as example of 140, 172–73
Antarctic, Scott's expedition to 140, 172–73
anti-discrimination *see* discrimination
Aristotle 18–19, 63

badness xv–xvi *see also* goodness
bodily integrity *see* integrity

charity 6–13, 16–17, 25
children
   moral development 19
   sense of fairness/unfairness 16–18, 19
circumstance
   equality and xix, 141
   value and xiv
commonality/commonalities
   equality of xix
   experience of, by particular social groups xix
   men and women 171–72
   modern era, of xix, 165–76
companionability as alternative to justice 35–38
conflict
   allocation and 22, 26–27
   injustice and 17

   moral conflict 27
   resolution of 22
consciousness
   false consciousness as to justice 6, 12–14, 33–34
   personal as political 19
consent
   absence of 56–60, 80–81, 109–22
   action and 80–81
   active mode of 83–85
   agency (acting) and 83–85
   current book's approach and contribution to legal literature on xvi–xviii, 58–59
   current book's content and structure xiii–xiv
   difficulty as to 62
   discrimination and 110–11
   explicit consent 75–76, 77, 78
   general lessons as to 109–13
   general senses of 109–13
   governed, of the 114–22
   by implication *see* implication
   implied consent *see* implied consent
   integrity and 59–60, 85–86, 95–96
   interaction and 81–83, 85–87
   interactions without consent 87–94
   law and xvii–xviii
   legality/illegality and xviii
   legitimacy of 75–79
   meaning of 54–55
   medical treatment, to 113–14
   negotiation as to *see* negotiation
   particular senses of 109–13
   particular setting of 109–13
   passivity and 83–85, 101–6
   place of 109–22
   present-day debate as to 200–1
   sexual relations, to xvii–xviii, 56–60, 107–22
   submission and 96–100
   unwelcome/unwilled events or circumstances, and 94–96
criminal law *see* murder; sexual offences
culture *see* social theory

decision-making
  current book's approach and contribution to legal literature on xix–xx
  current book's content and structure xiii–xiv
  ideal, and the 194–201
  law and xxn.12
  law as process of collective decision xiii–xiv
  living well, as to xix–xx
  value in 194–201
democracy, People's consent to be governed 114–22
detachment *see also* engagement
  engagement and 10n.8
  good, from the 23
  liability as to 207
  moral judgement, and 179–80, 181
  personal as political 18–19
  persons from value, of 43–45
  problem of 145–47
difference
  actuating of 150
  definition of people by their difference 138
  domination and 132
  elimination of 137
  equality and 131–32, 134–37
  extent of 139
  protection from equality 132–33
  recognition of 132–33, 150
  reconciliation with equality 137
  value of 138
difficulty
  consent, as to 62
  equality, as to 174
  good, as to the 26
  ideal, and the xix–xx, 194–201
  justice as to 15
  moral inspiration, as to 178
  relationships, in 4–5, 47–48
  respect for persons, as to 49
  value in 194–201
dignity
  integrity and 85–86
  women's 108–9
discrimination
  consent and 110–11
  equality and 138, 169–70, 171–72
  levelling down, and 142n.18
  recognition of 43n.27
  varieties of 110–11
  women and 142n.18
distributive justice *see* allocation
Dworkin, Ronald xixn.11, 184, 185–86, 190–91n.13, 192–93, 194–97, 198–200

engagement *see also* detachment
  detachment and 10n.8
  moral world, with xv
  value, with xv
equality *see also* justice
  betrayal of 128–31
  circumstance and xix
  commonalities of xix, 165–76
  critiques of paradigms of 137–40
  cultural function of 127
  current author's approach to 124–27
  current book's approach and contribution to legal literature on xvi–xvii, xviii–xix, 126–27
  current book's content and structure xiii–xiv
  detachment and *see* detachment
  difference and 131–33, 134–37
  difficulty as to 174
  discrimination and 138–39, 142n.18, 169–70, 171–72
  distribution and 139–40
  goodness/value relationship, and 127
  ideal of xix
  independent moral value, as 124
  inequality and xviii–xix
  integrity and 131–32, 194–200
  levelling down, and *see* levelling down
  mercenary ideal of 126–27
  moral flexibility of xix
  oppressive operation of 126–27
  personal position (situation), and 141
  present-day debate as to 200–1
  protection from difference 132–33
  purpose and 194–200
  Raz's theory of 124–26, 127
  reconciliation with difference 137
  shared experience, and 141–42
  suppression and 50–51, 147–51
  tempered claims of 131–34
  value of xix
  Walzer's theory of 124–25, 126, 128–34, 138–39, 147–48, 171–72n.35, 174–75
  women, of 142n.18
ethics
  current book's approach and contribution to legal literature on xv–xvi, xx
  ethic of care for women 12–13
  meta-ethics of value xiv–xvi, xx
everyday life *see* life
experience, equality and 141–42
explicit consent *see* consent

fairness
    childlike perspective as to fairness/
        unfairness 16–18, 19
    injustice and 16
false consciousness *see* consciousness
Farage, Nigel 18
fatal offences *see* murder
Finnis, John 120–21, 191, 198–99
Frankfurt, Harry xviii–xix, 175–76

Gardner, John 2n.1, 21n.14, 22, 24n.16, 39n.21, 54, 56, 63n.8, 124, 178n.1, 201n.16
gender *see* women
generosity
    justice and xiii–xiv
    love and 6–12
good, the (concept of)
    allocation and 22, 23–24, 26–27
    difficulty as to 26
goodness *see also* badness
    allocation and 26–27
    fallibility of goods and of 161–64
    groundedness of xiv
    justice and xvi–xvii
    value and xiv, xviii–xix, 127, 157–58
goods *see* goodness
government, people's consent to be governed 114–22
grounded worlds 178–86

Harrison, George 2
Hart, Herbert (H.L.A.) 185–86, 203, 204
health *see* medical treatment
homicide *see* murder

ideal (concept of)
    decision and 194–201
    difficulty as to xix–xx, 194–201
    equality, of xix
    everyday (life) and xiv–xv
    grounded worlds and ideal worlds, in 178–86
    living well, and xv, 187–93
    moral inspiration, problem of 178–84
    murdered testator, problem of (*Riggs v. Palmer*) 184–86, 201
ideal worlds 178–86
Ignatieff, Michael 29–30
illegality *see* legality
implied consent
    consent by implication 58–59
    legitimacy of 72–75
    morality of implication 65–72
    politics of implication 65–72

    sexual relations, to xvii–xviii
    structural features of implication 63–65
    understanding of implication 61–63
inequality *see* equality
injustice *see* justice
inspiration, moral *see* morality
integrity
    bodily integrity 85–86, 95–96, 113–14
    consent and 59–60, 85–86, 95–96
    dignity and 85–86
    equality and 131–32, 194–200
    justice and 16–17
    law as 185, 186
interaction, consent and *see* consent

justice *see also* equality
    absence of 4–6
    active mode of operation as to xiii–xiv
    companionability as alternative to 35–38
    conflict and injustice 17
    current book's approach and contribution to legal literature on xvi–xvii, 3
    current book's content and structure xiii–xiv
    descriptive overview and definition of 15–16
    difficulty as to 15
    distinction between persons 23
    distinctive value of xvi–xvii
    distributive justice *see* allocation
    fairness and 16–18
    false consciousness as to 6, 12–14, 33–34
    generosity and xiii–xiv
    goodness and xvi–xvii
    instead of love 2–3
    integrity and 16–17
    just allocation *see* allocation
    kindness and xiii–xiv
    love and xiii–xiv, 2–3
    lovingness of 2–3
    mercy and xiii–xiv
    morality and 19–21
    passive mode of operation as to xiii–xiv
    present-day debate as to 200–1
    primacy over other values xvi–xvii
    purpose of 25n.18
    Rawls' theory of 27–28
    reasons to seek and to prioritize xiii–xiv, xvi–xvii
    reconciliation with love 2–3
    respect for persons 39–52
    respect for value 25–26
    unfairness and 16
    unlovingness of 2
    worlds without justice 29–35

kindness, justice and xiii–xiv

law
   consent and xvii–xviii
   decision and xxn.12
   formative values of xiii
   integrity, as 185, 186
   legality (and illegality), consent and xviii
   present-day debate as to 200–1
   process of collective decision, as xiii–xiv
   protective interventions for women xviii
   responsibility and xviii
   theatre of the particular xix–xx
   value of xix–xx
legality (and illegality), consent and xviii
legitimacy *see* implication
levelling down
   concept of 142–44, 146, 163
   value pluralism, and 144–45
life *see also* living well
   everyday life, ideal and xiv–xv
   key features of xvi
   moral life, value and xiv
   morality and xiv
   purpose and 156
   time and place, within xvi
   value and xiii
living well *see also* life
   current book's approach and contribution to legal literature on xix–xx
   decision-making as to xix–xx
   difficulties/problems of xix–xx
   ideal, and the xv, 187–93
   morality and xvi
   'project' of xiv
love
   charity and 6–13, 16–17, 25
   generosity and 6–12
   justice and xiii–xiv, 2–3
   justice instead of 2–3
   justness of 2–3
   mercy and 6–12
   need for 2–3
   reconciliation with justice 2–3
   unjustness of 2

medical treatment
   consent to 113–14
   women's 103
men, women and *see* women
mental health *see* medical treatment
mercy
   justice and xiii–xiv
   love and 6–12

meta-ethics *see* ethics
Miller, David 125, 148, 173n.36
misallocation *see* allocation
morality
   children's moral development 19
   detachment from moral judgement 179–80, 181
   difficulty as to moral inspiration 178
   engagement with moral world xv
   equality and *see* equality
   first principle-level facets of xiv–xv
   implied consent, of 65–72
   justice and 19–21
   life and xiv
   living well, and xvi
   moral conflict 27
   moral inspiration, problem of 178–84
   moral life, value and xiv
   personal as political, concept of 18–21
   populist politics, moral aspect of 18
   value and xv
murder, Problem of the murdered testator (*Riggs v. Palmer*) 184–86, 201

negotiation
   companionship and 36
   consent and 55
   explicit consent, and 78
   implied consent, and 67, 69, 71
   non-consent, as to 87–94
   relationship and 4
non-discrimination *see* discrimination

offences against the person *see* murder

Parfit, Derek 39–40, 142–43
passivity
   consent and 101–6
   passive mode of justice xiii–xiv
people, the, consent to be governed 114–22
personal as political, concept of 18–21
personal circumstance (position), equality and 141
persons *see* social theory
place of consent *see* consent
pluralism, value 144–45 *see also* value
political theory *see* social theory
politics
   implied consent, of 65–72
   populist politics, moral aspect of 18
position (circumstance), equality and 141
practice, purpose of 199–200
purpose
   equality and 194–200

justice, of 25n.18
law, of 199–200
life and 156
practice, of 199–200
problem of 194–200
sense of 22–23, 156–57, 188
value and 155

Rawls, John 23–24, 27–28
Raz, Joseph
  commonality in the modern era, on 175–76
  consent, on 94, 115, 116, 120–21
  current author's tribute to xx, 203–8
  equality, on xviii–xix
  interdependence of value and social practices, on 158–59
  interdependence of value and valuers, on xvi, 152, 153, 156–57
  just allocations, on 22–23, 25, 26
  justice and respect for persons, on 43, 45, 48–49, 52
  levelling down and value pluralism, on 144–45
  personal as political, on 20
  problem of living well, on 187
  value, on 124–25, 126, 127
relationships (personal)
  in difficulty 47–48
  difficulty as to 4–5
respect for persons, difficulty as to 49
responsibility, law and xviii
Riggs v. Palmer 184–86, 201

Scott, Robert Falcon 140, 172–73
sexual offences, consent to xvii–xviii, 56–60, 107–22
shared experience, equality and 141–42
social theory
  access to value, as to xv
  cultural function of equality 127
  justice and respect for persons 39–52
  people's consent to be governed 114–22
  personal as political, concept of 18–21
  persons as bearers of values 22–23
  social practices, relationship with (concept of) value 158–61
  social practices, relationship with justice xvi–xvii
submission
  consent and 96–100
  unwelcome/unwilled events or circumstances, to 95–96
succession *see* testators
suppression 50–51, 147–51

Temkin, Larry 146n.21, 162–63
testators, problem of the murdered testator (*Riggs v. Palmer*) 184–86, 201
time and place, life within xvi
Trump, Donald 18
trusts *see* testators

unwelcome/unwilled events or circumstances, consent and 94–96

value
  allocation and 22–23
  badness xv
  circumstance and xiv
  consent *see* consent
  current author's tribute to Joseph Raz 203–8
  current book's approach and contribution to legal literature on xiii–xiv, xv–xvii
  current book's content and structure xiii–xiv
  decision-making, in 194–201
  difficulty, in 194–201
  engagement with xv
  equality *see* equality
  first principle-level facets of xiv–xv
  formative values of law xiii
  goodness and xiv, xviii–xix, 127, 157–58
  justice *see* justice
  law, of xix–xx
  levelling down, and *see* levelling down
  life and xiii
  meta-ethics of xiv–xvi, xx
  moment, and the xiii
  morality and xv
  persons as bearers of values 22–23
  purpose and 155
  second-level (meta-ethical) facets of xiv–xv
  social practices, as to 158–61
  social theory as to xv
  value pluralism, and 144–45
  valuers as possessors of xvi, 152–57
valuers *see* value

Walzer, Michael 124–25, 126, 128–34, 138–39, 147–48, 171–72n.35, 174–75
wellbeing *see* life
Wertheimer, Alan 55
Westen, Peter 54–55, 98, 124–25, 132n.8, 146
women
  articulation of gendered sexual and social circumstances 109
  commonality with men 171–72
  consciousness of oppression 13
  consent to sexual relations 112–13

women (*cont.*)
   dignity of 108–9
   disadvantaging of 138n.13
   discrimination and 142n.18
   equality of 142n.18
   ethic of care for 12–13
   explicit consent, and 75–76, 77
   implied consent, and 67–70, 72–75
   law's protective interventions for xviii
   male forcefulness upon 112–13
   medical treatment 103
   physical resistance to sexual assault 97
   recognition of capabilities of 141n.16
   sexual relations with 80